# IN THE
# COMBAT ZONE

# IN THE COMBAT ZONE

## An Oral History of American Women in Vietnam, 1966–1975

### KATHRYN MARSHALL

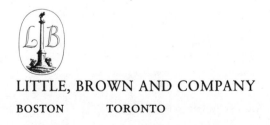

LITTLE, BROWN AND COMPANY

BOSTON          TORONTO

FIRST EDITION

*Library of Congress Cataloging-in-Publication Data*

Marshall, Kathryn.
　In the combat zone.

　Includes index.
　1. Vietnamese Conflict, 1961–1975 — Women —
United States. 2. Vietnamese Conflict, 1961–1975 —
Personal narratives, American. I. Title.
DS559.8.W6M37 1987　　959.704'38　　86-10580
ISBN 0-316-54707-7

RRD VA

*Published simultaneously in Canada
by Little, Brown & Company (Canada) Limited*

PRINTED IN THE UNITED STATES OF AMERICA

*For the women whose stories are still untold*

# Contents

# IN THE
# COMBAT ZONE

# Introduction

JUST as there is no "woman's position" on war, there is no single position on the Vietnam War in this collection of narratives. The women who went to Vietnam during the war years supported, opposed, and suffered the war. Some were intensely patriotic. Many believed in the war. Others felt hemmed in — they wanted adventure, and Vietnam was what was "happening." Others went for a sense of helping. A few were pacifists. And some, mostly Army nurses, did not intend to go. Nor were these women uniformly affected by their time in Vietnam. Some, on their return, did personal or political turnabouts; others committed themselves more deeply to the ideals that had sent them there.

This collection of narratives reflects something I saw last May, on the weekend before the dedication of the New York Vietnam Veterans' Memorial: women who had gone to the Vietnam War, both with the military and as civilians, were organizing.

There was much these women didn't agree on. Their backgrounds and politics were diverse, and the work they had done in Vietnam ranged from caring for orphans to decoding body counts. They argued over the term *veteran* and whom it should include, and they couldn't agree on whether the Vietnam Veterans of America or other, less formal, networks better served their common interests. In fact, they had little that could really be described as common interests except their desires to be recognized and to locate other women who had been in Vietnam.

Throughout the seventies, all they had had in common was that they had gone to the Vietnam War. Back then, when no one was sure there was even a way to talk, how could these women have talked to each other as "veterans"?

The impetus to try came some five years after the Vietnam War was over. It came both from within and in spite of veterans' organizations. Former Army nurse Lynda Van Devanter, then active with the Vietnam Veterans of America, began speaking out. Women counselors in the VA–sponsored Vietnam Veterans' Outreach Program began contacting other women, and the Disabled American Veterans began seeking out women who had been disabled in Vietnam. In California, Debra DeBondt, a Vietnam-era* Air Force veteran, started the Women Veterans' Information Network, while in Massachusetts Lough O'Daly, also a Vietnam-era Air Force veteran, started the newsletter organization Athena. Here and there, vet centers were seeing women for the first time. And after former Red Cross worker Jeanne Christie began digging letters out of trunks and making calls to distant time zones, women who had been in Vietnam with military support organizations and relief agencies began coming together. Finally, at the dedication of the Vietnam Veterans' Memorial in Washington in 1982, women who had been military in Vietnam and women who had been civilian began — tentatively — to talk. By May of 1985, when I did my first interview, they were talking in earnest.

According to the Department of Defense, between 1962† and 1973, some 7,500 American women served on active military duty in Vietnam. The Veterans' Administration, however, puts the number of military women at more than 11,000. For civilian women, there are no official figures. Independent surveys indicate that the total number of American women, both military and civilian, working in Vietnam during the war years is somewhere between 33,000 and 55,000. No one seems to have an accurate count. This apparent lack of data on the part of the Department of Defense and the State Department both serves as a reminder of government mishandling of information during the Vietnam War and points to the more general belief that war is men's business.

The best-documented group of women consists of those who served in the military. According to a 1984 study by the Senate Veterans' Affairs Committee, there were 36 women Marines in Vietnam, 421 women in the Navy, and 771 in the Air Force. The rest were in the Army.‡

Some 80 percent of the military women in Vietnam served in

---

* "Vietnam-era veteran," often shortened to "era vet," refers to anyone who was in the military, but was not in Vietnam, during the war years.
† This is the official DOD line. However, the Army Nurse Corps says three American women were in Vietnam on temporary duty in 1956.
‡ These figures, I suspect, will change.

the Navy, the Air Force, or the Army Nurse Corps. (The Marine Corps has no nurses.) All nurses were officers and had to be twenty-one to serve in a combat zone. Their tour of duty was generally a year; like all military personnel, they were rotated in and out of Vietnam on an individual rather than a unit-by-unit basis.

Navy nurses lived and worked on either the USS *Repose* or the USS *Sanctuary,* hospital ships that sailed off the coast of Vietnam, normally between Danang and the Demilitarized Zone. According to a Navy nurse who served on the *Sanctuary* in 1968 and 1969, "Only once did we go further south than Danang. This was January of sixty-nine. Chu Lai was a catacomb of VC then, and the Marines were going in there to clean them out. So our ship went along with this flotilla. It was a whole mess of ships — gunships, chopper ships, destroyers. I remember being on the ship and watching. The Marines would get dropped into Chu Lai and then there would be an explosion and then the Marines would be picked up — the choppers would get the wounded to us in maybe four or five minutes." Navy nurses were also stationed at the bases in Danang and Cam Ranh.

Air Force nurses cared for the wounded on in country evacuation flights as well as on evacuation flights to Japan, Okinawa, the Philippines, and the United States. Lieutenant Colonel Marsha Jordan, a flight nurse in Vietnam, described the converted cargo planes used for evacuation flights: "Inside the aircraft, as you walk in — you're coming in the back end — there would be stacks of litters. Visualize a commercial plane with no seats in it, poles all the way down the middle of the aircraft, and on those poles are brackets. We could put patients four high on those poles and brackets, so we would have them on either side of the aircraft. Then, along the sides of the aircraft — the bulkhead — we had more poles and brackets." Air Force nurses also worked at casualty staging facilities, or evacuation hospitals, in Danang and Cam Ranh.

The Army had hospitals as far north as Quang Tri, thirty-five kilometers from the Demilitarized Zone, and as far south as Can Tho in the Mekong Delta. These hospitals were classified as field hospitals, surgical hospitals, evacuation hospitals, and MASH (Mobile Army Surgical Hospital) units. In addition, the Army had convalescent hospitals and hospitals for POWs. Army hospitals, like all American military hospitals in Vietnam, were equipped for emergency surgery. At the smaller hospitals, patients were stabilized and shipped out; the larger Army hospitals, like the hospital ships, were equipped for major surgery. Most had Vietnamese wards, where civilians and, occasionally, POWs were treated.

Throughout the Vietnam War years, all branches of the service, except the Marine Corps, recruited at nursing schools. As always, the Army recruited most heavily. To a student nurse from a working class background, the Army's monthly check meant she didn't have to take out loans or get a job to cover tuition and expenses. It also meant two or three years in the Army Nurse Corps — and a possible tour in Vietnam. Although potential recruits, in many cases, had been told that a woman had to *volunteer* for Vietnam, in fact this was not so; young Army nurses who had no intention of going to Vietnam could, and did, find themselves in the war zone.

Other nurses joined the Army after they had been out of school awhile, many because they wanted to go to Vietnam. Still, most lacked adequate experience for the kind of nursing the Vietnam War demanded. Anna Mae Hayes, then Assistant Chief of the Army Nurse Corps, reported that 60 percent of Army nurses in Vietnam had had less than two years of nursing experience; of this 60 percent, most had had less than six months. Nor did the Army, or any other branch of the service, adequately prepare nurses for the carnage they would see in Vietnam.

In the Vietnam War, the small arms used by both sides were specifically designed to inflict massive, multiple injuries, as were the Americans' napalm, white phosphorous, and "antipersonnel" bombs. Furthermore, because the country was small, because Americans had an enormous number of hospitals, and because helicopters — those ubiquitous symbols of the American military presence in Vietnam — could transport the wounded to base camps in a matter of minutes, soldiers lived who, in earlier wars, would have died en route. Even nurses with backgrounds in trauma surgery were unprepared for the kinds of injuries they saw. Traumatic amputations of one or more limbs were routine. Blast wounds were often "so big," said Saralee McGoran, a former Army operating room nurse, "you could put both your arms into them." Becky Pietz, a Red Cross hospital social worker in Vietnam, described a soldier with fragmentation wounds so extensive "his whole body was like someone had taken a cigarette or maybe a hot ice cream scoop and just burned every other half-inch." Because napalm and white phosphorus burn flesh down to the bone, the burn wards — which more often than not were filled with Vietnamese — were particularly gruesome. A Navy nurse told me the burn victims she saw were "essentially denuded. We used to talk about fourth degree burns — you know, burns are labeled first, second, and third degree, but we had people who were burnt all the way through." Often nurses had no terms for either the operations required to save lives or the injuries. "We used to call them horriblectomies and horridzomas," the same nurse said. "Horriblectomies were when they'd had so much taken out or removed. Horridzoma meant the initial grotesque injury but also the repercussion of the injury — the tissues swelling and all that."

Nurses regularly saw GIs who had been wounded by "friendly fire." According to Saralee McGoran, "American artillery created the worst wounds. They would be black. Plus the blast wounds and holes they left were much larger than the other wounds that came in." In addition, nurses encountered diseases they had not been taught to treat: typhoid, TB, malaria, dengue fever, bubonic plague. Lieutenant Colonel Ruth Sidisin, who worked at the air base in Danang, said, "We saw diseases they'd told us people hardly ever got anymore." And, toward the end of American involvement, the larger hospitals established drug wards, where GIs were treated for marijuana, opium, amphetamine, cocaine, and — primarily — heroin addiction. Said a former Army nurse, "Nobody told me I was going to be taking care of so many strung-out motherfuckers. I mean, this was supposed to be a *war*."

Less well known are the 1,300 military women who did nonmedical work in Vietnam. Most were with the Women's Army Corps; over half were enlisted women. They were secretaries and clerks both at MACV (Military Assistance Command, Vietnam) in Saigon and on the larger bases. In addition, women worked as air traffic controllers, photographers, and cartographers. Women were in the Army Signal Corps. They also worked in intelligence and at other jobs requiring security clearance. Pinkie Houser, a personnel sergeant, did top-secret work with the Army Engineer Corps in Vietnam. Another woman talked to me at length about her time as an Army decoder:

"The Army had not had female decoders since World War Two. There were very few of them then. But they decided that women could carry more mental stress than males, so because of this factor they decided to try to get women decoders in the Army Security Agency.

"Now decoding is a mind-type thing. Your only tools are your brain, a red-blue pencil, a triangular-shaped ruler and paper. When they were training you, you'd get pieces of paper with numbers and letters on them and then you'd draw little brands and say, 'Well, this letter is repeated so many times and this letter here is repeated so many times, and this letter is only used once, so it has to be an $X$ or $Z$' —

"In Saigon I used to get messages. I would see body counts and stuff on paper. We would know when certain battles were being formed to take place and where recon units were getting ready to go into."

Civilian women often worked directly with the military. The American Red Cross had a field service staff that helped with arrangements for emergency leaves and generally acted as a liaison between soldiers and families. They also had an in-hospital staff. In addition, the American Red Cross sponsored the Supplemental Recreational Activities Overseas (SRAO) program, which hired college-educated women in their twenties to "boost the morale" of the troops.

During World War II, the SRAO women had been known as "donut dollies." They ran clubs and canteens in rear areas and — more to the point — drove to the front lines in vans equipped for making coffee and doughnuts. Although the name "donut dolly" stuck, in Vietnam SRAO women were also called "chopper chicks" and "Kool-Aid kids." Like the World War II donut dollies, they ran base camp centers where soldiers could play cards, play pool, hang out. In addition, they were paid to — as one former SRAO woman put it — "dream up crazy things to do." They put on style shows for the troops, organized art shows and sing-alongs. And — unlike the original donut dollies — the new donut dollies were "choppered" to heavy combat areas on an almost daily basis. There they served Kool-Aid, chatted with the troops, and led audience participation games.

Army Special Services also employed civilian women. Although their numbers were much smaller, Army Special Services women did the same kind of recreational work the SRAO women did. The USO, perhaps the best known of the military support organizations, hired singers and high-kickers to tour with the big shows headed by entertainers such as Raquel Welch and Bob Hope. And, during the Vietnam War, Armed Forces Radio hired its first woman disc jockey.

Civilian women were stewardesses on Air America and World Airways, which had contracts to fly military personnel and government officials in and out of Vietnam. In Saigon, civilian women were secretaries and receptionists at the U.S. embassy and other government offices; in Danang and Nha Trang, they worked at the consulates. Civilian women also worked as secretaries in the offices of American contractors* in Saigon. And women were among the hordes of free-lance journalists and foreign correspondents based at Saigon's Continental and Caravelle hotels. In the villages and smaller cities, civilian women did undercover work for the CIA. They also worked in Vietnamese schools, orphanages, and hospitals under the auspices of relief organizations such as the Peace Corps, International Voluntary Services, and USAID.

And American women worked with religious organizations. The Mennonite Central Committee sponsored schools and hospitals in Saigon, Nha Trang, Pleiku, and Can Tho. In Quang Ngai, the American Friends Service Committee ran a hospital as well as a rehabilitation center for amputees. Catholic Relief Services sponsored nutrition and medical programs in Saigon, Can Tho, Danang, Qui Nhon and Nha Trang; Church World Services sponsored similar programs all over South Vietnam; and the Seventh Day Adventists and the Christian Missionary Alliance ran Bible schools and hospitals.

Although some areas of the country were harder hit than others, there were no clearly delineated front lines or rear areas in Vietnam. In effect, the entire country was a combat zone. And, as with male veterans, the transition from the "high" of life in the combat zone to the everydayness of life in the States was depressing, difficult, and, in some cases, impossible.

On coming home, life in general seemed dull — all the women I interviewed agreed on this. In addition, most agreed that work was no longer as rewarding. Skills that, in the combat zone, had been painfully developed and finely honed were neither recognized

---

* A "contractor" was an individual who hired himself out to the U.S. mission, the Saigon government, or an American company to perform some job in Vietnam; "contractor" also refers to an American company with an office in Vietnam.

nor respected when women returned to "the World." Lynda Van Devanter, for one, in *Home Before Morning,** tells of being assigned to a hemorrhoid ward after a year in an Army operating room. Others who left nursing, like Saralee McGoran, told of performing doctors' work in Vietnam, while Lily Adams zeroed in on her estrangement from the nurses she worked with when she returned to civilian life. Jeanne Christie, who was with the SRAO, talked about the sense of self she'd become accustomed to in Vietnam: "Over there I'd had responsibility, power, ability. At home I felt I was a totally inept boob."

Relationships presented other problems. "One of the reasons those of us who were there will never get over Vietnam," Anne Allen, a journalist, told me, "is that we developed such deep friendships" — friendships many still craved but found impossible to duplicate. Other women described the emotional walls they learned to build in Vietnam. Others missed "the high of being a round eye [American woman] — the fellows worshipped us!" One way or another, on coming home to a country that didn't want to acknowledge them, a country weary of Vietnam, most women felt a vast confusion. "I'd been waiting and waiting to get back to the World," said a former Army nurse. "But when I got back, all I could think was 'I want to live in Nam.'" Life in the States seemed superficial and self-indulgent; they themselves felt displaced.

The need to talk was perhaps the single overwhelming need of the men and women who had gone to the Vietnam War. But if talking was hard for the men, it was harder for the women. Because their numbers were smaller and because they had worked for such a variety of organizations, the women were more isolated from each other than the men were. This is one reason many women who had gone to Vietnam ended up marrying or living with male veterans: at least there was someone to talk to, someone who — in the words of a former Army nurse — "made you know it had been real." On the other hand, once they returned to "the World," many women were so isolated they didn't even know any male veterans.

Most were also cut off from traditional channels of help. Women who had been with the military quickly learned that the Veterans'

* Her first-person account, published by Beaufort Books, 1983; Warner Books, 1984.

Administration had a history of ignoring women. Those who tried to join established veterans' organizations were often denied membership or shunted off into the ladies' auxiliaries. Furthermore, the force behind the organization of Vietnam veterans was all-male, and combat was the central issue.* Civilian women, even those who had worked with military support organizations, were legally ineligible for government compensation or benefits and technically ineligible for counseling at Vietnam veterans' centers.

"Civilian or military, these women were invisible," said Pam Nissman, an advisor to the Vietnam Women's Memorial Project.†

Officially, women who had been in the military in Vietnam hardly existed; civilian women, officially, didn't exist at all. Nor did these women exist in the popular imagination. From the early sixties until early 1968, media attention had been riveted on the shooting war. Even after the Tet Offensive, when media interest in the war shifted from the battlefield to the shape of the peace table, noncombatants' work in general, and women's work in particular, didn't rate news coverage. Nor did it rate in Hollywood.

Until *Purple Hearts,* in 1983, women were all but absent from Hollywood's Vietnam. John Wayne's *Green Berets,* released in 1968, was the first Hollywood feature about the Vietnam War. No women appear in it. After *The Green Berets* (which occasioned the picketing of movie theaters), Hollywood temporarily backed off from the war. But for a decade it turned out movies in which the protagonists were (male) Vietnam veterans. As Gilbert Adair notes, they "portrayed the returning veteran as incurably 'changed,' almost as much an alien as the faceless enemy with whom he had been in contact."‡ Typical was *Taxi Driver*'s paranoid, obsessed combat vet who stalks a vague evil less through the streets of New York than through some nightmare jungle.

It was a grim stereotype; the Rambo fantasy is even grimmer. But the point here is that, in the popular imagination, Vietnam remained a zone where no woman had been.§ Perhaps it was inconceivable that women had gone to such a dirty, confused war,

---

* Or, in the case of Vietnam Veterans Against the War, the issues surrounding the war itself.
† Begun in 1984 as the Vietnam Nurses' Memorial Project.
‡ In *Hollywood's Vietnam,* p. 84.
§ Vietnamese women, yes. But here we enter the realm not only of sexual but also of racial stereotype.

a war America had lost, a war that bore no resemblance to World War II movies; or perhaps no one wanted to confront the possibility that women, too, might have come back changed. At any rate, with the exceptions of one scene in *Apocalypse Now,* in which Playboy bunnies bump and grind for the troops, and one brief hospital scene in *The Deer Hunter,* Hollywood kept women on the homefront. Women did appear in the television series "M*A*S*H." But "M*A*S*H" was set against the background of Korea; its audience wasn't forced to make connections with Vietnam.

Even the 2.5 million American men who had gone to Vietnam were mostly unaware that American women (with the possible exceptions of Jane Fonda and Raquel Welch) had been there. For, unless he ended up in a hospital, odds were the average soldier wouldn't encounter a nurse. Also off his beaten path were the women who worked with Vietnamese civilians or performed any kind of nonmedical work. And sighting an SRAO woman was, one veteran told me, like sighting a rare bird.

Another explanation for both their invisibility and their silence is that, by and large, women in Vietnam were caretakers and helpmates. They had been trained to take care of people — wounded people, sick people, children. And they "did" for men because, in the military and elsewhere, that's what women did. By training and by habit they downplayed their own feelings and denied their own needs. The men's experiences, or the patient's or the child's feelings, came first. They were used to being minor characters, even in their own lives.

In addition, many women who had been to the war felt cut off from other women of their generation. "They'd been getting married and having kids," said a former SRAO woman, "while I was flying in and out of LZs [landing zones] and fire bases." Jill Mishkel, a former Army nurse, talked about joining a women's rap group: "The women in my rap group all knew I'd been in Vietnam, but we never talked about it — we were too busy talking about the terrible things our mothers did to us when we were three." There were other significant gaps. Younger women still in the military felt estranged from older military women, even those who had been in Vietnam. For, whether or not the younger military women acknowledged it, their lives had been touched by feminist politics. They were likely to be more outspoken. They were certainly more vocal about sexual discrimination and harassment and less tolerant of stereotyping, both of women in the military and of women in general. Yet there were enormous differences among the younger women as a whole, the main one being that some had been military in Vietnam and some civilian.

In the course of doing these interviews, I was repeatedly asked how I came to this book. In other words, what did the Vietnam War have to do with me?

The war didn't affect me directly until 1973. As a kid in the suburbs of north central Texas during the fifties and on through the sixties, I was essentially isolated from anyone who wasn't white and upper-middle-class. In the freshly bulldozed subdivisions around Dallas and Fort Worth — prairies of ranch-styles on streets with names like "Bunker Hill" — people's fathers were commercial pilots, test pilots, math professors, engineers. These were neighborhoods where the adults had barbecues and boozy, late-night bridge parties at which, as I got older, they talked more and more about the "Vietnam conflict." Mostly they talked about how we were winning it — "we" being white, upper-middle-class America.

I can't remember my friends' older brothers going to Vietnam. None of my relatives went — I had one cousin in the Air Force, but he wasn't in Vietnam. In high school my graduating class — the class of 1969 — was all white. Most of them, on graduation, went to Tarrant County Junior College or the University of Texas at Arlington. I went to Southern Methodist University.

There, in 1969 and 1970, my friends and I shared a studied apathy about politics. We didn't talk much about the Vietnam War, except to acknowledge that we didn't want to get our asses shot off, or we didn't want our boyfriends to get *theirs* shot off. Later, at the University of Texas, I made friends who were passionate and outspoken about the immorality of the war. But by then funds for the draft were being cut off and the troop withdrawal was accelerating; day by day, the war pressed against my consciousness less.

In 1973, in graduate school in California, I met someone who wasn't like the people I'd grown up with. Rick was from inner-city Chicago. He'd quit school in ninth grade and gone to work in a factory; in the late sixties he'd been drafted and sent to Vietnam. For three rough years, Rick and I lived together. By the time we went our separate ways, I had an emotional stake in the issues surrounding Vietnam veterans.

And the Vietnam War helped shape my writing. Like everyone else, I watched the war through the flat, nerveless eye of the television. I read about it in *Newsweek* and *Time*. But Vietnam War narratives weren't like the World War II novels I'd devoured in seventh grade, and they weren't like the World War II footage on Walter Cronkite's *The Twentieth Century*. No, unlike World War II novels and *The Twentieth Century* footage, Vietnam War narratives didn't give me any aesthetic pleasure, any sense of the real. They seemed deformed — fragments, images, severed pieces of plot. There was no way to order them, and trying only made the war — the world itself — recede farther and farther from me, leaving me with a weird feeling of dislocation: space would angle away, juxtapositions would become illogical, everything would seem simultaneously fixed and disturbed. After a while, the Vietnam War story became so jumbled and ambiguous it was not a narrative at all. It was a kind of nightmare geometry. And it overwhelmed and undermined everything. There was no organizing principle, no discernible narrative line — instead there was a web of stories, each as confused as my life was.

By the late 1970s, that feeling of dislocation had become a habit of packing up. Many of my friends from college lived the same way I did. We didn't move to take better jobs — we took jobs in order to move. We didn't know why we lived this way. All we knew was that things would never be the same again, that we had, so to speak, crossed the McNamara Line: we were in enemy territory. Living in America, we believed, could only be contrived by drugs — or by moving to ever remoter parts, places where we were less likely to feel passion or be forced to analyze our confusion, places where we weren't required to articulate much of anything; our ideal, it seemed, was an unpeopled universe. When my younger sister would ask me what this moving was all about, I would sense the gap between us. My friends and I were the cutoff point: unlike our younger brothers and sisters, we were close enough in time to our parents to remember their idea of America.

For instance, I remember being in elementary school and saying the Pledge of Allegiance and feeling safe. I remember memorizing, on my own, all three verses of the "Star-Spangled Banner." And I remember reading about the X-15 in *My Weekly Reader* on an afternoon in late spring, when a thunderstorm was turning the sky black and hail the size of golf balls was cracking the classroom windows — and feeling safe. I remember feeling safe. That's something our younger brothers and sisters don't remember.

And, mostly because of the Vietnam War, I had choices my mother didn't have. The feminist movement of the 1970s, which grew out of women's experiences in the civil rights movement and, more directly, the antiwar movement, brought about changes that allowed women to inhabit the world differently than they had a generation or even a decade earlier. Although I came to feminism by an intellectual route, my life, like many, was turned around by a conscious feminist awareness. For one thing, I felt I had the freedom to stay somewhere. Not that I felt any safer, but at least the terrain seemed less alien. I could imagine relationships that would be worth working for. I could imagine a sense of commitment. I could imagine what it was like to care who was President, to care about the arms race, to care in my gut what the fate of the world might be. As far as my work went, I knew I wanted to write about women. And I wanted to do more now than just assess the damage.

But how to explain the grip these stories have on me?

No book has been so hard to give up. No material has so thoroughly let me enter into the lives of others, and no material has so frightened me. For several years I'd been writing about women in extreme psychological and physical circumstances: women on Parris Island, women in South Africa, women in mental institutions. But I had never interviewed someone and been unable to shake her nightmares. I had never checked into a motel and piled the furniture against the door. No, I had never dreaded interviews the way I dreaded these or fled from people the way I fled from the twenty women whose stories are here and the many whose stories are not. Somehow, it all felt too familiar.

I couldn't share my feelings during the hours I sat listening. I had not been to Vietnam. I was an outsider. In the face of what these women were telling me, how could I say I, too, had lived in a war zone? How could I say they were taking me back — much farther back than I wanted to go? How could I talk about my father's World War II memories? Or his drinking, his rages, his death? How could I talk about my mother's silences? How could I talk about the time I was raped or the relationships I survived or the logic of violence by which I lived most of my life?

Inevitably, I feel closer to the women who believe, as I do, that

15

the Vietnam War was not only misguided but was also unjustifiable. And, of those women, a few talked with such power I couldn't let them go. I thought about them constantly, even when I wasn't working. I wrote to them. In response, I got long, passionate letters. Over the last six months, by phone, by letter, in person, I've at last talked out the connections between these stories and my own. In other words, I finally understand what the obsession has been about: in the process of collecting and editing other women's war stories, my own memories became more real.

Looking back now, I realize I may have met some heroines. But my stake isn't in heroines. Rather, it's in ordinary lives made extraordinary by a direct involvement in the war of my generation.

December 30, 1985
South Hadley, Massachusetts

After this interview, I'm not going to be in control of the aftermath. The aftermath is going to be in control of me. But I think the story needs to be told. And if it's going to be told, I want to be part of the telling because I was there and I know what happened because it happened to me.

— Becky Pietz

# 🌿 Debbie Wong (alias)

*Debbie Wong is an American of Indonesian-Chinese heritage. Her mother was a schoolteacher. Her father was a diplomat and a businessman.*

*Debbie's family was "always very, very staunch Catholic, and their primary concern was that I get a good Catholic upbringing. They didn't really care whether I got a good academic upbringing — I was just a girl, they said, who cares — they figured I'd just get married anyway."*

*In 1967, at seventeen, Debbie went on her own to Vietnam. Intermittently for the next three years she lived and worked in Saigon — "I was trying to understand why I had this burning desire to be in Vietnam."*

I KEPT TELLING MY FRIENDS, "I don't know what's going on, but I don't believe half those things printed in the newspapers." My friends were all going to these wonderful places for vacation, but I kept talking about going to Vietnam. Finally my friends just got tired of hearing me talk. "If you really want to know what's going on," they said, "why don't you just go?" They didn't think I'd do it. But their daring me really triggered it off.

My mother didn't think I'd do it either. At that point in time my father had been dead about a year and I didn't have a passport and knew I couldn't get my mother to sign the papers. But I managed to get a passport and went to the States for a week. Back here I got a visitor's visa from the Vietnamese embassy — it only permitted me to stay, I think, a maximum of a week in Saigon. But I knew I had to go, so I just went.

I arrived in Saigon with twenty dollars and no skills of any kind. Now, when I think back on what I did, I'm horrified — but at that point in my life, I believed things would work out. And, amazingly enough, they did.

The first job I got was with the *Saigon Daily News*. I stayed there a month and then got a better-paying job. It was with an American contracting company, an architectural engineering firm. Even after working for them for a year and a half, I didn't know much about what they did. Theoretically they were supposed to build bridges and maintain things, but it was obvious that something was weird. Our office processed piles and piles of papers, but what did the firm have to show for it? For instance, we were running generators, but why did we need three million dollars and all that paperwork to run one lousy generator? Well, anyhow, I worked as administrative assistant to the head of the firm, even though I couldn't type. They wanted me because I spoke English — they were hiring anybody who spoke English. That was the bottom line.

My first year and a half I learned a lot about private sector investments — that took me a long way toward getting my blinkers off. I also made a lot of friends in the military — the company I worked for was on a military base.

A lot of times, because of my Oriental face, my situation was really rough. Just walking down the street I'd get derogatory comments from the GIs. They thought I was a Vietnamese bar girl — only bar girls wore Western clothes, and I was always in blue jeans. The Vietnamese looked down on me. So a lot of the time I was getting harassment from both angles.

At first, my sense of curiosity was so strong that I was almost oblivious to the difficulty of my situation. In other words, nothing computed — the stares and comments just went straight through me. My primary thought was "What the heck is going on in this country?" This kept up for about my first fifteen months.

I led an almost frivolous existence. I don't know how to explain it — there was a war, but the war wasn't in Saigon. Saigon was an old French city. You had wonderful restaurants. You could change dollars on the black market and buy more things than you ever dreamed of. There were other things you could do that seemed to be, well, not right — but OK, like if you saw a jeep parked on the side of the street, if you wanted it, you just drove it off. Ha ha. That's just the way things were. Whoever the jeep belonged to would just go requisition another one, and somebody else would probably drive off with it. Paint it a different color, change the numbers. I myself owned three motorcycles during the time I was there, and every one of them got stolen. Finally I got to the point where I just expected my motorcycle to be stolen.

So it was a very unreal existence. Very unreal. I had money, I had identification cards that would get me in anywhere — working for an American firm, that was one of the benefits — so I could go all over the country. Even though I had Oriental features, I could thumb a ride on a helicopter any day of the week. I could go to Vung Tau, a beautiful little resort in the south, or I could go to Da Lat, a resort up in the mountains. It did not occur to me, at least not at first, that the situation was very unfair. I looked Oriental but I was not, and because I was not Vietnamese I had more freedom than they did — they were third-class citizens in their own damn country. First were Americans, then all the Third Country nationals, then the Vietnamese. I mean, they were born there, they loved that country and still love it, and yet they couldn't go anywhere without their countrymen stopping them and saying, "No, you can't come here. You can't go beyond the checkpoint because you're Vietnamese." When I could hop a helicopter and go anywhere in no time flat.

But my first fifteen months I was not aware of reality. Like once I went up to visit a friend of mine, he was a captain at Cu Chi. When I got on the helicopter I was wearing a little pink dress and little pink shoes — I wasn't dressed for a war, I was dressed for a tea party. Well, Cu Chi was barren, like a desert surrounded by trees, except that the trees were all way out in the distance. There were dirt hooches all over the place, not concrete buildings, just these hut things. And we had a little firefight — flares and rockets and tracers — and I thought it was all very exciting. So I spent two days at Cu Chi and then flew back down to Saigon, where it was still relatively safe.

My first fifteen months I went to embassy parties at least every other night. And the British used to have teas in the afternoon. Once, I remember, I was at the British embassy for tea and I heard this woman absolutely bemoaning the lack of caviar — "Oh, why is there no caviar?" I'm not a very good poet, but I later wrote a long poem about Vietnam, and that line kept coming up. As time went by, I was no longer comfortable at the embassies. The dinners were very extravagant and someone even invented this game called Counter-Insurgency — you sat around playing it at the dinner table — in which some of the guests were Charlie and some were ARVN [Army of the Republic of Vietnam]. A lot of other stuff went on at embassy parties, but I can only tell you off the record. . . .

Also during my first year I met a doctor who proposed to me.

He asked me to marry him and go back to the States forever and live in Kansas City. Well, he was a sweet, adorable man, but marriage was just the furthest thing from my mind. I was where I had to be and I knew I wasn't ready to leave. Because I'd come to find something out, to understand something. And, inside, I was telling myself, "You need to stay a little longer, because what you're seeing now is just veneer."

Not that I didn't try to leave — I did leave, I don't know how many times. I came back to the States, I went to Australia, Europe, Hong Kong. I kept telling myself, "This is it — you've had it!" But something kept pulling me back. It is so hard to try and describe it.

When I came back, I think it was the second time, I started getting friendly with the journalists in Saigon. They worked for papers like the *Washington Post* and the *New York Times,* also magazines like *The New Yorker, Esquire, Time,* and *Newsweek.* And if I thought the world I lived in was unreal — well, the world of the journalists was even more unreal. They lived in beautiful houses or apartments. They all had maids, something that must have struck them as very unreal, because, unlike me, they hadn't grown up with maids their whole life. Well, some of them knew their life was unreal and some of them didn't. Some of them would just go out in the morning and experience the war and then, at the end of the day, go back to the Continental and sit on the patio with a drink. Just like in a Somerset Maugham novel.

There were not very many like Sean [Flynn, the photojournalist and son of Errol Flynn], who had a real love for the Vietnamese. The only one I can really think of is Gloria [Emerson, journalist and author of *Winners and Losers*]. She had so much sensitivity and love in her, and that's why she's haunted today. I used to not understand when the men journalists — they were mostly men in Vietman, there were not many women journalists there — would say, "She's just your typical female journalist." I would have no idea what they meant. And when I finally coaxed it out of them the picture I got was a very negative one. "You have to be hard," they said; "you have to have brass balls, you have to have the right stuff." Well, I think now that a lot of it was jealousy. Gloria could get to the heart and soul of a story so naturally — whereas they could only try.

My second and third years were the more important years of

my stay in Vietnam. That's when I — and everyone else — began to see reality. It started with the Tet offensive. Suddenly the safe zone just is not safe anymore. Suddenly it's "Wait a minute! Something's wrong! This should not be happening!" Like you're walking down the street and you come across mutilated bodies. Or the little paper vendor you bought the *Saigon Daily News* from just the day before is dead now. The *Saigon Daily News:* it was probably the worst-written English newspaper ever printed, but I loved it. It was part of the culture. I used to sit on the patio of the Continental sipping a drink and reading it. And if, at the end of the day, the kid who made his living selling it had some copies left, I'd buy every one. Just to help him out — I thought of it as my contribution.

But my little paperboy was killed. And other things started happening, so that I became more and more aware, started wanting to try and do something. There was this whole colony of lost kids in Saigon. One little girl in particular I used to notice. She was about seven but she looked four. She just wandered the streets, living out of garbage cans. One day I said to myself, "I'd really like to get her out of Vietnam, get her into a nice, safe place." So I wrote my mother. I said, "There's this child who I can't adopt because I'm too damn young — they'd just look at me and laugh. So would you please adopt her?" My mother hemmed and hawed and finally said OK, she'd do it if I took care of all the paperwork.

I knew the traditional channels, the official ones, would have gotten me nowhere fast — by the time the process came to an end, who knew where the child would be? So I went to a guy I knew at the American Embassy and asked him to pull some strings. He kept telling me, "Well, we'll see what we can do . . ." Finally all I was getting was "We'll see what we can do —" so I said, "Look, if you're at a crossroads because of some legwork, maybe I could do it." And he said, "Debbie, why are you so worried about this child? There are hundreds and hundreds like her." "So?" I said. "So she's a gook," he said. "You've got to look at it that way . . . she's just a gook." "I'm a gook, too!" I screamed at him — I was hurt and angry; I was crying. "You're not a gook," he said. Then he said it again, and I said, "Look at my eyes! I'm a gook! I've got 'gook' written on my forehead!"

Looking back, I don't think he was trying to be detrimental. I just think he was trying to prepare me so I wouldn't be in shock.

Because, of course, I was never able to do anything for that child.

There was another child, another little girl, who really used to haunt me. When I first saw her she was about eleven or twelve. She lived in the doorway of a big apartment building and anyone who walked by there raped her. She was raped and raped and raped and raped, until finally she lost her mind. She'd walk down the streets with her dress lifted, showing her privates to anyone. When she was about thirteen she got pregnant. I don't know, after that, what became of her. But she used to haunt me — still haunts me. I ask myself why I didn't do something. There were a lot of orphanages around, I could have tried to get her into one. I don't know why I didn't. I could have but I didn't.

I would say that the Vietnamese gravitated toward me a lot more than toward non-Asian Americans. Like my maid — when I first hired her, I hired her alone. Then one daughter moved in, and then another daughter, and by the time of Tet the whole family was living in the kitchen and one little room in the back. My maid, during Tet, was really remarkable. On the third or fourth day of the fighting, when things had calmed down a bit, she asked me for money to go out and buy us food. Well, I don't know where or how she got it but she did. For several days she kept all of us fed.

Then, finally, I decided it was absurd for her to be the one risking her life on the streets. So I borrowed her Vietnamese clothes — I knew that if I went out in western clothes, I'd for sure get shot — got on my scooter and went out to the black market. I was not as talented as she was, though — she was coming back with fresh food, whereas I only came back with cigarettes.

At some point we were evacuated to this big building next door. I remember lying on the roof there all night long, looking at the tracers and the helicopters. I remember looking down into the alleyway and seeing people being shot. People were running around. There were firefights. For the first time, I knew the war had come to me. It was very real. Yet, at the same time, I wasn't afraid I would get killed. It's that personal fable, you know, that belief that you're immortal — I was still living with that.

I don't think I ever knew the true meaning of friendship before Tet. My maid was wonderful to me. And this guy I knew, a military policeman at Bien Hoa, came down a number of times in his jeep just to see if I was OK. "You're crazy to come here!" I'd say to him. But he just kept coming back, risking his life because he cared about me. For me that was a real awakening. I knew how scary it was out on the streets — your heart was pounding, you thought you were going to pee, you knew that, if anyone stopped you, you'd have a heart attack.

I left Vietnam again after Tet. It wasn't hard to get visas out. The main thing I remember about leaving that time was the airplane taking off. It didn't take off gradually — it went straight up.

I stayed in the States maybe nine months and was just a complete misfit. While I was here, in San Francisco, I dated this Jewish dentist whom I effectively managed to screw up. I mean, I was off the wall, a complete dingbat from the word go, just absolutely zippety-doo-da. I mean, I was out in the ozone somewhere, because my mind was still rolling around Vietnam. I couldn't communicate with this guy, didn't even try. He was in love with me. But all I could think about was Vietnam — I still wanted to put all the pieces together, still wanted to understand what the hell was going on. I mean, why were we — the Americans — calling Tet a victory? It wasn't a victory — they'd just come in and killed a lot of people and thought they'd made Saigon safe. Well, safe for what? The whole thing made me sick.

When I told the dentist I was going back to Vietnam his attitude was "You've got to get this out of your system, honey — you poor thing, you'll be home again soon!"

Well, I took off. And this time I had my real awakening. Because this time I met Sean.

Sean was a very, very remarkable man. I guess a good word to describe him is *Apache* — you know how Apaches are; they're wild. They're not like other people.

Sean knew Vietnam. He knew Vietnam and loved the people. He'd spend weeks out in the field with the grunts, knew the country better than they did. He was not like the other men journalists. And the troops loved him. They were always coming to the house looking for him. I'd answer the door and they'd say, "Just tell him so-and-so came by —" Everyone in Saigon knew and loved him — because Sean had a sense of loyalty to people that absolutely knew no bounds.

Actually, I had met Sean a year or so earlier. When I first met him, I couldn't stand him, would have nothing to do with him. He was still in his volatile period then — Sean was a very complicated man. In addition to being generous and gentle he had a violent streak. But when I ran across him again, in Bali, he was twenty-nine and very, very calm. He had gone to Bali to get over a beautiful Indonesian girl — he'd gotten in a little trouble because of her in Djakarta.

I remember sitting on the beach with Sean in Bali. I'd listen for hours while he talked. Never before had I heard anyone talk about the beauty of Vietnam. And I had never, till then, understood much about the politics.

So Sean taught me to see Vietnam differently — to see the country through his eyes. He also taught me that it was OK to be yourself, with all your foibles and imperfections, with all your weirdnesses and quirks. I remember once — we were lying in a hammock in the apartment — I told him that, all my life, I'd been taught to think you had to be perfect for a man to really care for you. And Sean said, "Well, there are things you do that bug me, but so what? Nobody is perfect. I'm sure there are things I do that bug you." Well, he hadn't done a thing to bug me, and the first thing that went through my mind was, "Oh no — what am I doing to bug him?" So I asked him what I was doing. And he says, "It doesn't matter, because it's a tiny, tiny thing." I couldn't believe it — I had never met a man who was so loving and caring.

Well, we went back to Vietnam from Bali and lived together a few months. I did not want to leave Bali, but Sean said we had to, we had to go back to Vietnam because the war was going to Cambodia. I remember we were having breakfast one morning when we heard about the American ship that had been hijacked up the Mekong to Phnom Penh. "Who are they trying to kid?" Sean said. "The war is going to Cambodia." And a few months later the war did go to Cambodia. So did Sean. We had plans to meet in Vientiane, but Sean never made it. As you probably know, he was captured. I never saw him again.

I went on to Vientiane to look for him. We kept getting reports that he'd been sighted moving first in one direction, then another. Nobody was sure. At first we thought it would be better if he'd been captured by the Khmer Rouge than by the others, but later, when we learned what animals the Khmer Rouge were, we stopped hoping that.

I remember, when I first learned he was captured, thinking, "Why did he do this? I'm going to kill him!" And then I started trying to figure out how I was going to find him. The American military didn't give a shit about him — he was just an expendable statistic, some asinine Yank who was getting in the way of their war. So I started knocking on embassy doors. I went to the Red Chinese, to the Russians, left CARE packages on their doorsteps. I went through all the diplomatic channels. I got a car with the Quaker emblem on it and drove from Saigon to the border and on across into Cambodia.

What I saw in Cambodia was carnage. Just carnage. One beautiful little village I had seen before the invasion was now destroyed completely. There were bloated bodies in the wells. Bloated bodies in the stream. Dead buffalo, even the buffalo — everything was deserted. I remember looking for Sean and thinking about how he'd taught me to talk with people. Villagers. I had learned to do that with Sean. Only I hadn't done it with the intensity that he had. I mean, Sean, that man could talk a bird out of a tree. He could talk to anyone and make them feel like they were special.

Then there came a period, after he was captured, when I made the rounds of opium dens. It was opium dens and more opium dens. Till I got to the point where, when I looked in the mirror, what I saw was the head of a skeleton. I was very thin, very drawn, very haunted.

Losing Sean was the beginning of the end. A number of my friends were shot — it seemed every time I turned around another one was dead or dying. After a few months I knew it was time to leave for good. I didn't want to leave — I believed Sean was still alive somewhere. But I had to. I had to come back here and try to pull my life together.

For years, in my inscrutable Oriental way, I just kept everything inside me. Most of the men I dated back here had not been to Vietnam. They didn't know what I'd been through, maybe didn't really believe it was possible to go through it. So I kept my distance. I associated off and on with the Vietnam Veterans Against the War, but even some of them didn't understand where I was coming from. I wanted, more than anything, the company of women, especially after I found out that — Well, after Sean was captured, it seems the big thing among the male journalists in Saigon was to see who could get Sean's princess in bed first. I did not find this out till much later, but when I did I was just livid. I said, "Shit on them — shit on men." That was when I started to develop friendships with women. It didn't matter to me at all that they hadn't been in Vietnam. I was tired of trying to cope privately — I wanted to learn how to be a human being again.

I don't regret having gone to Vietnam. Even though it was so traumatic for me, I wouldn't change one minute of it.

But I ache over Vietnam. I ache because it was such a beautiful country and we managed to cream the crap out of it. We didn't stop to learn about the culture, we didn't ask the peasants what they wanted, we didn't or wouldn't think. We made beggars out of an entire nation — a nation of very proud people — and then turned around and said, "Ha! Look at these beggars!" We didn't think for one minute that the people of Vietnam had any rights. We didn't even think they were human — it was "Gooks don't bleed, gooks don't feel pain, gooks don't have any sense of loyalty or love." And you know, we're making the same sickening mistake in Central America. As Sean would have said, "Come on, guys!"

I still have nightmares. I still wake up screaming and don't know what I'm screaming about until I calm down. And then I remember. In one nightmare I'm up in a chopper again with this guy who wants to impress me. He's making a sudden raid, swooping down to shoot at something. I don't know what he's shooting at — we're just swooping down toward a paddy field, spraying the entire area.

And Sean? If he were alive, he'd probably be in Asia somewhere. Or in Central America, covering the war. Or maybe we'd be in a hut on the beach, with banana trees, coconut trees, the sunrise. That was Sean's idea of heaven, and so what if it was unrealistic? He was entitled to that. Yeah, I like to think that, if he'd survived, we would have children. And that they'd all grow up to be Apaches, gentle Apaches, like Sean.

*Debbie Wong is a nurse.*

# Lieutenant Colonel (Retired)
# Ruth Sidisin

*Ruth Sidisin grew up in Roselle, New Jersey. Her father was director of traffic at the Jersey City railroad yard, "where he could see Lady Liberty from his tower window. His family had come over from Czechoslovakia, from a town about twenty-five or thirty miles south of Poland. At Ellis Island there wasn't a letter in English that was a 'zha,' so the name was just spelled 'zsidisin,' pronounced 'zhudician.' It sounded like 'sedition.' Then, when my father graduated ninth grade, he was so sick and tired of being at the end of the alphabet, the back of the bus, the end of the line with 'zs,' that he took the 'z' off and made it sound like 'citizen.' So we were patriotic citizens."*

*Ruth's mother, whose family came from Minsk, Russia, had been in the Red Cross during World War I. "She had helped out in the hospitals and did private duty after the war. And I wanted to be a nurse from the time I was three or four, when my brother cut his finger and I put a Band-Aid on it."*

*In 1949, after completing two years at what was then New Jersey College for Women, Ruth entered the Johns Hopkins Hospital School of Nursing. In 1955, three years after graduating, she joined the Air Force Nurse Corps and stayed in for twenty-five years.*

*A Vietnam volunteer, Ruth was stationed at Tan Son Nhut, at the 21st Casualty Staging Flight, from December of 1968 until December of 1969. She worked as a staff nurse and as charge nurse of the dispensary ward.*

I WAS NOT A YOUNGSTER when I went to Vietnam. I was thirty-nine when I went over. I turned forty while I was there. And when you're forty, you feel a long way from being nineteen, which was the average age of the people who were over there.

Being older than them was some help. At least I'd been around. At least I'd seen a bit of life and so forth, unlike most of the nurses in the Army and the young ones in the Air Force. They were just kids of twenty-one or twenty-two. Still, there was no way to prepare yourself for what went on in Vietnam. Lord knows I wasn't out in the boonies, but that didn't stop me from seeing what happened. Because in Vietnam every day was disaster day.

So age was some help, but not much. Neither was experience. I'd been in Japan. I'd been in Washington in 1963, was working the evening of Kennedy's assassination so I saw everything that happened when they brought the body back. Also I was in Turkey and in Tucson, Arizona. But not even working with earthquake victims or in the emergency room of a big hospital could equal what I saw in a single day in Vietnam.

There was a whole variety of just plain trauma. There were belly wounds, amputations, head injuries, burns. On top of that they all had infections and complications. They had things we'd never heard about in school — things some of the physicians had never even heard about — and diseases they told us people hardly ever got any more. Dengue fever. Malaria. Hepatitis. Bubonic plague. Bubonic plague they got from rats. Those rats were really something. I don't want to gross you out, but I have to tell you about this one guy who forgot to wash his hands before he went to sleep. It was in an area where there were lots of rats. Anyhow, this guy had just had a peanut butter sandwich, and when he went to sleep and dangled his arm over the edge of his cot, a rat went for that peanut butter — and ate most of his finger.

Some days you felt you'd lived a lifetime in just a week. Because Vietnam was not John Wayne on the beach at Iwo Jima. It was not ketchup on make-believe wounds. It was more like a grotesque form of "can you top this," because each time you thought you'd seen the ultimate, something else would come along.

I remember one young man with beautiful blond hair who came in blinded and missing one of his arms and both of his legs. He also had a belly wound. Well, thank God he couldn't see my face when he said, "Nurse, today's my twenty-first birthday." Because that was one of those times when you just couldn't have let them see it. When you smiled and smiled while you were there taking care of them so that afterward you could go home to your hootch and cry.

Now, there were, of course, some of the people who drank, but I think most of us just sort of got by by sharing with one another. Friendships, talking — I met the most beautiful people of my life in Vietnam. Plus some of us either adopted people or were adopted. Like I became a mom to the Security Police. Plus when I first got there there was this lieutenant colonel male-type in the next BOQ [bachelor officers' quarters] upstairs. I was real sick when I first got there, but after I'd sort of recovered a bit I was standing outside my door one day with my hair stringy from sweat. This lieutenant colonel came over to me and said, "You sure look terrible." I said, "Thanks a lot." Then he said, "No, I don't ever think I've seen anyone in my whole life who's looked so puny, like they felt so rotten —" Well, he scrounged some paint and came over to my room. It was a room that hadn't been used for a while before I got there, and it had this wall that at first I thought was green but that turned out to be mold. So he washes the walls down to get rid of the mold and paints them and rearranges the furniture, and then he gets the screen fixed so I won't be eaten alive by mosquitoes. After that he became a good friend. It was just a friendship type of relationship, nothing further than that. And it was like that a lot, sometimes in different ways.

I guess I don't know any nurses who weren't adopted by guys. And the things they did for us. They would find trucks with, shall we say, back doors that didn't work properly, so that steaks were always falling out of them just when they passed our quarters. Or chickens. Or hamburger. And my heavens, if they weren't used up ... Or maybe the guys would get a parachute and hang it between two hootches so we could eat there, get away from the boiling sun. Lots of little things like that. Or like what happened with me and the Security Police. They were the boys that guarded the perimeter, out on the edge of the base.

It started when I first got there. When I was sick and in a fog — you know, when I thought the mold on the walls was green paint. Well, every evening I'd hear the rumbling of heavy artillery going by. After a while — after I'd come to and started to realize where I was — I'd drag myself over to the door and wave at the guys. And every night they'd wave and yell and whistle at me, until one night when these sergeants came by in their jeep and stopped. "Ma'am, we're afraid the Security Police have sort of offended you." And I thought, well, if they have I sure haven't noticed it. So I said, "Oh, no, nothing like that." Then one of the sergeants said, "They've sort of taken to calling you Mom." And I thought, Good grief, if I'd gotten married right out of high school like all my girlfriends did, I'd have kids the age of those guys. So I said, "Well, look, I'm flattered. They can call me Mom if they want." And every night after that, unless I was on R and R or something, they'd wave and shout and yell "Mom!" Sometimes, in the mornings, they'd invite me over for breakfast. And once a month, when they had their hail-and-farewell barbecues, they'd come get me in Ruthie the Screaming Mini — the mini-gun tank they'd named after me. They'd come get me, too, on my days off. I'd have my steel pot on my head, my flak jacket and cammies on, and we'd ride out to the perimeter and just visit. After a while I really thought of them as my sons. They were beautiful boys.

The day I was due to leave some of my Security Police boys picked up this other gal, Captain Karen Baareman, and I in Ruthie the Screaming Mini and drove us down to the plane. They kept apologizing, saying, "Too bad the rest of the guys can't make it — too bad they're all asleep." Well, I'd been sitting on the plane maybe five minutes when I heard this announcement: "Major Sidisin, will you come to the front of the plane." So I went and looked out and — what do you think I saw? Trucks. Jeeps. Mini-guns. Big guns. All kinds of vehicles filled with my sons — maybe four hundred — who had come to see me off. Well, I tell you, I dissolved. I got off the plane and cried and kissed and hugged every one of them.

I don't know if you know it, but the heroines of all the nurses over there were the Army nurses. Those gals were terrific. Sometimes they'd come in to stay with us for a weekend or a night, just to get away from the field hospitals. I was always so struck by them — those young, young faces and ancient eyes, just like on the statues in Washington. Yeah, they were eyes that had looked into hell. Not that the Air Force and Navy nurses didn't work hard — but you know, the Army nurses just never got a break. And they were young gals. So young.

I don't mean this to sound foolish or anything, but the year I spent in Vietnam was the most satisfying year of nursing I ever had. Because you got to give good nursing care without all the Mickey Mouse paperwork. If you needed something, you didn't have to make out fifty-five forms in quadruplicate, you could just pick up the phone and call Danang. "Hey, we've just run out of such and such, you got any up there?" And they'd plop it on a plane and send it down. And those boys were the best patients in the whole world. Thinking about the Army nurses kept us going a lot of the time, but thinking about those dear, sweet boys got us through some of the worst.

Because no matter how much our feet hurt, we at least had feet

31

to stand on. No matter how much we had a headache, we at least had all the brains inside our heads. If our arms were aching from lifting people out of bed, we could at least remind ourselves that we had arms. Speaking of arms, I can remember seeing two guys, each minus an arm, pushing a guy that had no legs in a wheelchair. Yeah, if there was ever an example of brotherhood and helping and doing and love, that was it. I really feel very fortunate and very blessed that I was able to go to Vietnam and do what I could do.

I had some hard adjustments to make when I came back. I found myself thinking inside all the time of Vietnam but I could never show it. Plus I was taking care of patients who had not been through the same life experience that either I or the patients I cared for in Vietnam had. I'd find myself thinking inside, saying things to myself like, "What in the world is this person who just had a little old plain appendectomy making such a big to-do about? Why is this person who just had his gall bladder worked on so worried, when there are people over there with all these god-awful things wrong with them — and they're busy worrying about their buddies, or helping other people?" This is why it was good I stayed in the military after I got back. I could call up one of my friends who'd been over there with me when the feelings and emotions got to be too much. I could say, "Hey, you know, I'm having troubles." And she'd say, "What do you mean?" And I'd say, "Every time I walk on the ward I keep seeing guys I was taking care of in Nam. I find that, inside, I'm very impatient with these people I'm taking care of over here." And she'd say, "Well, we're all feeling that way," and I'd tell myself, "Ruth, you have to remember that these people have not been through the same things as the people you were taking care of over there, so you have no right to judge or let this guide the way you feel about them. Because you can't possibly expect someone who has never seen an elephant to know what one looks like." And then I would be all right.

Sometimes, in my mind's eye, I still see things I saw over there. Like the blond kid I was telling you about. Or the little Vietnamese kids and their families going through the garbage. They used to climb up inside the garbage trucks, with the rats and mice and everything. But mostly I see our kids, the guys. Because there are things you can never rub out, you just learn to live with them.

When I first got back I had insomnia a lot. Plus I was afraid of noises — like a car would backfire and I would jump ten feet in the air. And I remember one time I was standing at the front desk of a hospital talking to the gal who was making appointments. Some workmen were changing the ceiling in the entranceway of the hospital, you know, from the old-fashioned vault-type thing to the dropped ceiling, and one of the plastic panels fell. Well, I almost gave myself a concussion diving under the desk. Things like that. But you learn to carry on.

For a long time I thought I'd put Vietnam behind me. But in the last two years I've cried more tears than I have in the previous quite a few. I think what it is, a lot of the stuff that I had bottled up because I was busy — I think it finally hit.

But I consider it an honor to have served in Vietnam. Even though I certainly did not agree with the business overseas of visits to Hanoi by certain unnamed individuals, and even though I think everybody's son and daughter should have served equally. No, there was no excuse for some things that happened over there. But I've never regretted going into the Air Force or going to Vietnam, even with all the things that happened. In the end, you have to forgive. I figure I've got too much to do in this world to harbor hatred. You can't harbor love and hatred in your heart at the same time, and I'm too busy trying to make my own little corner of the world better to waste time on people who don't deserve it to be wasted on. Because you never know how much time the good Lord gives you, so you might as well make it worthwhile while you're here.

The gist of it is that I'm so glad they're finally recognizing that there were women over there. And that the women saw as much as the guys did, but in a different way. This should finally end the idea that a woman is supposed to give and give and give, and make everything nice-nice, and be an Earth Mother and console everyone all the time without receiving emotional support themselves. Because if you believe women don't need to be replenished, you're a fool. That kind of thinking is just a bunch of garbage.

Yeah, staying in the military made a whole lot of difference as far as attitude and adjustment. Because in the military there were other gals and guys to replenish and affirm you. The young ones that got out at old Travis [Air Force Base], spent maybe a year Stateside, were processed out and sent home — they found that nobody gave a darn, that they had no one to talk to. It was almost as if they had been on Mars and come back to reality. Or as if they'd been in reality and come back to Mars.

*Now retired, Ruth Sidisin lives in Sumter, South Carolina, where she is active in church and civic affairs. She is a member of several veterans' groups, including the Vietnam Veterans of South Carolina and the Veterans of Foreign Wars. Ruth is an active organizer for Vietnam veterans and frequently speaks to veterans' groups on the role of women in Vietnam.*

# Pinkie Houser

*Pinkie Houser was born in Autaugaville, Alabama, and grew up on a farm near there. Her father raised cotton. Her mother took care of the nine Houser children, of whom Pinkie is the youngest.*

*"On the property where we lived there were three black families, and we were all related. There was also this white family. We all grew up together, got along just like we were one family. Autaugaville is really just a little family town. Both my parents were from there. There's even a street named after us.*

*"My brothers and sisters had to pick cotton. But by the time I came along, I didn't have to. I don't know if it was because I was younger, but my family was overly protective of me. Because of the fact that they bought everything for me, they wouldn't let me work while I was going to high school. And believe it or not, on junior prom night my brother and cousin were waiting outside for me, to escort me back home behind my date and I in the car.*

*"So my family being overprotective was one of the reasons why, when I finished school, I decided to leave home."*

*In 1964, after graduating from Autauga County Training School, Pinkie joined the Army. She volunteered for Vietnam in 1968 and in September of 1969 reported to Long Binh, where she spent a year as a personnel sergeant with the Army Engineer Corps. Her work was classified.*

W HEN I FINISHED SCHOOL I went to Chicago and stayed with a brother and sister there. I had just turned seventeen because of how my birthday fell — you know, we graduated in May and my birthday wasn't until October. Anyway, I got there and they were getting ready to send me to the University of Illinois. Only I wasn't ready to handle college. So I took off one day while they were working, and up on West Madison I found this recruiting station. I went in, talked to the Army recruiter, took the test, and they sent the paperwork home to Alabama for my parents to sign.

That night I talked to my mom. She told me to do whatever I wanted to do, if it was to benefit me, and they would sign the consent. My brother and sister were very angry. He had just gotten out of the Air Force, and of course he was telling me all the bad things about the military. But I'm a pretty headstrong person. I said, "Well, it's something I want to do. If I don't like it, then I can get out." But I signed up for three years.

I took basic at Fort McClellan, Alabama, and AIT [Advanced Individual Training] at Fort Leonard Wood, Missouri. From there I went to Fort Eustis, Virginia, and was there about a month. They had put me on a levy for Fort Knox — a levy is you hold a MOS [Military Occupational Specialty] that is needed at another post. If there is an abundance of this particular MOS at one fort, then they will select so many persons to be transferred. So I was selected to go to Fort Knox.

That march they had in 1964 in Alabama — I had just gotten home on leave that Saturday afternoon and they had walked through Saturday morning. They came right through where I live, right in Autaugaville. They came from Selma right through Highway 14, which took them right into Montgomery. Which, because of that, a lot of people said, "If you had been there, would you have joined the march?" I said, "Nope, I would not have." They also used to say, "Tell me about in Montgomery, if you rode one of the buses, you rode in the back instead of sitting up front." Well, at the time I wasn't riding on buses, but if I had been I wouldn't have sat at the back. The way I look at it, my money is the same as anyone else's.

When I was at Fort Knox — they were very prejudiced up there — I'd go in these stores, like in a shopping mall, and she'd take the money out of my hand when I paid for something but then when she gave me back my change she'd lay it on the counter. I'd look at her, and one time I said, "That item I just bought. I don't want it — in other words, give me back my money. It's just as good and the same color as anybody else's. If you can take it from me, you can hand it back to me" — I'm that way now. If you have to put my money on the counter, I don't want your product. I can easily go someplace else.

But you ask what didn't seem right to me personally to have joined in the march that day — I'm going to give you an easy copout. For one thing, I was in the military and couldn't partici- pate, and for another, my folks wouldn't have let me done it. But even so, I wouldn't have done it because it's against my policy —

even if they came through Columbus today, I still wouldn't do it. Now, I'm sure probably my friends would feel differently, but it's not going to accomplish any more by me being out there marching. Because the world is not going to change. It's going to always remain the same. And you go out, you try to do something — you know, you bust your butt — and you're either going to get killed or you're going to get hurt. I love myself too much for that. You know, I just wouldn't do it. I really wouldn't. So that is how I felt about the march in sixty-four through Alabama.

But about sixty-five, sixty-six, the Vietnam War came around, and I don't know, for some reason I wanted to go. By that time I was the company clerk with the WAC [Women's Army Corps] Company at Fort Knox. Which, a company clerk, you can say is the first sergeant's assistant, but even though I only held the rank of PFC I was acting first sergeant for, I don't know, numerous times — when she was absent, it was just like I was in command. Well, I did my job so well that, when I came down on the levy for Germany, they took me off four times. I didn't want to go to Germany. But, like I said, I was dead set on going to Vietnam.

I was at Fort Knox four years. I went from a PFC to an SSG E-6 within that period. Then I reenlisted for six years to go to Vietnam. Well, when I was home on leave they called me and said there was a P.R. job in Washington at the Department of Defense. If I had taken that job, they would have changed my orders and I would not have gone to Vietnam. But I don't know, I just wanted to be there in the war. I felt like I wasn't serving my country enough by being at Fort Knox. I don't know, it's kind of hard to explain, but like I said, once I make up my mind to do something, I do it. A lot of times I don't know the reason, but this was something I had to do.

My parents didn't want me to go. Still, again, they said, "If it's what you want to do, do it." So, after thirty days' leave, as the time got nearer and nearer, of course, you know, the nerves start getting to me. But I left, went over from McCord Air Force Base in Tacoma, Washington. I was with the 101st Airborne out of Fort Campbell, Kentucky — there were about three hundred GIs on the flight and two of us females. They couldn't fly us into Long Binh because it was too late at night, so we landed in Danang and stayed in the nurses' barracks. The next day they flew us to Bien Hoa and bused us into Long Binh. I tell you, when I got there, I just sat and looked and said to myself, "What am I doing here? Here I came all these thousands of miles — why am I here?"

The first three weeks it was kind of rough. I didn't really know anyone, and the girls in the WAC company just weren't too friendly. But then one night I was laying in my bed and all of a sudden my bed started moving — it's, like, three in the morning — and I jump and say, "What's going on?" And my roommate says, "The B-52s are bombing about fifteen miles from here." You know, my bed was going from here . . . and then it would come back over here. . . . And the next day I went down to the PX [Post Exchange] and bought me a carton of cigarettes and, of course, beer — which was fifteen cents a can. Before that, I didn't smoke, I didn't drink. But after I started drinking beer I started knowing some of the people.

So anyway, they took me up to Misery Hill, which was USAV — United States Army, Vietnam, that's how it is — and I was assigned from USAV to a unit called USAEV, which is United States Army Engineers, Vietnam. It consisted of fifteen officers and one enlisted personnel, which was me. There was another unit in our outfit that also had a female E-6. Her name was Jackie. With a total of thirty men in that command, we were the only women, and both of us were black.

The mission we had was top secret. What we did, I can only say we handled the power and the bridges throughout Vietnam. The section I had with the fifteen officers did something different than Jackie's did. Which, you know, we couldn't talk about what we did because of the defense. I had a clearance that said whatever went on, it was for me to know and nobody else. Because if it was for everyone to know, then I wouldn't have the clearance.

When you have that type of top secret clearance, I could of went out and talked about it. But then I would have been put in a situation like these people that were spies. They could have clarified me as a spy because I shot off my mouth. Even though the war is over, I can't tell about what we did. Like I was talking the other day to a guy, and he said, "Were you at Long Binh?" I said, "Yes." He said, "Well, can you tell me where we had all of our heavy power? Because I know you know." I said, "No, I couldn't tell you that." I said that was something I couldn't say, and I think you can basically talk to anybody and they'll probably tell you the same thing.

I can tell you I'd go out sometimes with the officers. We'd fly to Pleiku or Danang or wherever we had to go if there was a problem with a bridge or power. I could put it like, say, I was maybe more like a secretary, I could put it that way. You know, I'd take notes on what's wrong with this or what's wrong with that. So we more or less inspected, and I took notes. When we went out, I had to wear a bulletproof vest and a .45. The .45 wouldn't fit around my waist because we couldn't get the straps small enough, so I had to put it across my shoulders. I carried the .45 on my side. Because I was only weighing like ninety or ninety-two pounds, the vest weighed almost as much as I did.

We worked from six to six, or however long it took to get the job done. Even in the office, when I worked there, it was six in the morning until six or seven at night. I was called "personnel sergeant" — the MOS I had was 72-Hotel — but it really didn't have anything to do with what I did over there. It had nothing to do with it. In the office I did all the typing, and at night the ribbons and carbons and all that had to burned. In addition, I was my colonel's driver, which that job I took upon myself. I had a civilian-type jeep, but it was green like the Army jeep, and when we would get off in the evening time, we would go over and talk to the troops at the Twenty-fourth Evac [Evacuation Hospital] and see if we could bring them anything.

So we'd bring them things, to bring their morale up. Because some of them were just down, they were really pitiful. What I really couldn't understand . . . I don't know, some of the things that I seen, some of the things I heard — I think they will stick in my mind as long as I live.

Like bodies of the GIs. Eighteen-year-old guys. What the Viet Cong did to us, and how they did it to us. Things that they had no reason to do, except that you're an American — You know, I can understand why we did a lot of things that we did because of what was done to us. I saw, in the hospital, bodies that were not recognizable — like I say, we could walk out of our back door and be in the main entrance to the hospital. There were guys that were, like, in helicopter crashes, or Charlie may have taken a grenade and threw it into their hootch — the Viet Cong, they were mean, evil people. They had a POW camp at Long Binh also. It was like a hospital — these people were supposed to be sick — but an American could walk by, like females, and they would grab ahold of the fence and be talking to us in Vietnamese. I'm sure they'd be cussing us out. You know, we didn't understand what they'd be saying, but it was like if they could have gotten ahold of us, they would have killed us right there. And I shouldn't say this, but I'd just pick up a rock and throw it at the fence.

It wasn't only that I was scared. It was just that we were trying to help them, you know, and they didn't want it.

It was a war we shouldn't have been in — which everybody, military and nonmilitary, said the same thing. We didn't have any reason for being there. But the fact was we were there, and we did the best we could.

You had to be careful when you went to downtown Saigon. Like we'd go down maybe to eat in the Air Force mess hall or something. If you saw a little three- or four-year-old kid, of course you give them a candy bar — that was just something that we did because the little kids liked chocolate. But the little kid could have a satchel on him full of live grenades. If he didn't know how to pull the pin, they may push him out somewhere in a crowd of GIs, and the kid would explode. Or a lot of times, if they were big enough — five or six years old — they would take it and pull the pin and they would throw it so it was always in a crowd where only Americans were.

I never saw anything like this happen. But a lot of the officers in my section did. Like they'd be down and they'd come back and they would tell us, you know, about what happened.

The worst thing I think that I encountered in Nam was the smell of human flesh burning. I don't think you have ever encountered that and I don't think you want to, but it is an odor that's hard to explain. Once it gets in the nostrils, it would stay there I guess for two or three weeks. Maybe it could be just in your mind that makes you smell it, but you know, the hospital was right in back of us. They had this big old incinerator about the size of my neighbor's little shed back there and each morning, I guess when they amputated, they would go out and they would burn it. Try to eat breakfast after smelling something like that — no way, you just couldn't do it. You never got used to something like that. And the whole country itself, it smelled bad — you know what a paper mill smells like? I think for the whole thirteen months I couldn't get used to the smell of it. When I first got there, it was just like you'd gag because it smelled horrible.

So you want to know what were my feelings toward the Vietnamese: well, I didn't like them at all. I shouldn't hate them but again I think I have a reason to because of the war. Personally, I don't even eat Oriental food. Because when I was over there we had a Vietnamese restaurant down the street called Loon Foon and I'd gotten so I really liked the sweet-and-sour pork. Only it just didn't taste like the pork over here, you know. It was kind of hard. Well, I come to find out their delicacy over there was dog and cat. That's what they cooked in those restaurants. And I found out the other day, they took a survey here, and ninety percent of the Oriental restaurants in the U.S. cook dog. That's why I won't touch it. My brother-in-law used to tell me, he was in Korea, he'd say he went out back to tinkle one night over there, and he looked up on the clothesline and there were big old rats that had come out of the woods. They had them hanging by their tails, had the tails tied.

Getting back to Nam, I can think of times when we'd be asleep — say, maybe eleven, twelve o'clock — and to hear incoming rounds, that's kind of hard to explain. You can say it sounds like a cannon — it makes that boom sound — but it also makes another loud sound that you can tell if it is incoming or outgoing. We had — I'm sure you've heard the nurses talk about bunkers — OK, we had those. Sometimes we'd sit from four to six hours in those bunkers — yes, I have sat, say, from four to six hours. And what we did was, we sat there and drank beer and talked. And then it's work time — you just go to work in your clothes without taking a shower or anything.

You see, at Long Binh there was the ammo dump, which is where they kept all the ammunition that supplied the troops in Vietnam. It was a humongous deal — all you could see was just mounds and mounds and mounds. The ammunition they kept under the ground, and Charlie was always trying to blow up the ammo dumps. It was right by the barracks, too — the ammo dump is here, the barracks is here, and there is a highway running here. So we got the majority of the incoming rounds.

On Christmas Eve, 1969, about seven o'clock at night, we were all standing outside laughing at the Christmas presents we'd gotten — we'd gotten gag gifts and stuff like that — when the rounds started coming in real close. Well, that night we could hear the shrapnel actually hitting our bunker. Now I was scared and praying that night. I think that's the first time that I had really, really been scared. This was worse than the B-52s.

When we went to bed at night, you always take your boots and your pants and you fix them like you were in them. In other words, you had your pant legs inside the boots. Because when you got in them, you just slid in. You had your helmet, your web gear, and all that that you had to put on, too.

When things weren't hot at night, we could party. We had everything we needed right there at Long Binh, which was big, was really like a city. We'd get movies in from the States before the people here would see them — we had first crack. So there was like a big patio with a big screen that they had painted white, and it was our movie screen. We also had a little club the engineers had built us, one for E-5 and above, another one for E-4 and below. I know you have heard of the saying, enlisted and officers cannot associate together because it's fraternization. Well, a non-commissioned officer and a lower-rank enlisted person, they cannot associate — supposedly — together. So you had to have the two sets of clubs.

But you know, after work — I'm talking generals on down — it was like everybody was the same. The officers would have parties and they would invite the enlisted females over. They would barbecue ribs, chicken, and they would supply all the liquor and beer. One time, I remember, some guys got all tanked up and here I am with my boots and fatigues on, and they say, "All right, it's time for Houser to go in the pool!" I say, "No, I can't swim —" And they say, "You're swimming today!" and throw me in the water. But I didn't drown because somebody was there.

We also had our own female softball team. We used to play the nurses and beat them and oh, they'd get mad at us for days, they really would. They were the same age as we were, you know, but they acted a lot older. I don't know if it's because, you know, the job they had. I do know I could not have been an Army nurse over there.

One thing that happened over there that really hurt me, was my general, his aide, and — there must have been at least six generals and their aides — they were shot down over Pleiku. They were aboard this UHI, which was, at that time, the largest helicopter the Army had. Well, they were coming back from checking the bridges and power and it was just dark and they were shot down. Killed, every last one of them. I tell you, I don't know, that got off with me so bad. I cried a lot, I really did, because by that being such a small command, the general personally would come in and talk to me, you know. So I knew him quite well. He wasn't one of them that threw me in the pool, but I worked for him and it really hurt me really bad. Every day he'd come around, he and the major, and they would of course chat with us two girls. So it took a while, like, to go back to the office, because you'd go back to work and know he wasn't there. Then, because I was personnel — I used just a little bit of my MOS — I had to process their records for the insurance and all that to go back to the family. I say that was rough, it really was. It probably wouldn't have hurt me so bad if, like the commanding general of the National Guard, I see him once in a blue moon. But my general, and Captain Booth, his aide — nice-looking guy, I think he was from up north — I seen them all the time. And who knew something like that would happen? It just really blew my mind.

The other thing was, Jackie and I were going out with them that day. But all of a sudden I changed my mind. I didn't want to go because we had something going on back in the company — I don't remember what it was — so Colonel Jack says, "Well, you know, if you don't want to go, we can take care of it." I don't know, for some reason I just had a feeling not to go.

So it was thirteen months and time for me to go back to the States. I wanted to stay in Nam longer — I wanted at least two years there — but my mom took sick. I'm sure that command was still there later, and I'm sure I would have still been doing the same kind of work. But after she took sick, I got a compassionate reassignment to Fort Benning, Georgia.

You know, when you go overseas to do a tour, you get thirty days of leave with pay — that's something Uncle Sam gives you, and you get the same when you come back. So I used the leave time by being home.

At home, my mother said I was a totally different person. She said it seemed I had grown up overnight. I don't know why — well, I do know why. It's just I had a lot built up in my mind with the things I'd seen, you know. I just basically wanted to be alone. While I was around the house my mom would be talking to me trying to get me to say something. She'd say, "Well, what was it like over there?" And I'd say, "Mom, I just don't want to talk about it." I really never did talk about it to my folks. My brothers and sisters would tell you right now that they don't know half of what I've told you because I just didn't want to talk about it. And they never pumped me with questions after I told them I didn't want to talk.

So I used to get in my car and I'd just drive. Go anywhere. A lot of times I'd go to the river and sit for hours and hours, all by myself — wouldn't even take my dog with me. I'd stop by the store and pick me up a couple of six-packs and put them in the cooler and then I'd just go sit and think. When I sat by the river I'd think about things in general that I'd seen. I would question myself as to really why I went to Nam. I would think how, when I went, I wasn't really knowing what to expect — I didn't expect to do or see half of what I had done. And I don't know, I felt older for some reason. I was twenty-four when I came back, but it just seemed like I felt like I was a thirty- or forty-year-old woman.

My girlfriend would get mad at me. She would even tell me I was crazy a lot of times, because she'd be talking to me and I wouldn't answer. I really wouldn't hear what she'd be saying to me. Because my mind, I had to bring my mind back from Vietnam to the States.

I was at Fort Benning for about a year and a half. Then, when I had ten months left in the Army, I went to Fort McClellan, Alabama, and was an instructor there. The Women's Army Corps was still in existence, and Fort McClellan, you know, was the only all-female post. Well, I was put on orders as a OOF — double-O Foxtrot — which is a drill sergeant. Only when I got there, I had made up my mind that I was not going to babysit any troops, not after what I had just gone through. So when I reported in, I said, "You can give me whatever you have, but I just flat refuse to be a drill sergeant." I guess they thought I was drill sergeant material — I was, but I didn't want it. They didn't give me too much flak, because, like I said, once I make up my mind to do something, that's it.

But after my ten months was up, they said, "If you're going to reenlist, you have to reenlist as a OOF." I said, "No way." They said, "Well, then you're going to have to ETS [resign: Expiration of Term of Service]." I said, "Fine with me — I'll just get out." So I got out and, three weeks later, a girlfriend called me — I went to Vietnam with her but she had a totally different time from what

I did — and was congratulating me. Well, she didn't know I was out. She was congratulating me because I had made the E-7 list, primary zone, which meant I would have been promoted probably within the next three or four weeks to an E-7. And they wouldn't tell me this. That's what really made me so mad when I got back here to Columbus — I went to Benning and they told me that if I got my records from McClellan they would just reenlist me there. That way, it wouldn't hurt me in making an E-7. But, you know, they wouldn't release my records from McClellan. They were mad because I wouldn't reenlist for a drill sergeant.

I tell you, one of the reasons I didn't like Fort McClellan is because I don't like working for a woman. Working for a woman is totally different than working for a man — and it's worse in the Army. I had roughly eight years in, had been to Nam, and those second lieutenants that didn't know anything would come and try to boss me around. That would get on my nerves; it really would. Also, they didn't treat you fair. That's why I didn't want to stay there with them. I didn't like it.

You know, I never ran into any racial problems until I entered the military. Like I said, I grew up with this white family. And I went to an all-black school. My girlfriend, she ended up going to an integrated school, but I graduated in sixty-four, the year before they integrated. But of the military, Vietnam was the worst, and the worst of all were the brothers — the black guys over there. If you didn't have this black wristband — you've probably seen it, all it is is a shoestring twisted together — if you didn't have that on, you were Uncle Tom. Well, I don't want to say the names the brothers called white people, because I just wasn't brought up that way. But those guys were wild. You knew they were wild just to look at them.

Even the girls, they would look at me like to say "What are you hanging around with the honkies for?" And I would put it to them bluntly — like I'm saying it right now — "When you start paying my bills, when you start giving me money, then you can tell me who I can see and who I can talk to." I said, "They may be a honky to you, but they're my friends. If you don't like it — lump it." Because I like everybody as long as you treat me right. But when you start talking racial, I don't get into it, you know. I don't particularly like it. I have actually told people not to come to my house no more. Because I feel like, I'm paying for it.

Anyway, I think in the military and in Nam the Northern background had a lot to do with the brothers and the girls not liking white people. Because we had a lot of people from Chicago, a lot of people from New York. There was even one girl — I think she was from Cleveland, Indiana, or someplace like that — and she just did not like whites. We never did see her hanging around.

Before I tell you about moving back to Columbus from McClellan I'll tell you some more — since you asked — of what were my feelings about the Vietnamese. Like I said, I didn't like them at all. We had one Vietnamese clerk, she'd come in whenever she wanted to, and I tell you, she didn't do nothing. And every time she didn't come in, we'd get rockets at night.

I don't know what it was, if she was working for Charlie or what, but she'd come up to me and she'd say, "Miss Lynn won't be here tomorrow." I'd say, "Why?" She'd say, "VC come tonight. You get rockets tonight." I'd say, "Nah — no rockets tonight." She'd say, "Rockets tonight. Miss Lynn won't be in tomorrow." And no kidding, we'd get ate up that night with rockets.

I don't know, but it was like she was working for them — every time she said Charlie was going to hit, he hit. And how she was being paid, I don't even know that, I really don't.

Well, she would tell us every time and sometimes she wouldn't show up. I remember one day — this was in the day — I was sitting at my desk and this humongous rocket came in and shook the building. My colonel came out of his office, looked for me, didn't see me. He yells, "Houser!" I say, "Yes, sir!" Well, I'm under my desk. We had an underground shelter, but there wasn't time to go down them stairs.

You could be in country six months, a year, two years, and you'd hear an incoming round — you'd run. Once — you remember that education center I was telling you about? — I saw how the iron from these rockets actually pinned a woman colonel there. I mean, those things have points on them like needles. Some of it is this long. . . . Some of it is longer, even longer than this. . . . It comes to a point and it had this woman pinned in her wall. I guess she was standing up when it came in and she was pinned against the wall with this metal in her. It got her through the heart and all.

That night after the all-clear came, everybody rushed up to the education center where the colonel and all lived — it was like a mixture of male and female officers living in the same area — and we just walked through the rubbish and was looking at it and stuff. So we heard the officers talking and anyway, we went in, and sure enough the rocket had hit her hootch at almost like a dead angle. One side of the wall was standing. And sure enough, she was pinned to the wall.

I boo-hooed. I cried. I threw up because I had never seen that before. It was horrible. All my fear came back. My knees were knocking, you know, because I had never seen nothing like that, and the education center just looked like a tornado had gone through it.

So this Miss Lynn, I used to tell her all the time, I'd say, "You VC?" She'd say, "No, Miss Lynn not VC." I'd say, "Oh, yes you are. How do you know every time we get hit by Charlie? You're out, how do you know? You're VC." "Oh, no," she'd say, "Miss Lynn not VC." And you know, that's all she'd say. She came from a kind of wealthy family, was what they called French Vietnam-ese — they had plain Vietnamese and they had French Vietnamese that were a lot prettier than the normal ones — and she spoke English with a French accent. But we all used to say that Miss Lynn worked for Charlie.

I know it's wrong, but nothing gripes me more than to see an American man married to one of them Vietnamese. I just don't see it, I really don't. I never got up the nerve to approach a guy to find out why he did marry one of them.

Like this guy, he used to live right over here. He was a young guy, black guy, came back from Korea. While he was over there he wouldn't send any money home for his family, so she had to go out and get a job and all the kids got part-time jobs after school. Well, he comes home with a Korean woman. It was a Sunday afternoon. It was raining. He threw his wife out, threw his kids out, threw their clothes out. He was married to that black woman and he drove her and their kids out in the rain. They moved somewhere up on the hill. I don't know if they moved out of the [trailer] park or were made to move out. But just the idea of that —

You know, I had to duck in my trailer several times while this Korean shot him one night. I kept hearing — bam! And she was talking to him in Korean and he was running around the trailer. Well, I hit the floor, you know, because I thought the shots were coming this way — that's what we did over there: you hear a shot and you hit the floor. Finally I go out the back door and ease around to the front. She's chasing him around the trailer with a gun. She shot him. He left and was gone for about two months, and when he came back his arm was in a sling.

They're still together. I see them every once in a while. They've got this little black Korean baby now. The wife and kids aren't up on the hill anymore; I don't know what happened to them. But like I said, I thought it was terrible. Guy throws his wife and kids out in the rain to marry one of them — I can't understand why, you know, they'd want to marry one of them.

But getting back to Nam, those people were not used to inside plumbing until the Americans got there. They would take a roll of toilet paper and I don't know what they thought it was, but they'd use it and put it in the toilet and wouldn't flush it. They'd just keep putting, putting — and you've got to go in there to go to the bathroom and the toilet paper would meet you at the door. And the smell — I've gone out behind the buildings between the jeeps lots of times because I just flat refused to go in there.

I think the Vietnamese lived a lot worse over there than the way they live here. Say, take the bare ground, like you see the bare ground out there. Well, the lower-class people, you know, they'd take this tall strawlike stuff that grows and that was weaved somehow and put that up as sides on the bare ground around these four poles. On the top would be maybe an old pasteboard box, and you could see all in it because they had no front door. It could be pouring down rain — all we got was monsoons, it would rain four months, six months, all at one time — and you'd see them just laying on the bare ground in all that mud. You know, no beds, nothing like that. And all they'd eat would be rice. Or they'd take these fish and they'd wrap them in these leaves and they'd bury them in the hot sand until the fish actually rotted. Then they'd dig it up — it was what they called *nuk mam* — and eat that with the rice. And when they're eating it, you'd better be two miles down the road. Because it smelled horrible.

Oh, one day we were sitting in the office and I kept smelling something that was horrible-smelling. The colonel came out and I said, "Sir, what is it that stinks so bad?" And he said, "I don't know." We got to looking and we kept hearing these Vietnamese laughing in this utility room, which has got a big sink and all the mops and brooms and stuff. Well, we find them in there with a hot plate and a skillet — they were catching these roaches that were this tall and that long, and putting them in the frying pan to kill them. And they were eating them, you know. That's what we kept smelling, roaches being burned. And they'd eat them.

We just looked at them. The colonel unplugs the hot plate and just takes it away from them, because they had stunk up that whole building — we couldn't open the windows, you know, because it was air-conditioning, and I bet that place stunk for three days.

They would eat anything. They ate worms and stuff. I'm serious. I don't know if they ate American food or not. Like my mama-san, she'd make me so mad because all that old grease and stuff from that old rotten fish mixed with rice — well, she'd do my uniforms and instead of using spray starch, she spit. And wherever she spit, I'd have little grease splotches all over my uniform. I told her not to do it, but it didn't do no good — she acted like she didn't even understand English.

I couldn't get myself another mama-san because that one was assigned to me. She was good, but I'd look at her and tell her about my uniform, "Look at this — number ten! You make *beaucoup* mistake. Uniform looks bad." And I'd show it to her and I wouldn't have it for maybe a month. And then she'd get carried away again and I'd tell her again. You know, eventually it would come out. But I tell you, she was something else, my mama-san. She had nine kids and they were all like stair steps. I have no idea how old she was — it's hard to tell how old they are because they look older than they actually are, and she was a lot shorter than me. She was a little bitty thing. And, you know, she was real nice. She wouldn't steal from me or anything. I would leave four hundred, eight hundred bucks in my fatigue pockets when I changed at night. I'd take off my rank and I'd take off my patch and I'd just throw my uniform down. And the next day she would have that wad of money in her hand, and she would go, "Baby-san" —all she called me was baby-san — "You *beaucoup* number ten. You left in pocket — that a no-no!" And she'd give it back to me and it would all be there. She'd never take it. I used to give her extra every month, twenty or thirty bucks, because she had so many kids and she had like thirteen of us girls that she had to iron for.

While she would be working for us, the papa-san would be out in his rice paddies gathering his rice. And their cows were ugly. I think they call them water buffaloes, but they didn't look like the cows over here. Their dogs didn't look like our dogs. They had the face of a dog but they really had the face of I guess you could say a kangaroo. And they were old, brown, dirty. Looked like they were tiger-striped, all of them. And they didn't sleep like our dogs. They had to be propped up against something, so they'd lay almost in a dying cockroach position, with all fours up leaning on whatever they were leaning on. I don't know, but they were ugly. We adopted this one and, you know, we'd bring it scraps and stuff out of the mess hall and it would eat it. But oh, it was ugly.

I think the only reason they didn't get our dog and eat it was we had a shepherd, too, that the MPs had given us. I guess that dog must have been about eight months old. But if it didn't like you, it would bite you. So they couldn't mess with our dogs because that shepherd didn't like Vietnamese women. I mean, it would chase them in the daytime. We had to keep it tied up. But I know they got a little kitten that we kept in the orderly room. I think they ate it. You think I'm lying, don't you?

Those Vietnamese were something else.

Well, I got out of the Army in July of seventy-three. I moved back to Columbus, drew unemployment for about three months, then I got a job writing radio commercials. Also, the day before I went to work at my new job, I enlisted in the Georgia National Guard. I had gone down to this unit on Victory Drive, an engineer outfit, and at that time they were not taking females because it was a combat outfit. Then they call back and tell me the state has authorized them to take females. So I stayed there for maybe six months and then they reassigned me to a unit up in Atlanta. It's noncombatant, a personnel outfit. The section I'm in is called an augmentation team, and our job is like, if our unit is activated — say to go to Lebanon or something like that — we'll stay behind. We'll process all the dependents that are assigned to my unit. Then, once that's completed, we'll go to where the unit is, to be their personnel center. Because, you see, somebody has got to maintain the troops' 201 — personal history — files.

So that's where I'm presently assigned, to headquarters in Atlanta, but I work out here on Victory Drive on weekend drills. We have a pretty good-size armory out there. We've got all the jeeps, the trucks, all that — just like a regular Army. Once out of a year we go to Fort Stewart, which is around Savannah, for two weeks of active-duty training. Believe it or not, while I certainly work full time at [radio station] WPNX, I make more in a weekend with the National Guard than I make in a week at WPNX. That's because of my rank, an E-7. At one time I was the highest-ranking woman in the National Guard in the state of Georgia. Now they have eight female E-7s, but they're not black. I'm the only black female E-7 still.

I'd say about twenty percent of the guys in the Guard are Nam vets. And the rest of them which — I tell them flat to their face — a lot joined to beat the draft. A lot of them are draft dodgers, and I don't like having too much dealings with them, not at all. And like these people that took off to Canada — I won't have nothing to do with them.

Because, you know, if another war came up, I would go. I would volunteer for it even if they didn't send me. Women can do it. We go through the same training. Why send us through all this training and then don't let us utilize it?

Just like I was telling the guys in the Guard, I said, "If you all think you're going to leave me behind — uh-uh. One way or the other, I'd end up where you are." That's just me. I guess I'm just an adventurous person. I don't know if I ever would want to be right on the firing line. But if I was told I had to, then, you know, I'd do it.

*Pinkie Houser, the highest-ranking black woman in the Georgia National Guard, is also the traffic director and receptionist at radio station WPNX in Phenix City, Alabama. She lives in Columbus, Georgia.*

# Leslie McClusky (alias)

*Leslie McClusky grew up in Columbus, Ohio, where her father owned a chain of supermarkets. She wanted to be a nurse "at first, because of the Cherry Ames books. I read all of them when I was a child. Later I became aware of a real desire to help people." Leslie's family was "very traditional. I did not know any women who worked outside the home." Nursing, to Leslie, seemed "like something to fall back on. The other options were teaching or secretarial work. And then you got married. And that was the end of it."*

*Leslie decided to join the military and go to Vietnam "because I felt I had had a sheltered life and wanted to grow up. Going to Vietnam, I felt, would be a maturing experience." She was in Vietnam from December, 1970, to November 1971. Most of her tour was spent at the 91st Evacuation Hospital at Chu Lai, where she worked in triage as well as in the intensive care unit and on the postoperative and medical wards.*

I WAS FIRST going to join the military in 1967. At that time I had a guarantee to go to Vietnam. But I made the ultimate mistake of telling my family before I was actually sworn in. Never in my life have I been bombarded by so much negative reaction.

Three years later, in early seventy, I decided that I really wanted to go. I was twenty-four. I still wanted to go for the same reasons, and I was very sorry that I hadn't gone before. So this time I didn't tell anybody until two weeks before I was leaving for officers' training school at Fort Sam Houston, Texas. There was the same outpouring, but now it was too late. If I'd been strong enough the first time around, I would have done it that way then.

At that time the Army was taking nurses for fourteen months if they would agree to go to Vietnam. Apparently they weren't getting enough to enlist for two years; they wanted people who had been out of school for a few years and had some experience. I was assistant head nurse in a surgical intensive care unit and had had three years of real critical care experience. I'd taken care of a lot of trauma from automobile accidents, stabbings, and things.

Little did I know that did not prepare me in the least for Vietnam.

I enjoyed basic training. It was the first time I'd ever really been away from home. I developed a pretty good sense of humor — you have to with the military; they take such ridiculous little things so seriously — and didn't really think of myself as being in the Army. Nor did I really give much thought to Vietnam.

It wasn't until the night we were leaving that I began to realize what I had done. And I was really sorry. I remember being in the airport and feeling like a little girl.

I had my big duffle bag and a suitcase, and I was wearing my uniform and my first lieutenant's bar. There were no other women around, and nobody was really smiling. I waited with all these young men to get on this chartered plane. My remembrance is that it was a real crowded plane — they had put seats everywhere — and I was stuck in between these two guys. One of them was really big. Nobody was talking. And there wasn't any liquor because it was a military flight.

In Alaska, our first stop, everyone got off the plane, went to the bar and had a few drinks. In Japan everybody drank again. Through this whole flight, I was never able to sleep, even though I'd had a few drinks and had brought some sleeping pills with me, because it was all very crowded and awful, and I felt awful. I didn't know what was coming up. I was scared and I felt very young, even though I was one of the oldest people on the plane. Most of the guys were eighteen or nineteen.

In Alaska I saw there was one other woman on the plane. She was sitting way in the back. I could have talked to her, but I didn't.

We landed at Bien Hoa. Bien Hoa had been rocketed the day before, so there was this mad dash to get us off and get us going. And they really meant going. This big truck came to pick us up. We were supposed to pile in the back, and here I am in my little skirt and heels — I couldn't get my feet into them after twenty-three hours of sitting, so I was carrying my heels. And I had to get my duffle bag and all my junk onto the back of this big truck that I could hardly get myself up onto. In those days I smoked two packs a day and had never dreamed about jumping up onto a truck.

There was no letup. They took us in these trucks to this room, where you were briefed. All the officers went into one room, the enlisted people into another. We got a speech about what we weren't supposed to do, and we changed our money and then they took us to get our orders. It was absolutely nonstop. Right away we were in fatigues. And then I was in this place — it was a barracks for women — way in the back with a guard out front and barbed wire all around it. I was given a blanket and two sheets and was supposed to try to sleep.

This other woman from the plane came in, but we didn't talk. We were both, I guess, so lost in our own thoughts. And she was older than me and seemed real hardened. This was her first time in Vietnam, but she was a captain, had been in the Army awhile. To me she seemed sort of callous. She used a lot of language that fit in with the guys. I didn't talk that way.

This building had six or eight cots in it. The light bulbs were bare and hung down. I don't know if it was clean — in Vietnam everything seemed filthy. And it was hot and dry and there were bugs everywhere.

I had been moving around sort of like a zombie but doing everything I was supposed to do, certainly acting like I was all right. Until I went to the outhouse. It was a thing in the back with these slits you had to sit on — it wasn't exactly a flush toilet — and when I sat down a frog jumped on my leg. For some reason that was the trigger. I just burst out crying. I didn't know what I'd gotten myself into, why I was there, or what was laying in front of me. And I was just completely exhausted.

I couldn't stay in that building, so I went up to the officers' club. As soon as I walked in I knew I'd made a mistake. It was all men. This other woman was there, too, but I didn't fit in with her. So I got a drink and went outside and met some guy and sat in a bunker. We just sat there and talked. I remember I wanted my mother.

This was not exactly the best night of my life. But the worst was yet to come. Because the worst day was the day I came back home.

After three days I got orders to go to the Third Field Hospital in Saigon. The Third Field was not at all what I had in mind. It was in the city and we wore white uniforms and we were mostly taking care of Vietnamese civilians and some sort of VIPs. I didn't like it there. I didn't know anything about the Vietnamese. The Army gave us absolutely no orientation to their language, their customs — the women would squat on top of the toilets — and here we had wards and wards of Vietnamese. It was very confusing. I hadn't gone there to help minister to them. In retrospect I guess I feel different. I remember there were a lot of women and children. The children, most of them, had been severely injured with mines.

Saigon itself was a very interesting city. It was dirty and real crowded, but it was so alive. There were cars, taxis, motor bikes everywhere, and on the black market you could get anything you wanted — cigarettes, decent hairspray, Breck shampoo. It's strange now to look at all the stuff on TV about Saigon, because the city looks so sterile, like it was made out of plastic models.

I was at the Third Field about a month and a half. We worked twelve hours a day, six days a week. I knew I was in a foreign city and I knew I was in the military, but mostly it just seemed like some kind of missionary camp. We weren't taking any casualties. So my experience just centered on trying to get by in this totally new environment. I thought I managed pretty well for someone who didn't think she could get by anywhere.

Our chief nurse was a pretty weird woman. When I put in for a transfer we had an argument. She started telling me that I was no longer a civilian, that I was an Army officer and that I would take orders. And that I would respect her. Well, I didn't respect her. I thought she was a little crazy. She loved the Vietnamese and used to take their clothes and wash them. It seemed to me the Vietnamese were all she cared about. And she was real petty and did everything she could to keep the nurses from dating enlisted men. Anyhow, she got me transferred to Chu Lai. She thought it was punishment. But at least it was different, so it was all right with me.

Chu Lai is in the northern part of the country, right on the coast. The camp was on a cliff overlooking the ocean. It was very beautiful there. And it was all Army — Chu Lai was the base camp of the Americal Division, so there were about forty thousand men stationed there.

The first guy that I saw wounded was a kid who had had his leg blown off. He had shrapnel everywhere, too. I had never seen shrapnel wounds, just like I had never seen a traumatic amputation. You know, I'd seen normal amputations under sterile conditions. But I had never seen a guy with big, black, pitted holes everywhere and a makeshift tourniquet over the amputation site. He was conscious, too. A sweet young kid. I had no idea what to say.

There were lots of others being brought in at the same time. I didn't know what to do, so I just quit functioning. That's when a corpsman sat me down and poured me some coffee. You know, the corpsmen are the people who deserve a lot of credit that I'm not sure they've gotten. They really knew what to do. They were real compassionate, too. Anyhow, after about ten minutes I said, "Shit — I'm supposed to be in charge here. I have to get some IVs, get some blood going, see who's hurt worst, who has to go in first." Only I couldn't look at anything.

But I knew that I still had eleven months to go. That I couldn't just sit there folded up in a chair not functioning. So I got up and did what I had to do. Only I didn't connect with anything. I just did it. What I didn't realize at the time is how fast a total emotional numbing sets in. I did my job well and was able to show compassion, but I worked hard at not feeling compassion. Of course I saw the kids, and of course I reacted appropriately. But it was all external. Only in the last six months have I been able to really see them, or see them again. This first kid, especially. Over the years, whenever he would flash in front of me, I'd just turn him off. I could not deal with that memory or any of the others.

There was another kid, I remember, who had had two legs and an arm blown off, probably by a mine. And the kid who was blind. You know, I've blocked so much of it that I don't remember anyone's name, even though I know I called them by their names at the time. Since I went to the Wall, though, I'm remembering more and more of them. It was at the Wall that I first was able to cry.

I remember these two other guys who had malaria. They came in real dehydrated and vomiting with real high temperatures. And they acted just like little boys — little boys who were sick. I remember how I tried to make everything better, only I couldn't give them back anything they had lost. I never felt I was good enough, that what I was doing would make up for what they were going through. So most of the time I felt real inadequate. And you can't imagine what that takes out of you.

It's true there was a lot of drinking and a lot of marijuana use. But I don't think there was that much drug abuse among medical people. Pot and alcohol, yes. No one used anything when they were working.

But when you weren't working — well, I drank. And I smoked.

Because, really, there was nothing else to do. You couldn't go downtown and take in a movie. You could go to the officers' club and see war movies, and I actually think I must have seen every damn war movie that was ever made. There was this group of us, medical people and helicopter pilots and gunners, and we'd sit around and watch this stuff. That was OK. Except that, in real life, it was real helicopters and real outgoing fire and real incoming.

We got rocketed at Chu Lai. At first it was scary. But I have to tell you that, after a couple times, you just get used to it. You always had a flak jacket and a helmet on the foot of your bed. The procedure was, when there was a rocket, you put on your flak jacket and helmet and ran to the bunkers. If you were working, there was a jacket and helmet above every patient in bed. What you were supposed to do was get them on the guys who couldn't do it themselves and then roll them underneath the bed. It would usually be just at dawn when we got rocketed.

The first night I went to the bunkers. That's when I knew this was bullshit. After that I actually got under my bed once or twice, but mostly I just stuck my helmet on my head. Because they usually weren't hitting anywhere near us. And you learn to know the difference between incoming and outgoing fire.

There was a two-week period in the middle of my tour when I was sort of a basket case. I wanted out so badly I didn't think I could stand another day. And I didn't know what to do, how to deal with it. I worked every day, but I quit talking to people. After work I'd go straight to my room and sit there thinking how I could go home. First I thought I would get pregnant, but that would take too long. Or I could break a leg, only I wasn't sure that would get me out. And of course I could really go crazy, but then I would have to deal with that. Finally, after two weeks, it was over and I felt fine. So I just went back and ended the next six months.

This other stuff happened to me, too. While I was at Chu Lai, I remember, I started to really hate the Vietnamese. I had grown up real liberal — as far as I was concerned, I never had a prejudiced bone. When I first got in country and everybody was talking about the "gooks," I thought they were really insensitive. Then I started hearing about things that happened. Then I started seeing the results.

Before long I started thinking of them as gooks, too. I had no love for them. Women, children, it didn't matter — I didn't want to take care of them. When helicopters would come in and there would be Vietnamese on them, I'd say to myself, "Shit. I do not want to go waste my energy taking care of them —" Now I'm happy I never acted on what I felt. Maybe I wasn't extremely kind, but I never did anything to hurt anybody, and I took care of them all physically, even the prisoners.

And then one day I suddenly realized what was happening to me. I was on the ward, doing something for one of the POWs, and I said to the guard — the prisoners were always guarded — "What are you sitting there with that M-16 for? Do you really think this guy is going anywhere?" I was thinking how crazy it was. Also how I never looked at them, never looked at their faces. So this time I did. I sat down and really looked at this Vietnamese as a human being. And what I saw was a fourteen-year-old kid.

I really had not cried at all, but I almost cried that day. I wanted to — wanted to cry because of what I knew had happened to me. That's when I began to see the whole thing as insane.

I started looking more at them after that. One night when I was still feeling mostly negative, there was this baby that was brought in. I said to myself, "What are we going to do with a Vietnamese baby? I don't want this baby here." I didn't want to take care of her, because I felt the same about her as about the others, even if it was a baby.

The kid wasn't really sick, but she was crying. I had to feed her, so I went and plunked this bottle in her mouth. I wasn't really looking at her. But I had to sit there and hold her — there wasn't much else to do — so after a while I started to look at her. And that time I did cry. How, I wondered, could I ever come to believe I hated a baby? I had lost all perspective, and I knew it. I also knew the numbing process was starting to wear off, but I did not know how I was going to deal with all these feelings.

Well, my year was ending. Like everyone else, I had a short-timer's calendar and short-timer's syndrome. You know, people would walk around saying, "Five days left. Four days left. I'm so short you can't see me —" And then you have your urine test to make sure you're drug-free and then you're on a plane going home. And you think it's going to be wonderful.

The flight home was certainly much louder than the flight over. I was the only woman. Everyone had thought to bring liquor. So we land in Seattle, and there's no ceremony, no one waiting to tell you what a wonderful thing you've done. I get a steak dinner, a little money, and my discharge papers. That's it. I'm out of the Army. And all of a sudden I don't know why, on the plane, I was saying, "Just get me home." Because I don't have an apartment anymore. And I feel very strange. Yeah, how strange I was feeling — that was really the only thing I knew.

I didn't know anybody in Seattle, but I stayed there for a while. Then I went to Chicago, which I had never been to, and stayed a few days there. I just wandered around, kind of. Then I went to New York, where my sister lives. She didn't know I was coming or anything. I remember I woke her up.

Everything was very strange.

I remember my brother and sister wanted to go out to dinner. I mean, they were really trying, but I was sort of in shock. All I kept thinking was that I didn't care where we went to dinner — What is this about going to dinner? Except for on R and R, I haven't been in a restaurant for a year. I kept looking around thinking how incredibly superficial everything was, how nobody really understood what's going on. And I wanted to scream. I didn't want to go to a restaurant. I didn't even want to be here. All I want, I'm thinking, is to go back to Nam.

In New York I got a job working in a recovery room. I knew I had to have a job where I'd have minimal interaction. Because I just could not deal with any more people who were hurt. I wanted to do a mechanical job, get my money, and get out of there. And that's what I did for a long time. I went back to school and became an anesthetist so I would have less interaction with patients. I had no more to give. I didn't care. And gradually, you know, over the years, that emotional numbness took its toll.

And then, one day about seven months ago, this thing happened. I was giving anesthesia to a guy who had had some prior trauma in different areas of his body. After the surgery we were talking and I said, "I recognize you." It turned out we belonged to the same athletic club. So I asked him how he'd gotten injured before and he said he'd been a Marine in Vietnam. That's when I said, "I was in Vietnam, too." And I couldn't believe it. Because for fourteen years I never told anyone.

This guy — he's a policeman — said, "Gosh, I've never met a woman who was in Vietnam." Then he said, "You women were great." And instantly I felt very close to him.

It had been a long time since I'd felt close to anybody.

One day he was on duty and driving by the club in his patrol car and I'm outside and he said, "I have something I want you to read." So he went home and got this book. It's *Home Before Morning,* which I had never heard of. I took it home and started to read it. Only I couldn't read it. Because every time I read a page I'd start to see things and start to cry. I kept saying to myself, "I can't believe this. I can't believe someone else is feeling the same things I am." Because, all those years, I'd thought I was the only one.

I had never come in contact with any veterans. Meeting my policeman friend — he was the first.

So I went to the Vet Center, which, before, I never felt had anything to do with me. The guys there greeted me like a long-lost sister or something. I couldn't believe it. They were just wonderful. They had all these things organized, too.

In November — this past November — I went down to Washington for the dedication of the Monument [the Vietnam Veterans' Memorial]. I had absolutely no idea what to expect. But when I saw all those guys, I felt so at home. It was, in a good sense, like being back in Vietnam. You know, you had on grungy uniforms again and everything was very recognizable and you were with people you felt truly comfortable with. Because those guys greeted me so affectionately and warmly. And you know, you just don't think of some big brute of a guy, an ex-Marine, coming up to you with tears in his eyes, hugging you, thanking you, being so open about his feelings.

I was afraid because I knew the dam was trying to burst. But I went over to the Wall [the Memorial]. I sat down and looked at all the names. And suddenly I couldn't stop crying. I was crying so hard I couldn't get up — every time I tried to get up I'd start crying again. It was as though I was never going to be able to stop. And I'd always had this thing about self-control and nobody seeing me cry.

So I was sitting there, trying to get up, when this big black guy came over and put his hand on my shoulder. "It's OK," he said. I looked up at him and couldn't talk. He backed away then — backed away but stood next to me. Finally, when I was able to stand up, I went over to him and saw tears in his eyes and he put his arms around me and I was hugging him. I couldn't believe it. And this was just the beginning.

I didn't know what to think. I was just a wreck. So I stayed with him awhile and then I went and sat on the grass. These other guys came over then. They had all been there. They just came over and they were all so gentle and we sat around and talked. It was unbelievable. It was really like being home.

*Leslie McClusky lives in Dallas, Texas.*

# ❦ Cherie Rankin

*Cherie Rankin grew up in West Palm Beach, Florida. "I'm the product of a divorced family. My mother, who was a very independent, very self-sufficient woman, separated from my father when I was eight, so my brother and I grew up primarily raised by her. Our religious background was fundamentalist, and that ultimately had conflicting influences on me."*

*After graduating from high school in 1964, Cherie worked for two years. "Then I went straight through college for four years, graduating with a degree in social work and psychology. When I was in my senior year of college I got involved with some of the antiwar demonstrations. Now, in my family, with our religious background, demonstrating against the war would not have been an acceptable thing to do. So I didn't tell anyone in my family that I had some real concerns about what was going on in Vietnam."*

*Cherie was in Vietnam with the Red Cross's SRAO program from September of 1970 to September of 1971. She was based in Danang, in Cam Ranh, and Phan Rang.*

WHEN MY YOUNGER BROTHER enlisted in the Marine Corps and was sent to Nam, I was concerned about him. I didn't understand how he could go over there and kill anybody. We were brought up to believe life was important, that you respected people's lives. I thought to myself, "If I were a man, I could never do that — go over there and pull a trigger." The more I thought about it, the more I wondered what it was doing to him. That's when I realized I wanted to do something to help. I did have a sense that the war was wrong. But I couldn't get away from the feeling that there were guys over there like my brother — guys who grew up with apple pie and country, guys who did what they were told and didn't question it. I didn't want to support the war, but I wanted to support those guys. So what was I going to do?

Around that time I heard about another woman, an acquaintance of mine in college, who was going to Korea with the Red

Cross. I'd never heard of such a thing. When she told me she'd had her pick between Korea and Vietnam, I said, "You're kidding. What are you talking about? Tell me more about this!" She told me. I was very excited.

So I contacted the Red Cross and went for the local interview. They supplied me with information about the SRAO program, and it sounded exactly like what I was interested in. So I pursued it. They flew me to Atlanta and put me through five hours of interviews. By the time they finished with me I was sure they had some kind of incredible screening process and that only top-notch women were going to Nam. Later I found out that everybody they interviewed went.

I came back from the last interview feeling like I wanted to go. But then I had to deal with the reality. First of all, what did this say about me? I talked to some of my friends, asked them if my going would be a statement in favor of the war. In the end, though, I made my own decision. Going to Nam met my needs. I wanted to go. I wanted to find out for myself what was going on, and I wanted to help if I could. I also wanted the adventure.

Then it was telling my family. My mother was excited. I found out she'd always wanted, during World War Two, to go be a donut dolly in Germany. She thought my going to Nam was great. Of course she didn't know about my political bent. My father supported me, too, though he had been in Africa in World War Two and wanted me to know something about the reality of war. So we had a long father-daughter talk before I left. He wanted to prepare me not only for the hardships but also for the kind of stuff I could expect from men over there. Because I was a virgin; I had dated a lot, but I strongly believed in my morals, my values. So my father felt I should know something about the other side of life — it was a heavy little talk.

The only member of my family who didn't know I was going was my brother. He was already over there.

Now what's interesting is that around this time a Red Cross woman got killed in Nam, shot by a GI. Both sets of parents hid the newspaper articles from me. I found out when I was at Homestead Air Force Base getting my shots. The guy giving me my bubonic plague shot said, "Did you hear that one of the women was killed over there?" I said, "No." My stepmother was cringing in the other room. I found out all my parents had decided not to tell me, but without any of the others knowing. But anyhow, my brother was the only person we weren't telling that I was going over to Nam. We all had a sense he'd go out of his gourd.

So we went to what I call boot camp in Washington, D.C. There they taught us how to do these programs we'd be doing over there. But we didn't get any political orientation. We didn't get any idea of the realities per se. All we were taught was what our job would entail.

I can't remember how long the flight to Nam was. Forever, it seemed. But I remember when we landed in Saigon. It was night and they were under a blackout, so there were no lights on the field. Just as we approached, they turned on the landing lights. Then, when the plane stopped, we were rushed off. We ran to the processing hut, which was also blacked out — I remember they opened the door and we sort of ran and hurtled in. It was very, very hot. And it was pitch night outside. And now here we were in this foreign country after having been on a plane for three years. That's when I began to think, "Gee, we really may be in a war here."

I remember somebody didn't have her passport right — there was a mess-up with her. But finally we were all processed. Then they took us off to our hotels in downtown Saigon. That was an experience! I don't remember the name of our hotel, but of course it wasn't Western. I had a little small room with filthy sheets and a very interesting bathroom. I think the toilet was on the floor — a squat toilet. I remember asking my roommate, Joyce, "Hey, what do you do with this?" Also, a Vietnamese man slept outside our door, on the floor. That was our security.

I think we spent a week or so in Saigon. We were oriented to the country, indoctrinated about the culture. We learned about the differences between American and Vietnamese culture, and how we would fit in. And there were women who had been in country awhile to help orient us. That was a little more useful and helpful than anything else we got. Also, we got a sense of the places we could choose to go, the locations we could request.

I knew my brother was in the First Marines, near Hoi An, which was outside of Danang. So I requested to be based in Danang, where I could see him. My brother and I, at that time, hadn't seen each other for about two years — maybe it had even been three, because I'd been off at college and he'd been off at boot camp.

Anyhow, we just hadn't connected, hadn't seen each other. So I requested Danang and then called my brother from Saigon. I called him on what they called a land phone — that was a trip-and-a-half! I'm calling from Saigon, which is quite a ways south — I had to go through all these relay places to get to where my brother was at. There were all these military guys relaying the calls: "Are you an American?" They kept asking that. So they were getting the story. And the story was: "She's trying to reach her brother — she hasn't seen him in two years!" Anyway, I finally got through to his unit and there was like total silence. On the other end was this guy who, when I said I wanted to speak to Doug and that this was his sister calling, said, "I beg your pardon, ma'am . . . Your brother? Would you repeat that? Your brother? Goddamn — your bro'! Excuse, me — man! Man, your brother is Doug? Well, he's not here, he's out fighting." "Well, would you please tell him his sister called?" "His sister — you're sure of that?" I say, "Yeah! Tell him his sister called and she's going to be in Danang, at Freedom Hill —"

So I got sent to Danang, to Camp Baxter. Our center was at Freedom Hill, which was this huge, huge mountain where they had a PX, a big USO center, a Red Cross center, stores, basketball courts, all kinds of recreation stuff. And, on my first day at our center, my brother showed up. It was funny — we opened the door and in he walks! I forget what he says — something like "My Lord!" But he had on his jungle fatigues, his ammo. We made him check his guns at the door. It really was a real incredible shock, though, to see my brother in all this war stuff, especially after not having seen him in two or three years. I remember how I went tearing across the room. I grabbed hold of him and was hugging and kissing him — all the guys lined up behind him, they wanted to be next — and he was just eating it up. He'd already been in Vietnam eight months.

After that, any time they needed resupplying, my brother's commanding officer would let him come to the rear. So my brother would come to Freedom Hill and go back to the hootch with us. He had twelve girls — Freedom Hill was the biggest unit in the country, with three mobile units, three base runs as well as the center — to fuss over him. I guess you'd say he was adopted as the mascot of the units while he was there. And he loved it. He really ate it up.

One time, I remember, my unit flew out to Hoi An. My brother's unit was right nearby, and we saw each other out in the field. Actually, a firefight was going on. I was in an illegal place at the time.

My brother and I hadn't been close before Nam, but in Nam we were very, very close. This is how it was with almost every man I met over there. There were no barriers — you were instantly close. I mean, guys would come up and talk to you about the most incredible personal stuff, from diseases to lovers. Guys would come back from R and R and show you pictures of their prostitutes. With pride. I remember — it's funny to think about it now — covering pictures of their prostitutes with contact acetate. Covering them so they wouldn't get wet when they were out in the bush. I'd be sitting there thinking to myself, "No one in a million years would believe this. . . ." But there I was, protecting some guy's picture of his prostitute while he's giving me a detailed description of his R and R. It was just as though I was another guy — not just another guy, but a close male friend. So they would talk to you about their diseases, their lovers, their problems at home, their families, their wives, their mothers. . . . They would talk to you about what was going on in their units. It was just instant intimacy. And you met all sorts of guys. All races — guys that, back in the States, you'd never be connected up with.

Speaking of races, we had a race riot at Camp Baxter. There were big differences between the officers, who were mostly white and educated and had officer privileges, and the infantrymen — they were mostly black, poorly educated, and without the privileges the officers had. As far as I could see, the blacks were not treated fairly or equally. For one thing, they were given a lot of the shit details. In general it was a micro-society at Camp Baxter, only with all the stresses of a normal society exaggerated. After the race riot we had to have armed guards sleeping inside our unit. We didn't know who we were more afraid of — the guys who were rioting, or the guys who were sleeping in our unit.

Also, at one point the perimeter was violated by the VC. Our hootch was out near the perimeter, and one night there was all kinds of banging on our door. After that there was all sorts of other stuff that went on, security-wise, so they finally decided they better transfer us from Camp Baxter to the more secure Twenty-fourth headquarters.

In terms of the war, Danang was the worst spot that I was at. They called Danang Rocket City, because it was always being rocketed. The first night I was there, seventeen rockets hit our base. I heard the alarm, jumped out of bed, and ran to the bunker — Those bunkers! You don't want to go in those bunkers at two o'clock in the morning, because you don't know what's in there. Snakes. Crawling things. They were like swamps; I mean they were gross. Just gross. After that we decided we didn't like going to the bunkers, so what we would do was pull the mattress over us and get under the bed. You just got used to sleeping that way, right through the rocket attacks. I mean, you just said, "Forget it about the bunkers," and slept underneath your bed.

Other things happened while I was at Danang. Once we did a run to Khe Sanh, right up by the DMZ. The helicopter pilot got off track and we ended up over Laos, where we could easily have been shot down. Once we got on a helicopter with a lot of wounded guys, and once we got on a helicopter we weren't supposed to be on. It was filled with body bags. And, out of Danang, we ended up on some fire bases that came under fire. Once I was with my friend Joyce on a fire base and Joyce — she had her movie camera — started filming the incoming. I yelled, "You idiot!" and some GI grabbed her and she fell. But she has it on film, just as she's going down. It was crazy, I mean, it was so out of reality for us. "Oh, this is a war! Oh, look at the war movie! Wow!" Kind of like that. It was crazy.

Another time we'd flown out to a fire base and the unit had moved, so someone sent for a jeep to pick us up and take us to where they'd moved. We weren't supposed to do that — if the place hadn't been secured and cleared, we weren't supposed to go there. Well, of course the guys didn't know any of these rules, and we don't know half of them ourselves. So we go by jeep and get caught in a crossfire. Only we'd gone too far to turn back, so we went on to the unit. As it happened, I got to see my brother — the unit I ended up at was his.

And I was on a fire base once where the NVA would pretend to be rice-paddy farmers during the day and then at night they would get into their uniform and play soldier. This one fire base had this big telescope. I asked a GI what it was for, and he said, "We watch for NVA. We watch where these farmers go when they leave the field, because they often turn into soldiers." Then he says,

"Here — look!" So I watched this farmer through the telescope for ten or fifteen minutes. Pretty soon he went into this little wooded area and came out with a uniform on. I said to the GI, "Come here!" You know, I couldn't believe it wasn't a setup. I knew it wasn't, I knew he hadn't planned that little incident just for me, but it just didn't seem real — until we were getting incoming and they were calling for our chopper to get us out of there.

What else happened at Danang? Well, we had Army-Navy games. Football. We were the cheerleaders. And Danang was where I barely escaped getting raped. Just after I left Danang, a girl was actually raped. Right in our hootch, too.

OK, what happened to me was this. I used to do volunteer work at Sacred Heart Orphanage. Whenever I could, after work, I'd go and help the nuns out. I'd play with the kids, take them stuff I'd had sent through my family and my church at home. It was wonderful. But OK, this happened on the road from the orphanage. It was a long deserted road that I had to walk, and it had big trees on either side. And our main form of transportation during off-hours was hitchhiking. We hitchhiked everywhere in Vietnam. Can you imagine that? It's weird to think of all the stuff we did, just as a matter of course. When we were on duty, we always traveled by chopper or truck or cargo plane or whatever, and we always traveled in pairs. This was both for security purposes and for morale. But when you were off duty you traveled by yourself and you traveled whatever way you could get there. So hitchhiking was no big deal. It got to be a normal way of life — you'd go down the road and you'd get picked up by a jeep full of guys or something.

So this day I was walking to the orphanage and this deuce-and-a-half [a two-and-a-half-ton truck] passed me with two guys in it. Then they stopped and said, "You want a ride?" I said, "No thank you, I'd prefer to walk," because my whole life I've always been very perceptive with being able to read vibrations from men. So then they went real, real slow. They followed me to the orphanage. They were delivering something there, but then they just hung around. So I had a feeling about these guys. They should have been long gone, but they were waiting to follow me again.

Now here's the conflict: you're supposed to be nice to the guys. You never know if you're the first American woman they've seen, so you always tried to be friendly. So when they stopped again and asked if I wanted a ride, my instincts told me not to get in the truck, but my professional self said, "Now what are you supposed to be doing here in Nam?" So against my better judgment, I said OK. That was a big mistake. They put me in the middle and one guy started to drive and the other guy started to molest me. His hands were everywhere — up my dress, in my panties. I was biting him and yelling at him. The other guy, the driver, was getting a little nervous. But they were both saying things like "Well, you do this all the time. You give it to the officers for free — what's the matter, you gonna charge us?" And I kept saying, "Stop it — I don't deserve to be treated like this!" I was trying to be very cool and rational, but finally I said, "If you don't take your goddamned hands off me I'm going to scream my lungs out and I'm going to file a report, and besides, I could be your sister! I have a brother here!" One of the guys was black and was making a racial issue out of it, too.

I don't think they were dangerous in terms of hurting me physically. They weren't threatening me with their weapons. They just thought I was a loose woman and that I'd been doing it and it was no big deal. That was the idea a lot of guys had about the Red Cross women.

Anyhow, I made myself real to them. The driver started getting more and more nervous and said to the other guy, "Maybe she really doesn't do this —" I finally knew I was reaching them. That's when I said, "Look, you don't deserve to have this on your record. It's bad enough being stuck in this place, bad enough having to be away from your families. You don't need this." So he stopped the truck and said, "Let's let her out." The other guy said OK and opened the door — but I had to crawl past him and he was all over me.

I got out. They sped off. I was shaking — I was as furious and indignant as I was anything else. And then I thought, "Oh, God, I've got to hitchhike —" I got picked up by five guys in a jeep and all I could think was "Ha, I don't need this!" But I got back to the unit all right. Then came the conflict about what to do. I felt I really did understand the men's perceptions of us. It's reasonable to think "What would healthy, intelligent American women want to be running around in a war zone for — unless they're making money out of it?"

There were so many rumors. Millions of rumors about the Red

Cross women — every guy claimed he'd had it with one of us. I don't know if any American women were over there as prostitutes, but I did have guys come up to me with money in their hands and say, "Here — how much are you getting now?" And I know of a couple cases of women who were what you might call very promiscuous and indiscriminate. So there was a general sense of what our reputation was. Plus we're talking about guys who got pulled away from their homes and families to fight a lousy war that no one cared anything about and that wasn't being fought in a way that they could understand. And then there were guys in the rear having all these things pulled on them, and half of them would be drugged — well, maybe not half, but a lot of them. So I understood what would cause them to act that way with me. In spite of my anger, I understood.

That's why I was in conflict about whether to report them or not. My reason for wanting to report it was so that, if these guys were dangerous, the same thing that happened to me wouldn't happen to another woman. Or to me again — I went to that orphanage all the time. But if they weren't dangerous, I didn't want to do anything to screw up what was already a bad experience for them. I was in real conflict. So I talked to my friend Joyce, who at that point was my acting unit director. We talked as friends, not on an official basis, and then we went to see a lawyer on the base — I think he was a judge — who we were friends with. We talked informally. Finally I made my decision not to report the incident.

I had something else happen at Danang that was pretty unsettling. The unit at Freedom Hill had a lot of guys who had just come into the country and hadn't been assigned to their regular units yet. There was one guy brand-new off the plane, starched fatigues, the whole nine yards. He was just a fresh-faced little baby, a sweet dark-haired kid. I don't remember his name but I do remember playing gin rummy with him. Well, the next day he got sent out to his unit. It was the 101st Airborne up there in Quang Tri. Now at that time the Red Cross didn't have a separate unit in Quang Tri. So every week two of us would go up there for a week. Well, the day that guy left it was my turn to go to Quang Tri. So I went up there and on one of the days we were working in the hospital, which was really more of a MASH [Mobile Army Surgical Hospital] unit. We were entertaining the guys, doing our activities, you know. And there, on one of the wards, I saw the dark-haired kid with half his face blown off. Tubes were sticking out all over him. He was sort of semiconscious, so I went over and held his hand. I was in shock. I was really in shock. A couple minutes after I left, he died.

Do you know I came back from Vietnam and never talked about that kid? I felt nothing when I came back. Absolutely nothing — no reaction at all. It's only been in the past year that I've started to get in touch with my feelings.

There were some good things, though, about being at Danang. The guys out in the field, on the fire bases we'd fly out to, were the most enthusiastic, the best to program to. The Marines were wonderful — there was nobody in the world to program to like the Marines. I guess they got the shit so knocked out of them in boot camp and the shit so knocked out of them in the field that they just gave us all they had. For instance, one of the main games we'd do with them was slamboard. You'd divide the guys into teams — it didn't matter what the subject was, it could be cars, it could be sports — and the teams would be given little cards with answers on them. Blue cards for blue team, red cards for the red team, whatever. The cards had Velcro on the back of them. And then you and the woman you were programming with would ask a question and the guys would have to find the answer on the card. Then they'd run up to the board and slam it on. The first team to get up there got the points, you know. Well, the Marines out on the fire bases — the Marines were wonderful! They'd get so into the energy of the game they'd forget everything else and be tearing up to that board. The boards, as you can imagine, had to be helicopterproof, bulletproof, and especially menproof. Those guys would come flying up to those boards, hit them with all their weight. They really were getting all their aggression and stuff out, you know.

I did love working in the centers. I loved the one-to-one — you could come and sit down with a couple guys at a table and play cards. You could just talk. You could shoot pool with them. That was good. What I did not like were the parties — I hated all that social junk. When I was off duty I either spent my time at the orphanage or I went back to the hootch and hibernated. I hated the party circuit. My impression was that — now this is just my impression — the officers thought we were theirs. At parties they would monopolize us. So I avoided parties like the plague, especially the generals' messes, which really were the worst. Some of the women, of course, loved to party and did it all the time. It was part of our job. Every week your unit of women would have a meeting that would last half or all the morning and you'd plan your social agenda. All the invitations from all the officers or all the units would come in, and we'd have to send representatives to all their parties. It was just constant. I hated it, used to trade off lots whenever I could with the women who really liked to party. I didn't like being in a social situation surrounded by all these guys. Usually I would just hang with two or three guys that were either good buddies or quasi-lovers. These were usually the guys who went to the orphanage with me. Or they might take me to the beach and protect me from everybody else so I could be left alone. But I hated those parties because I hated being on display.

After Danang I was sent to Cam Ranh Army. Now Cam Ranh was a rear area, so to speak, and it was really tough to work with the guys there. Yeah, Cam Ranh was really the pits. I was sent there as one of four new women whose job was to rebuild the Red Cross unit, because they'd had some horrendous things happen at Cam Ranh. One of the women had died. She had a rare blood disease that had been complicated in Vietnam. She died. And then there was a woman who skipped the country. She just got on a flight and went to Thailand or something. Plus the women had gotten into smoking pot and having guys over at their trailers, which was breaking all the rules. Now my opinion about those rules is that I was glad we had them. They gave you some sense of safety and security and privacy. Your job itself was grueling enough — you were constantly being put in situations with men who were horny as hell. Men who were angry, who had had all sorts of miserable things happen to them, who were disoriented for all kinds of reasons. So there were many, many times when you were physically, emotionally, and psychologically threatened, just in the course of doing your job.

So if all the women obeyed the rules you had some sense of protection because the guys learned to respect you. And it was important that they respect you — otherwise not only could you not do your job, but you weren't safe. Now for the most part, the women I worked with obeyed the rules. At least they did when they were on duty — really, they were terrific, very professional in a potentially chaotic situation. If they had affairs when they were off duty, that was their business, as far as I was concerned. I myself chose not to be very sexual while I was in Vietnam. I made that decision before I went — I didn't want to get involved in a very intimate relationship over there because I didn't think it was going to be very real. I did find one guy with whom I fell in love. We continued the relationship after we got back to the States, but I did stay within the limits I set for myself while I was over in Nam. Not that I was against a woman having relationships — I thought that was natural and normal and fine. But you just had to use some discretion about it. Otherwise — well, you got into all sorts of stuff. And that was what had happened at Cam Ranh Army and why we were sent in to clean up.

Cam Ranh Army was so horrendous I almost quit and went home. I mean, we'd go to the unit to program and the guys would be on drugs. Also, they weren't used to the women doing their jobs. We'd show up and they'd just look at us like "What are you doing here?" The women who had been there before us just hadn't gone to work if they hadn't felt like going. And at night they'd have very public parties in their hootches and they'd be smoking dope. And often, at Cam Ranh Army, they took us for prostitutes. They just assumed that's what we were — you spent a lot of energy proving you weren't over there making money. It was horrendous. The women who had been there before us had just made a joke out of the SRAO. I think Saigon actually fired two or three of them. Anyhow, we were getting obscene phone calls. And you'd go to program and the guys would just be stoned out of their minds. Now, none of this happened at any other place I was at. Like I said, Cam Ranh was in the rear, so most of the guys there hadn't seen any action. It was harder for those guys, because they had more time to think. They felt inadequate because they weren't out in the field fighting. Also, it was a heavy lifer area, an area where the military was expecting spit-polished boots and all that. And those guys just couldn't relate.

Yeah, I did have a lot of guys proposition me at Cam Ranh, and it was more than just your typical "Hey, honey — you wanna?" I mean real nasty, aggressive propositions. Out in the field again, it was different. I have no complaints about how those guys treated us. They were wonderful out in the field. Oftentimes they were more afraid of us than we even thought to be of them — I mean, they hadn't taken a bath in six months, hadn't said anything that was more than four letters long in terms of their vocabulary. And here were these American women plopped down on their fire base — sometimes they would just stare at you, follow you around and stare. That's why the programs were such wonderful icebreakers.

On Christmas, I remember, we had our very own helicopters for the day. There were six of us, two in each helicopter. We flew out to the fire bases with bottles and bottles of champagne, also hot food and mail. And we'd land where these groups of guys were waiting to go out and fight and we'd just pop open a few bottles of champagne and the guys would go "Huh? Huh?" and then we'd get in the helicopter and fly away again.

We did have our favorite units. One of them was out in Hoi An. They were always stoned, absolutely always stoned, and sometimes they were hostile. But somehow we liked them. They were way out in the boonies, those guys.

The things we got used to! Like, out in the field, we'd brush our teeth out of helmets. And you learned how to go to the outhouse in twosies, you know, sharing the outhouse with another woman. One time I was on a fire base and they built this little outhouse for the women. It didn't have a roof. Well, when this other woman and I came out of the outhouse we got a standing ovation! There were guys up on the hill with binoculars, all clapping when we came out of the outhouse. What do you do in a situation like that? Well, you smile, that's what you do. Another time we were in a helicopter flying over a group of guys who had just come back from the bush. Now they had what they called shower trucks, which were these big flatbed trucks with a couple of shower nozzles rigged up. All the guys would be herded naked, like cattle, onto the trucks for these group showers. Well, the helicopter pilot saw we were coming up on them and wanted to embarrass us — or embarrass them, we never figured it out, but anyhow, he wanted to get his jollies. And here we're leaning out the door of the helicopter, waving at the guys below, and my long blond hair is flying out of my helmet — Well, the guys are waving, and I'm waving, and then we figure out what's happening — It was so funny, it really was. They didn't know whether to wave or cover themselves.

Another time I was sort of flying the chopper. That was illegal, totally illegal, but the pilots were always asking us if we wanted to fly. I was pretty afraid of it, but one time I said, "OK, fine —" so I got up there and he's showing me what to do. Just as I'm getting behind the stick we get a radio message — another chopper with a full bird colonel in it is coming within range. Well, if we'd gotten caught, this pilot would have lost his wings for letting me behind the stick. So we just drop. We just land in the middle of this jungle and out come all these GIs, thinking we're the rescue chopper picking them up. And then they see me in the pilot's seat and just stop everything and stand there staring. They were in total shock — totally disoriented. I mean, what's this? Right away we took off again. So they figured out that we weren't their bird, that we hadn't come to take them to safety or take them out to fight.

There were some real funny things like that. And the strangest things, in Nam, came to seem normal after a while.

OK, let me tell you about the fashion shows in Cam Ranh. Our center there was named Steppin Groove and it was located in the section of Cam Ranh where the guys were leaving the country, DROSing. These guys were just there to get their urine tests to make sure they didn't have any drugs in them, just waiting to get processed to go home. So we put on a fashion show for the guys at the Steppin Groove Center. We modeled civilian clothes. The show was such a success the fire marshals had to come — the place was absolutely packed, so packed it was a fire hazard. Then the generals at Cam Ranh got wind of it.

Well, this one general decided a fashion show was a wonderful thing. He decided we were going to put on a fashion show for thousands — not hundreds, thousands — of guys. He wanted the Air Force as well as the Army in on it, and he wanted all the Red Cross women at Cam Ranh, both on the Air Force and the Army side. He wanted all these guys and he wanted all eight of us. So he got together with these other generals and they had a — what do you call it? — a gangplank built. A walkway. And they had the military band and they set up stadium lights and they built stadium seats that would hold three thousand. So there we are in our little hot pants and miniskirts being paraded in the middle of the night in front of three thousand horny guys. Well, they played music and then at the end of the show we had to go out and get guys in the audience and dance with them. They were afraid to come up and dance with us onstage — except for the ones that were drunk or stoned. They came up. They were grabbing us. And we were nervous. When we'd had the fashion show in the center, the small show, we more or less knew the guys. But this big show was a lot different. It was scary — as far as we were concerned, it was out of control. I mean, it really was a bit much — displaying us in that way.

I don't remember any major trauma happening, though. The insult of the year came with the Bob Hope Christmas Show. He sent word, or his entourage sent word, wanting to know if we would like to be the dressers, to help the women backstage. We were highly indignant. We said, "No, we're service people, too. We want to be entertained." So we went to the show. It was in this huge stadium filled with thousands and thousands of guys. And when we Red Cross women walked into the stadium — we came in together, and we were still in uniform because we'd come straight from work — we got a standing ovation. All the men suddenly stood up and started applauding us — it was just incredible. We were all sobbing. That was really a wonderful thing.

The Bob Hope Christmas Show was actually very controlled in comparison with the USO shows that came around. The USO shows were obscene. Obscene! The entertainers, most of whom were Thai or Japanese, were really like strippers. Sometimes we were billeted with women employees of the USO — not the entertainers — and got to hang out with them. However, the Red Cross discouraged that. According to Saigon, all USO girls were wild and naughty, while we were — quote unquote — nice and proper. Ha! Those were just Saigon's stereotypes. I made one good friend in the USO — we still see each other, even after all these years.

So there are the bad memories and there are the good ones. There are also the ones that are some of each: like once, at Cam Ranh, the perimeter got overrun with VC. I was on my way home — I'd worked the swing shift at the center, and the center was a significant distance from where we lived. So this other girl and I were coming home in our jeep and all of a sudden the place was crawling with Military Police and military guys. They pulled our jeep off the road, and this GI pulled me out, threw me down into the sand and jumped on top of me. A firefight was going on — I don't know how long it lasted, but this GI was laying on top of my person the whole time. Protecting me. Then, when the firefight was over, he picked me up, brushed me off, and put me back in the jeep. I never knew who he was.

Like I said, I did not like Cam Ranh, being on the base there. Cam Ranh really, totally did me in — I cried a lot when I was there. I was depressed. I wanted to go home. I even told Saigon I was going to quit, so they told me I could have my pick of locations. I went to Phan Rang then, finished out my time there. Phan Rang was fine. But by then all I could think about was leaving Nam.

I was luckier than some of the women I worked with. Nobody that I was intimately buddy-buddy with got killed — that I know of. I did have a guy who used to write me with such regularity that when I didn't hear from him I went looking through all the hospitals till I found him. He had a very severe case of malaria. That was scary. And my brother disappeared for a while, and that was very scary. But I didn't lose anybody. My friend Joyce had lost her fiancé before she'd come to Vietnam — he'd gotten killed, and she decided to come. And another woman in the unit got engaged to a pilot while we were there. He got shot down and killed. But I myself, I didn't lose anybody.

The hard part for me is that I met so many men and just don't know what happened to them. Some would hang around the center regularly, month after month — but I can't remember names, I can't put names to the faces. The ones I was closest to I know came back OK, but there are all the others. . . .

So you come back and people ask you, "What was it like over there?" How do you answer? How do you tell someone it was the most wonderful and the most terrible experience of your life? I mean, you can't possibly make people understand what it was like, so you don't talk about it. After I got back a lot of people, even my good friends, never knew I'd been in Nam. I felt I just couldn't talk about it except with people who had been there.

Eight years after I got back I went to see the movie *Coming Home*. I am not a hysterical person, but I became absolutely hysterical. I started to sob uncontrollably. I felt this incredible, intense pain, emotional pain, and I couldn't handle it. That episode scared me so badly I decided I was never going to read about Vietnam or talk about Vietnam, ever. But whenever the subject of Vietnam would come up, in any situation, tears would come to my eyes — I knew I had a lot of stuff there. Only, you see, my pain didn't make sense to me. I had always minimized my experience in Vietnam. I always told myself, "Hell, you weren't a guy. You weren't fighting. How can your experience have been so tough? You don't have any right to feel that way!"

77

Well, about two years ago, when they started networking for the women who had been civilians in Nam, I started reconnecting with other women. I started sharing some experiences. I started to get in touch with my feelings — with a lot of the fear, for one thing. I realize now that I must have been afraid many times over there. Also, in the last year or two, my brother and I have started talking. I really think I've worked through a lot. Now I can read about Vietnam — as you can see, I have gobs and gobs of Vietnam books on the shelf over there. And I'm able to talk pretty freely now, without a lot of crying or pain. Now what I feel I need is recognition. There is a sense of wanting to be identified as having been in Vietnam. Not because I supported the war. No, I want to be identified because I feel that what I did over there was valuable. I want to be proud of that. Because for so long I was ashamed. For so long I was afraid people would think I supported the war.

Let me end by telling you what happened to me last May, at the reunion in New York. I'd only been there a few hours when I started getting sick. It was horrendous — I couldn't cry, but I had this terrible headache, and then I started throwing up. I threw up and threw up, and when that was over, I was OK. The headache went. The depression went. I just threw it all up out of me. Later I told my therapist what happened and she said, "That's a normal response. Because your experience in Vietnam made you sick."

That's how I understand it. It was terrible and it was wonderful, but it made me sick. I'm better now — I've worked through a lot of my issues. In fact, I'm starting to call myself a civilian veteran — something I never felt entitled to call myself before.

*Cherie Rankin lives in Norwood, Massachusetts. She is a clinical social worker specializing in the treatment of alcoholism.*

# Julie Forsythe

*Julie Forsythe grew up on a Quaker dairy farm near Medford, New Jersey. "A lot of my youth was spent milking cows and raking hay." On her father's side, Julie traces her Quaker ancestry back to the early eighteenth century. Her mother, who was a pacifist during World War II, comes from a family of Congregationalists.*

*In 1972, a year after she graduated from Oberlin with a degree in religion, Julie accepted an offer from the American Friends Service Committee. "It was a rehabilitation project in Quang Ngai — a civilian center for Vietnamese amputees, burn victims, paraplegics, and quadriplegics. The job seemed like an absolute natural for me."*

*Unlike most Americans in Vietnam, Julie became fluent in Vietnamese. She also stayed through the change of government: "most Americans call it the fall, they call it the liberation." In October of 1975 she returned to the United States with a doctor she'd met in Quang Ngai.*

YOU NEVER get over the sense of green and flowers in Southeast Asia. Coconut palms, mango trees — the villages are really beautiful, especially where the mountains come down to the coast. And Saigon. You know, the earliest Western travelers there — the Portuguese were there in the sixteen hundreds — talk about walking on the roads out of Saigon and being entirely overwhelmed by the smell of orchids. Because, you know, the trees were just everywhere full of orchids. Of course, by the time I got there the Americans had done a fairly nasty job.

That's why there were so many diseases — the whole economy was wrecked. For instance, the U.S. came in with bulldozers and plowed down the hedgerows, right through the irrigation system. We messed up the fields and left Agent Orange in the hills, so every spring there were floods. Yeah, all the wells were messed up, too — you can't just wreck an environment the way we did and not leave a lot of nasty footprints. Typhus. Bubonic plague. Polio. All kinds of diseases from lack of public health and a completely destroyed economy.

Yeah, it used to be a beautiful country.

I wasn't prepared for a lot of things I saw. Like the prison wards. Or once I was in surgery and they were doing amputations — this was right after I got to Quang Ngai — and I nearly passed out. Horrible. But the kids were the worst. Up to forty percent of our patients were kids — we saw about a thousand people a year — because the kids are the ones who take the ducks out and take the water buffalo down to the river. And some yo-yo leaves a landmine in the path and — pop! That's it. No, I wasn't prepared for how many kids were so badly damaged.

A lot of them came in with no arms and legs. And we saw kids with neck injuries from shrapnel, so that they were entirely paralyzed. At times we took over the hospital's burn unit, where we saw the kids who'd been napalmed. Napalm is really grim stuff. What's so disgusting about it is that only oil stops the burning. Water doesn't stop the burning, so when kids get hit with napalm they run into the river and the stuff keeps burning — they keep burning. And listen, the most disgusting thing you've ever seen in your life is a child who's just totally burned. Right down to the muscle. It's very, very painful, and the treatment is brutally long. It's almost impossible to undo that kind of damage. Maybe under extremely sanitary conditions — which we didn't have — and with horrible, really horrible, scar tissue.

Other burns we saw were due to black marketeering. A lot of airplane fuel was ripped off from the Air Force and sold as cooking fuel. And when it ignited — whooom! Really disgusting, those body burns.

We did the best we could for our patients, under tough conditions. There never seemed to be enough of us, though. The center had a Vietnamese staff of sixty. They included the prosthetists, the physical therapists, the people who made limbs, a maintenance department, a schoolteacher, a social worker, a nurse, and a physician's assistant. The Americans were my husband, Tom — he was the doctor — a physical therapist who was training the Vietnamese, a husband-and-wife team who were codirectors, and me. I did all the jobs that fell in the cracks.

My position was great, because I got to relate to everybody. I got to take patients back to their homes, for instance — which meant I was out in the countryside much of the time. And I did the books. I emptied the trash. I made trips to Danang to get pipe — we made all our own wheelchairs out of electric conduits, American military surplus. So I'd always have to go to the black market and scrounge. And let's see. I learned to make legs from a Vietnamese who'd invented the paddy leg. You know what a paddy leg is? Well, suction is a terrific force, and if you're going to work in a rice paddy with a prosthesis on, the foot will be sucked off. So this guy invented a very, very small foot that you could screw on, with a suction-release valve on the bottom. That way people could still go on being rice farmers even if they were amputees.

And we did nutritional evaluations. I remember once Tom and I went up to the mountains to do an evaluation on a hill tribe. It was pretty desperate — they were pretty much living on leaves. Not long after we got to the village a woman came out of a hut and grabbed me. "I want to show you a picture of my son," she said. "He was killed in the fighting." So I went inside. She showed me the picture, and then she started keening and weeping. And there was nothing I could do. Nothing but sit very quietly, listening to her. So that's what I did. I just sat and listened.

I don't know why that memory jumps out any more than the others. Because things like that were so much a part of what went on.

Or another time. One of my other jobs was taking tourists around. My Lai was very close to us, and it was a place American tourists often wanted to go. Not that there were a lot of tourists, but occasionally people would come. Reporters, for instance. So I'd take them across the ditch to My Lai. And one time we were standing there when some Vietnamese kids came up and stood with us. "Well," I said to the kids, "is there anything you want to say?" And one of them asked, "Why do you Americans think this place is so different from any other place?" You see, My Lai had been blown up seven times. And there we were, Americans, focused in on a single moment in what we think of as history.

Oh, the stories. Like you're planting rice and a bullet goes astray and — bang! — you're a quadriplegic. Or I could tell you a story about a woman who went home and poisoned her son as soon as they left the center. The child was a paraplegic and she couldn't take care of him with all her other responsibilities.

But let me go on to the liberation. Tom and I are in Saigon. And suddenly the whole country is changing hands. We make tracks for Danang by the first plane we can get north, and there's no one on the plane but us — everyone is going south, of course. But I had the severance pay for all our people, and it was very important to me that we end things at the center in a clean manner.

We make it back to Danang. That's when we find out there's no way they're going to let us near Quang Ngai. It had already been liberated.

In Danang people were going absolutely bananas. I remember nothing but mass hysteria — people hanging off the wings of airplanes, all that stuff you read about. The roads were jammed. It was almost impossible to get anywhere. This was the end of March, 1975.

All of a sudden Tom is told by the Buddhists to stay in Danang — they need doctors — and I'm told to get out. So I'm packed up and put on a refugee barge, hauled way out to sea. It was the damnedest thing that ever happened to me. There were all these hundreds of people trying to get on the barge. People pushing each other off. Mothers losing babies overboard. People throwing possessions over, throwing each other's possessions over, people coming up in rafts and getting pushed off by people who were on the barge. For twenty-four hours that kept up. I just stood on the barge like a total sardine. Waiting.

You never forget something like that — a big, flat barge in the middle of the high seas, very hot and impossibly crowded. All this hysteria, this pushing and shoving. Finally a freighter — it was a supplier, a U.S. ship bringing weapons in — pulled alongside and unloaded us up these little ladders. I remember the woman who wouldn't get off the barge. She just sat there in the middle after everyone else had gotten off, screaming, "I want to go home! I want to go home!" The Marines hosed her down and hauled her onto the freighter. Then they took all of us to Saigon, where I made the decision to stay until both Tom and I could get out of the country.

Saigon was encircled at that point. Every night, as soon as it got dark, the Viet Cong would start lobbing mortars in. But, from my perspective, Saigon wasn't bad at all. Maybe I was just used to military action by that time. Yeah, Quang Ngai — now that I remember it — was pretty hot. There was always shelling at the airport. The small bridges were blown up all the time. And I got so used to our ammunition dump blowing up I learned to sleep right through it. Compared to Quang Ngai, Saigon seemed safe.

So I just hung out in Saigon for a few months. I walked around and talked to people. I remember I read a lot.

On May nineteenth I was interrogated. It was Ho Chi Minh's birthday. There was this big march downtown, and I was just dying of curiosity — the communists love parades, all that kind of show. So I go downtown and watch it. And when I get back there are these two NVAs sitting in my living room with their AK-47s. "What do you think you're doing?" I said to them. They were only kids, maybe fifteen. "We're taking you away to be interrogated," they said. But there wasn't any jeep to take me away in. So we had to sit there and wait.

While we're waiting, I get these kids to tell their stories. They were southerners. They'd hidden in the caves during the bombings. And believe me, they'd seen a lot of hard stuff.

The interrogation? Well, I sat in a room and answered questions. It lasted a few hours. Four, maybe three. These particular guys, the ones who interrogated me, were actually very polite. They offered me tea. They'd heard of the center at Quang Ngai.

I wasn't afraid during the interrogation. Other things, by then, had scared me a lot more than that. Like, I was afraid of helicopters. I was afraid of the unclean water. And I always got in the habit of checking out paths, of asking, "Is it safe to walk here?"

I'd give my eyeteeth to go back and see what the Vietnamese have done. I sincerely hope they're not as militarized now. I'm sure things are desperately poor and probably still incredibly beautiful. But whatever's happened, it's their country now, and I'm glad of that.

*Now married, with two children, Julie lives on a communal farm near Putney, Vermont.*

# Mary Stout

*Mary Stout grew up in and around Columbus, Ohio. "I went to Catholic schools all my life — even nursing school was a Catholic school." Her mother worked in the home; her father "was a blue-collar worker. Actually, he owned his own business, distributing gasoline in a very small town." Mary enlisted in the Army in 1964, during her last year of nursing school. In 1966 she volunteered for Vietnam. She was assigned to the Second Surgical Hospital at An Khe, which was moved to Chu Lai in May of 1967. At An Khe Mary "did a little of everything"; at Chu Lai she worked in intensive care.*

M Y FATHER wasn't too hot about me joining the Army. What finally brought him around was I offered to have the nurse recruiter come talk to him. I thought that if anyone could convince my father, she could. Because the first thing that struck me when she came to talk to our class was that she was a perfect lady.

Which is what I was brought up to be. You know, we had the nuns. When I was in high school we even had to curtsy to them. So being a lady was, you know, very serious. And I think seeing the nurse recruiter really changed my father's idea.

It was 1964 when I signed up and 1965 when I graduated. At that time, there wasn't really much news about Vietnam. I didn't know what was going on there. And I had no idea that Vietnam was going to be a major part of my life.

In basic training I realized that everyone was a little bit bitten by the war bug. We spent a few days in a field-type hospital with mock casualties and all that kind of thing. You started to get the idea that this was the kind of nursing you were supposed to be doing. So a lot of people volunteered right out of basic training.

With me, what happened was that at Fort Ord, my first duty assignment, I met Carl Stout, who is my husband now. I knew we were going to get married, so when he got orders to go to Vietnam, I volunteered to go. I thought it would be important for us, for our life together, that I had that experience, too. It just seemed like Vietnam was going to be a real important experience in his life, and I didn't want to be cut off from it. I remember when my orders came through and I told my parents, my father asked me point-blank if I had volunteered.

Carl didn't get to Vietnam until the middle of December because he had to go to jungle school in Panama. I got there the first of November. The Second Surgical was in An Khe then, which is up in the highlands. An Khe was the base camp of the First Cav., but they were at that time pulling away. The area was pretty secure and there wasn't a lot of action there. So we were working eight-hour days, five days a week, and doing a lot of surgery on civilians. Then, in May, the hospital was moved to Chu Lai.

The Army was defending Chu Lai then because they were moving the Marines north, more toward the DMZ. Chu Lai was getting hot about the time we got there. Almost immediately we started twelve-hour days, six days a week. At first I was on the post-op wards, but after two or three weeks I went to the chief nurse and said I really wanted to work in intensive care. I guess I just felt I was ready to take on that challenge.

I learned pretty fast that you had to separate yourself emotionally from your patients in intensive care. Still, you remember particular people. Like this one guy who had been in an APC [armored personnel carrier] and they hit a mine and the gasoline exploded. He was the only one who came out of it alive. But he had terrible burns. We just expected him to die, waited for him to die. He was right across from my desk — we always kept the worst ones near the nurses' desk — and just looking at him I felt so helpless. I knew we couldn't evac him because he'd go into shock, and I knew I couldn't talk to him because there was nothing I could say. And he was conscious. I felt so guilty. Even after I got back I felt guilty about that guy.

I never could face death. Whenever we had patients die, I'd have to leave the ward or at least make sure I was at the other end when they came with the body bags. Because if I didn't have to look at the body bag, it seemed that person wasn't really dead. I just never could deal with the death part of it. And I'm not sure, you know, how I reconciled that.

Like I said, I tried to separate myself emotionally. But I remember faces; I even remember names. There was one guy named Johnny Darling — I remember him because he was in Carl's unit. A lot of times Carl's unit was in the Chu Lai area. Whenever I was off duty and the choppers would come in, I'd go straight to the emergency room and see what unit they were. I always had this fear that one day Carl would come in. I mean, I had a lot of confidence that he would take care of himself and that everything would be all right. But still, I always had to go and make sure he wasn't there.

Johnny Darling had stepped on a mine and lost both of his feet. The night he came in I walked over and started asking the units if anything had happened to Carl's company. And I remember this big black sergeant saying, "Oh, you're Lieutenant Reis. Don't worry about Lieutenant Stout. We're taking real good care of him." But, you know, I was always scared that something would happen to Carl.

We had a lot of people come in with missing arms, legs, hands: you name it, it was gone. We had one sergeant — I think he lost both legs at the hip, plus a hand and an arm. And he was blind, had a head injury and lots of internal injuries. I guess it was a mine of some kind — that's the kind of damage a mine does. That guy we did surgery on — even with all those things wrong, he was still alive. It was absolutely amazing.

So I think we did wonderful, wonderful work. I can't even imagine anything else I could have done where it would have felt more satisfying. In Vietnam I worked harder than I ever have, and I did more good. Thinking back, it sometimes amazes me.

There was one time, though, that I just got so overwhelmed I thought I couldn't take it anymore. It all had to do with this one patient named Steve.

Steve had a lot of internal injuries, but he had been through surgery and was doing really well — I didn't separate myself from him because I didn't think he was going to die. Also, I liked talking to him. He was fun to be around. I don't remember what we found in common now, but he was just one of those people I felt especially close to. Anyway, I came to work at seven o'clock one night and his breathing was pretty bad. I talked to the nurse who was on duty, asked her what the doctor had said. Now Steve's particular doctor was the only one we didn't have much faith in — maybe that's one of the reasons I got so close to Steve, because I was worried about his surgery. The corpsmen called this doctor the Butcher. And believe me, he deserved that name.

So the other nurse said the Butcher had been in to see Steve and had said he was just fine. Said we were supposed to just suction him — Steve had, among other things, a chest full of real rusty phlegm. So we keep suctioning him and suctioning him and he isn't totally feeling well, so I call the Butcher, who says he's just been up to see him and asks if his breathing has changed since I came on. I tell him no, it's really about the same but it's not too good. And then the head of the hospital walks onto the ward.

The head of the hospital — we were always real paranoid about him coming on the ward, because every time he came, someone went into cardiac arrest. I mean, this wasn't a joke. This was a kind of frightening thing. Anyway, he came on the ward and walked up to Steve and said something to me about his breathing. And Steve was talking to this doctor. And all of a sudden this doctor, the head of the hospital, says, "He's going into cardiac arrest." And he died, just like that.

We were on him right away — suctioning, bagging him. We put in a trachea tube, did everything we could, but we couldn't bring Steve back. And so finally the doctor turned to me and said, "This is all your fault. He should have had a trach, you should have known that —" Well, I had never had to make a decision about someone having a trach. That was one of the things we relied on the doctors for.

They came to take Steve off, like they did everyone else. I left the ward. But I had to work through the rest of the night. All I know is, I did it in a kind of fog. Because when I was walking off the ward before they brought the body bag, I was saying to myself, "Never again will I become close to anybody."

At seven o'clock the next morning I went straight to my room. I had a bottle of Black Label that I had bought to take to Carl. So I sit there contemplating it, saying, "If you drink that whole bottle right now, you'll probably die." And just then Carl's battery commander, who I had never met, knocks on the door. "I just stopped by," he says, "to introduce myself and tell you that any-time you want to come to the battery, we would love to have you." I asked him when he was going back, and he was going back right that minute. So I grabbed my steel pot and left. I didn't sign out or anything; I just got in that helicopter and went to spend the day with Carl.

When I got back that night, I went down to the club. That was something I did real often. At night, when I couldn't sleep, I'd go and throw down a couple of boilermakers. Anyhow, that night I went down and was sitting at the bar — just sitting there by myself, not talking to anybody — when the hospital commander comes up and sits down next to me. "Well," he says, "I'm glad you can be here at the club having a good time when you just killed somebody." And I get up and walk fast out the door.

The officers' club sat up on a cliff. There was a road that went down to the beach. I walked down the road and walked into the ocean, just kept on walking out. And then somebody — to this day I do not know who, or where he came from, or how he saw me — grabbed hold of me, picked me up, and carried me back to the beach. He just sat there and held me. God knows how long I cried. I just cried and cried and told him about Steve. I don't remember this person saying anything except "It's going to be OK."

For a long time he held me. Then he walked me back up the hill. And, you know, I don't think I even looked at him; I don't think I could even have seen him in the dark through all my tears. But I do believe it wasn't anybody that I knew.

Steve is something that never left me.

Because once I got back from Vietnam, I could not take criticism at all. Carl would come home and say something about the house, or the meal wasn't right, or just everyday kinds of little things — not that I didn't take the criticism, but it was like a lance. It was very, very painful. And I would have this image of Steve.

I would, well, not so much see Steve as feel him. Feel his actual physical presence. It was like Steve was there and things were the way they were when he died. It was the same feeling, the same feeling I had when he died — a feeling of helplessness and absolute uselessness. I'd think, "You didn't do this right, you didn't do that right, you didn't do right for Steve." So I was living with these terrible, terrible feelings of guilt. In my mind, I was seeing Steve all the time.

It wasn't just Steve I couldn't put into any perspective. It was Vietnam, the whole experience. When Carl and I first got home, nobody asked about Vietnam. Or if they asked, they asked the political kinds of questions. Of course, this was sixty-seven and the antiwar protests were starting and everything was becoming negative about Vietnam.

I got out of the Army when Carl and I got married. The Army

wasn't too good about assigning people together then, so it seemed like the best thing. It was strange for me, though. There were times when I felt very insignificant. Like, for the first couple of years after Carl and I got back, we would go to parties and the guys would tell war stories. Once, in Long Beach, the Petroleum Club had a big party for Vietnam veterans, but they were only honoring the men. Carl always told people, at parties and things, that I was a Vietnam veteran, too. And they would say, "Oh, you are?" And I'd say, "Yes." And that would be the end of it.

About three years after I got back I became aware that something was going on with me. Carl and I were in Wichita, Kansas, then. He was going to school at Wichita State. I was feeling very dead, because I wasn't doing anything with my mind except taking care of babies, so I decided to go to school, too. But I was feeling lots of pressure and lots of stress and seeing Steve all the time, and after a while it got to the point where I was almost immobilized.

I was taking this psychology course and really liked the instructor. One day I told him about how I couldn't take criticism — Carl was, you know, getting upset about having to take care of the kids when I was trying to study or go to school. So I told the instructor this, and I told him about Steve. Steve was with me all the time then; everything was the way it was when he died.

So, with this instructor's help, I started to deal with the guilt. In lots of ways, I got over it. But the memories are still there — the memories of the guilt and pain. And the memory of the loss. Everybody who was in Vietnam — particularly the nurses, but the guys, too, and even people who didn't serve — has one name on the memorial that epitomizes the tragedy of Vietnam. And for me that name is Steve. I can't find his name, and I can't remember his last name. For a while there I struggled real hard to remember it. But the most important thing is that Steve would never have wanted me to feel guilty about his death.

Three or four years ago Carl went to Korea and I was on my own for the first time. That was when I really started dealing with all my Vietnam stuff, because suddenly I had all the responsibility. I was always wondering if I was doing the right thing, if Carl would approve, if he would be angry — there was a lot of pressure and a lot of responsibility that I had never faced by myself before. That's when Vietnam was on my mind constantly. I'd be trying to concentrate on something, and suddenly I was thinking about Vietnam. So I decided to see if I could get in contact with some other veterans.

The first time I ever met another Army nurse was through the VVA. The chapter called me up and said this woman was coming down to the office and would I come talk to her. Well, I didn't want to talk to this woman — I was doing fine talking to the guys. Because my feeling was that I didn't want someone to open up all those places. I didn't have to deal with my things with the guys. They don't understand a woman's feelings. They don't understand about losing patients, about taking care of people and then having to see them die — the medics, maybe, and the corpsmen. But talking to another nurse, I knew, was going to open up some things. So I hemmed and hawed and finally went down and met her.

Well, we kind of skirted around. We talked about the rats, you know, and about the living conditions. But we weren't really, either of us, talking about the patients. When you start talking about the patients, that's where the hurt begins.

So I was driving her home. And I remember her saying something about a patient, mentioning someone's name. And I said, "Who was that?" Then she really opened up and I pulled the car to the side of the road. "My God," I said, "you've got one, too. The name of my patient was Steve." And we sat for a long time and talked.

That's how I started putting a lot of pieces together. I'd remember an incident and what hospital it happened at, whether we were in An Khe or Chu Lai, what the weather was like. For a while it seemed like I wanted to remember every minute, because I had spent so much time blocking all the memories out. Now I'm real content knowing the memories are coming back and that, when they come, I'm able to deal with them.

I don't want there to be another Vietnam.

Still, if my kids want to got into the military, I'll encourage them. Because I think the military is a good opportunity, especially for women. It's one of the few places women are treated equally. And if my kids want to volunteer to go to a war, I'll encourage them to do that. But it better be a war. I don't want any of these conflicts.

That was the problem with Vietnam — we didn't declare war, so we didn't get the country behind it. I don't know, if we'd declared war, whether we could have won or not. But declaring war would have changed the whole perspective of the country about the people who served there. Because the most damaging thing to us wasn't the war experience. It was our perception of that experience after we came home.

I have to tell you I was more frightened in this country after we came back than I ever was in Vietnam, even when we had mortar attacks and rockets were going off. Just before Carl and I were going to Wichita so he could go to Wichita State, we heard about a ROTC instructor in Syracuse whose house had been fire-bombed. I told Carl, "Grow your hair long, wear a moustache. Don't tell anyone you're in the military," because I was frightened of the antiwar protesters. I was frightened for my children.

It wasn't safe here. This was supposed to be home, and if you'd gone and served your country, it wasn't safe.

I believe the war was wrong, wrong from the concept of we'd been warned it was a war we shouldn't get into. High government officials made decisions against the best advice of the military. The military knew it was a war we were going to have a hard time winning, and the government just didn't listen.

I've always blamed the government. When I was over in Vietnam I thought we were right to do what we could to keep them from becoming a communist country. Now I think it was inevitable that Vietnam would go communist. And if we hadn't interfered, Vietnam would be in a lot better shape than it is.

But I still think service to your country is service of the highest order. I've never been ashamed of having volunteered.

*Mary Stout is National Membership Director of the Vietnam Veterans of America and Staff Advisor to the Vietnam Veterans of America Special Committee on Women Veterans. She and her husband have three teen-aged daughters.*

# Colonel (Retired)
# Eunice Splawn

*Eunice Splawn was the third of six children in a Southern Baptist family in Spartanburg County, South Carolina. Her father, a farmer, "had been on the front lines in World War I. He expected his sons to have to go to war — my older brother was a Korean vet — but of course he didn't expect his daughters to. When I joined the Air Force, I didn't think about ending up in a combat zone. I also had no idea I would stay in twenty years."*

*Eunice finished high school at seventeen, nursing school at twenty. "After I graduated I went to work in Michigan at the University Hospital in Ann Arbor for about six months. Then I went to Florida for about four months. After that I went to college at Bob Jones University, which is a very regimented, fundamentalist school. But I also wanted to travel, and I knew there was no way I could go and do all the traveling I wanted to do and still keep my seniority as a nurse."*

*In 1961 Eunice joined the Air Force. She received orders for Vietnam in 1967. From January of 1968 until January of 1969 she was stationed at the 22nd Casualty Staging Facility at Danang, where she was head nurse on a dispensary and casualty ward. In 1970, after working stateside for twenty months, Eunice returned to Vietnam as a flight nurse with the 57th Air Evacuation Squadron.*

I WAS IN MY EARLY THIRTIES when I went to Vietnam. I may not have been wiser, but at least I was older than a lot of the people — I'd been overseas and away from the tightclose-knitness of home. So it wasn't as difficult for me as it was for some of the younger ones, the ones who came straight out of training and went.

Still, I went over not really knowing what was going on. All I knew was, I was going over there to take care of patients. I don't think it really dawned on me that I was going to a combat zone until I stepped off the aircraft in Danang. I tripped on the steps coming off — I was in high heels, because we had to be in our class A uniform, which means a short, tight skirt, jacket, and high heels. I caught a heel in the step of the aircraft and walked right out of my shoe.

That was when I turned to the pilot — I was the last one off the aircraft — and said, "You know, my mother doesn't know I'm over here. I really don't want to be here. Can I go back with you? If I just get back in the aircraft, nobody will know the difference!"

He got very upset. He kept saying, "Honey, I can't do that. I'd take you back with me if I could, but I can't. I'm very sorry." The man thought I was serious. I wasn't that serious. But I had looked out and seen people in flight jackets and helmets carrying M-16s. It was then that it dawned on me where I was.

Before 1968, there were only male nurses at the base in Danang. When us eight girls came, of course, there was resentment. I don't know if there was any from the doctors — I didn't get any of their feedback, but I did get some from the male nurses. Their idea was that not only would they have to take care of male patients during a rocket attack, they'd have to take care of us. Well, during the Tet offensive we had one male nurse who was so scared he actually beat the patients to the bunker. We had to send him out within a couple of days — he couldn't take it anymore.

Our unit was a casualty staging station. This means we were set up to stabilize patients that came in off the field or from the hospitals or wherever. We got them after their initial treatment, so our job was to get them stabilized and on the aircraft to Cam Ranh Bay, Japan, the Philippines. We had minor surgery capacity in our unit and could do emergency stuff, but we didn't do big surgery, like they did at the Army and Navy hospitals. Our patients were kept — at the maximum — only overnight. It took me a long time to get used to this. I was used to seeing day-by-day progress with my patients. So it was very frustrating — we never knew whether our patients lived, got better, made it back to the States, or what.

My ward, at times, would have as many as seventy patients on it. I'd have to take care of everything myself, with just a ward master and one tech. One day, I remember, we handled over a hundred and sixty patients. We had them in the hallways, we had them laying on stretchers everywhere, we even put some of them across the street in the USO building. Looking back now, I wonder how we did it. But we managed. The patients helped take care of each other — the ones who could walk would get up and help.

The nurses' quarters were away from the hospital. We were up in the compound with the fighter pilots, the helicopter pilots, the senior NCOs, all your officers and doctors and all. I often thought if Charlie ever hit the compound and wiped it out, you would have nothing left there. The base would be gone — all you'd have would be techs and people who couldn't fly aircraft or take over the running of things. Fortunately, Charlie never hit the compound. His main rockets and things came in against the flight line. He'd walk the rockets up the runway, trying to hit the planes.

After the start of the Tet offensive, I remember counting about thirty rocket attacks. Finally I decided to heck with it — I didn't want to count anymore.

Like I said, when I first got there, things were fairly calm. Then, a few days before the start of the Tet offensive, I kept hearing people saying, "Tet is coming." And I kept saying, "What's Tet?" They told me Tet was this big holiday, but I still didn't know what it was, so it didn't make that much difference to me.

The day Tet started, I had no patients on my ward that needed anything. So we carried some of our supplies down to the Catholic and Protestant nurses at the provincial hospital; they could not get supplies, so we took them our needles and they boiled them down and used them again. We also took them other things, whatever we could spare. Anyway, I went downtown that day with the crackerbox ambulance. The guy riding shotgun had a rifle with him. He was real jumpy — every time a firecracker would go off, he'd jump four feet in the air. Of course, I didn't understand why, because I'd only been there fifteen days.

Well, we came to a corner. On this corner is a Vietnamese soldier in the ARVN uniform. He's approximately twenty feet away from me. I looked right at him and never in my life have I seen such hate in anybody's eyes. I remember thinking, "Hey, why is he hating me? We're over here to help them." I figured it might have to do with my being a female, but I really couldn't figure it out. Then, the next day, I found out that there was an entire squadron of Viet Cong in Danang. They'd infiltrated by wearing the ARVN uniform.

So that first day I was very, very close to a Viet Cong.

After the offensive started, I stood in the back of my ward and watched planes come in and strafe the village behind us. The Viet Cong had gotten through the village, but the Marines moved in behind the hospital and held them until an air strike could be called in. That was when I decided the Marines were really who they claimed to be. Before that I'd always thought they were just a little bit overrated — they were always telling you how great they were — but after that, I went to bed many nights saying, "Thank God for the Marines."

It was around that time that I Corps, up the road from us a small distance, was almost overrun. One of the guys from the ambulance group said to me, "Come on!" so I went. I remember going up to a place close to I Corps headquarters where they had a big cement landing strip. It was lined up, row after row, with Viet Cong people that had been killed the first night of Tet. How many I saw, I don't know. But I remember a Marine gunny [gunship] sergeant came in to see me and was extremely upset — he had realized that some of those bodies laying out there were women, and he was afraid he had possibly killed a woman. I explained to him that when someone has a gun and is shooting at you, you don't look to see if it's a man or a woman. This was very difficult for him to accept.

The first two days of the Tet offensive, we worked something like thirty hours without sleep.

I remember going down to the hospital. It was night, and the area was not secure at all — there were fires everywhere, and rockets and mortars were dropping all along the runway. Some of the girls were running on ahead of me. When they passed the wing commander's trailer, a guy said, "Halt! Who goes there?" One of the girls said, "We're nurses. We're on our way to the hospital —" I distinctly heard her say that, but apparently he didn't. Well, I had just gotten past the guy when I heard the loudest sound of my life — even with all the rockets and sirens, I heard him move the safety catch of his M-16. I stopped dead still, right in my tracks. Very slowly I turned to him and said, "We are nurses. We are on our way to the hospital." And this little voice said, "OK, ma'am." I realized then how scared he was — how close we'd come to getting mowed down by one of our own guys.

That night at the hospital, the chaplain and I crawled around underneath beds with patients who were not able to go to the bunkers — you took as many as you could to the bunkers, and the ones who could not go to the bunkers, you put them on stretchers and got them underneath the bed. Some of them were mental patients, guys who had just broken under all the strain. Myself, I'm sure I felt some anxiety, but there was so much to be done I didn't have time to feel it. For one thing, I was in charge of the ward and had to set up the triage area. So you had to triage — you had to decide which ones were critical, which ones had to be treated first, which ones would make it and which ones wouldn't. And you had to get their medicines attended to, and get their dressings changed. You had to get them bedded down if they were going to spend the night or get them set up to go on the ambuses if they were going out on air evac — during Tet, we'd get three or four flights out before midnight, because somewhere near midnight was usually when Charlie would start hitting us.

So you constantly had something or other going — you didn't have time to stand around and worry about the next rocket attack. You just kept working as long as you could. At one point during those first thirty hours we were told to get a few moments' sleep, and some little guy said, "Here, ma'am, take part of my mattress." For ten or fifteen minutes I shared a mattress with someone, I don't know who he was. But there was no way I could get any sleep.

After Tet, I ended up with a bad case of bronchitis. I was kept in the hospital for a short period of time, but I couldn't get myself to rest and relax because there was too much work to be done. I was always getting up to help them make beds and get the patients in and out. Of course, this was contrary to what the doctors wanted me to do. Finally they let me go back to my quarters to get as much rest as I could. Then I went back on duty half-days — for the first three or four the hospital commander picked me up at the end of my shift. On about the fifth day, when he came and said, "It's time for you to go off duty," I said, "I'm sorry, sir, but there's no way I can do that. There's nobody else on duty and too much work to do!" So I more or less worked my way back to health after Tet.

The whole year I was there I worked very closely with my corpsmen. I would know instinctively when one of the patients had gotten to them: I'd look in and one of the techs would be fighting tears and swallowing, and I'd go over and say, "Hey, go take a coffee break and come back when you can handle it." They did it for me on one occasion. I looked down and saw this guy who was about seventeen years old. He had both eyes out, and he was clutching a Purple Heart. I remember standing there thinking, "My God, that Purple Heart means nothing —" Just then one of my techs came along, put his hand on my shoulder and said, "Go take a coffee break, ma'am. We'll take over till you get back."

I remember some children being on our ward, kids that had been on the *Repose* or the *Sanctuary*. They had already been taken care of but we had to hold them on our wards until the military was able to get them back to their villages. One of them was a cute little girl who loved to play poker — she had been taught by the Navy corspmen exactly how to win, and she would cheat something terrible. The guys never could win with this little girl — it had to always be she or I winning. We had another child that had shrapnel wounds on the face. The sores, which had an odor to them, were not totally healed. One eye was blind from shrapnel, and she couldn't see very well. The other children didn't like being around her.

This particular child was on my ward for two or three days, and I had to give her baths and feed her. She couldn't understand what I was saying to her, but she understood the tone of my voice, and she understood touch. Each time I'd go away to take care of the other children, she would cry and reach for me. Well, the day she was supposed to be shipped out to her village, I took her down to the flight line. We were standing there when a plane went over — I had to cover both her ears, because she was terrified of the sound. Finally I got her on the aircraft. There, of course, I had to leave her — it was very hard for me to walk off with her still crying and reaching for me.

You could lose your heart to those little children. You looked into their faces and you really saw what the war was all about.

Of course, I'm talking about the injured ones. There were others that you didn't trust. When you went out into the villages on MEDCAPs [Medical Civil Assistance Program], there were children who would absolutely rip the watch off your hand. It was not uncommon, either, for them to come up to you and throw a Molotov cocktail. The Viet Cong, of course, used children for their own purposes. It was a sad situation; those children didn't have much of a life ahead of them. When our year was up, we could leave. But there was no way those children could leave, because it was their country.

I was fortunate to meet some of the best of the elite Vietnamese.

The Vietnamese wing commander's two young sons were on my ward — we did circumcision on them just as a goodwill gesture — so the commander invited me along with the doctors to their house and they took us out to a French floating restaurant. Another time I was invited to one of their squadron parties. These Vietnamese and their friends were very intelligent people. The commander himself was fluent in five languages — he made me feel kind of dumb.

I also met a few of the Vietnamese helicopter pilots, who came in as my patients. Some of them spoke very good English. All of them were very appreciative, of course, of the fact that we were there. One particular Vietnamese had been injured actually going back for an American. He didn't think it was at all unusual for him to go back for the American — the American was in trouble and my patient went back and ended up with burns.

We also had Koreans on our ward — some of them were very stoic individuals. I had a couple of Koreans who were mental patients — I don't know what happened to them, whether they had head injuries or had just broken under pressure. The bad thing is, we sent the Korean mental patients back to their country not knowing whether they were going to be killed when they got there or what. To the Koreans, having mental problems was a very bad loss of face — they would kill each other if one of them went crazy when they were out in the field. I mean, they would absolutely sacrifice a person rather than give away their position.

I also had a few American patients who had worked in intelligence; they were the guys who had gone out and infiltrated into the villages. I remember one young man because he asked me if there would be a place for him in the States. "I'm a trained killer," he said. "What can I do when I get back to the States? There's no job for a trained killer in the States." Then he told me that the first time you kill someone, it's very hard. You worry about it, you have nightmares. The second time, he told me, it's a little easier. By the time you get to three, four, five, you enjoy what you're doing.

I had no answer for him. All I could tell him was that, hopefully, he would get some kind of deprogramming.

For all of us at the Twenty-second CSF, it was an emotional year; you lived on your nerve ends. You were confined to a small place and couldn't go anywhere. But you talked, you listened, you found people who cared about you. All in all, you helped each other get through.

On your days off, of course, you really had nothing to do. Us girls, we'd do our laundry and our hair and all the little things that girls do. The guys — well, they couldn't work on cars and they didn't have the other stuff that guys have as their pastime. So a lot of times they would come in and talk to us.

You listened to the guys over there because you realized you were a kind of a stand-in for their sister, their mother, their girl-friend. For instance, I remember hearing a lot of stories from fighter squadron pilots. A lot of times — they wouldn't admit this — they were very scared. They'd come back after making a trip north and bombing and stuff, and you could always tell: they'd get a little bit more rowdy, or they'd want to talk. This got to be a problem at times. Very rarely did you get to sleep through an entire night — if it wasn't Charlie hitting us, or planes taking off, it was a fighter pilot banging on your door because he wanted to talk. Finally the wing commander had to issue a warning to all the guys that the girls needed their sleep and couldn't stand there and listen to all their problems all the time.

One time, on one of our days off, my friend Sandy and I went with one of the crews of a 123, or Caribou. They were taking some supplies in to a Special Forces camp. So we're in the air and I'm listening to one of the Jolly Green rescue pickups that's coming in on the headset, when all of a sudden we start going into a corkscrew landing — I'm holding on to the side, wondering why I'm getting so dizzy. "Hey, why are you doing this?" I said. "Well," the pilot said, "Charlie shoots at us sometimes and this maneuver makes us harder to hit." That didn't make me feel too good. Then, when I looked down at the runway, there was no runway. We just landed in the middle of a field and hopped over the rocks and things.

When I got back, I kind of got chewed out by a couple of friends who wanted to know what I was doing in the middle of the countryside like this. But as far as I was concerned, it was not any more dangerous than going out on some of our MEDCAPs.

One day we went out and set up MEDCAP in one of the villages when all of a sudden we heard some shots. Finally we realized this was one of the South Vietnamese shooting at his own people — he thought the guy was going AWOL or was a draft dodger or something. Sometimes, in some of those little villages, it was kind of strange. It was also a little difficult taking care of the villagers, because some of the people were very sick. You would have people with heart conditions which you couldn't treat that well because they were like children — some of them would go and switch pills. If you gave one a red pill and the other one had a blue pill, then they'd go switch. So you had to be very careful with this. Also, you couldn't give them soap that was wrapped up because if you did they wouldn't use it for what it was supposed to be used for. They'd take it and sell it on the black market. So there was a lot of politics and stuff that went on.

Of course, we knew all the time we were over there that there was a lot of politics going on back home; we knew it was a political war. But, being nurses, we also knew what our job was.

Now this is something I didn't know until I'd spent my entire time over there, but most doctors who went to Vietnam, at least in Danang, went with a big supply of birth control pills. I do remember the doctors seeming to think the nurses belonged to them. For instance, once we went to visit a little squadron of Marines. They were kids, young kids, who'd built a beautiful little clubhouse with scraps of lumber. So we went over one night, because they'd asked the nurses to come to the dedication of the clubhouse. When we came back, one of the doctors said to me, "What were you doing over there? Let them get their own girls — we have our girls; they can get their own."

I was very angry. I informed that doctor that we were in Vietnam to do a job — we had to work with him and the other doctors, but that was it. We didn't belong to them. I also told him that, for once, it was very nice to go somewhere and be treated with the utmost respect and courtesy.

I think we had only one or two doctors who were not married. Several of the married ones were dating nurses, but I was not going to date a married one while I was there — getting hung up on a married man was just asking for trouble. It was hard enough dating a single guy. For instance, I was dating a guy from the Jolly Greens and many times he would have to go out on rescue missions. When I would get angry at him, I'd want to say, "Hey, look — go away and leave me alone and never come back." But I knew that if I really said this and then he went out and got shot down, I'd have to live with the guilt. I didn't want to take that chance.

Coming back home to a military environment insulated me a lot from the trauma that people went through who got out after their two years. In the military, you were always running across people who had been there, people who understood. So you were not running into all the hate and the indifference. If I wanted to talk about Vietnam, I could. Vietnam wasn't something that I had to keep hidden. Now many other people, your neighbors and so on, didn't want to hear about Vietnam, but that didn't make that much difference to me. Because, if I needed to talk, I could always find somebody who had been there.

After I had been back here about twenty months, I went over to the Philippines as a flight nurse, flying in and out of Vietnam. My first flight was into Danang. That was when I realized how much I'd put behind me; I had a lot of memories come back. But then I put the shell around myself again so that I would not be bothered by memories.

When I'd gone over the first time, in sixty-eight, there was a lot of fighting going on. In seventy, when I first got back, we were still taking care of a lot of casualties, though we weren't seeing the intensity that we'd seen in sixty-eight. When I finally left Vietnam in seventy-two, we were bringing out loads of drug patients.

These "golden flow" flights were hard getting used to. Here we'd been taking care of casualties, and suddenly we have a group of immature personalities — you would almost have to babysit an entire planeload of kids. When we first started to set up these flights, nobody knew what to expect, so we had guards on board in case they got rowdy or had flashbacks. Fortunately, that type of thing didn't happen much. We did have a little difficulty at first because the patients were oversedated and you couldn't go all the way to the States with them — a couple flights had to be diverted back to the Philippines. So, by seventy-two, things were very different than they were in sixty-eight and even in seventy.

I don't remember having any dreams of Vietnam after I came back. I'm also sure that I'm not suppressing anything in my subconscious somewhere — I may have dreamed a couple times about the people I knew over there, but I don't remember ever dreaming about any of the bad times I had with patients. You know: patients all over the place and you trying to take care of them, trying to get them on the aircraft before the rocket attacks. No, I don't remember having any of those bad dreams. So I feel that I was very fortunate that I could get rid of my anxieties while I was over there.

I guess I cried more during my year in Vietnam than in any other time in my life. Very rarely did anybody know this. I usually cried when I was in my room all by myself. Then, after my good cry, I'd be ready to go back and face it all again.

The little guys flying missions and wading through rice paddies, of course, had it the hardest. I've cried a lot of tears for them. After we got back, they would tell me about some of their hardships — about how, back home, they got tired of being called names. I would talk to them, tell them that this was a period of time when America did not like itself. But year by year I've seen a little bit more openness and a little bit more acceptance of these guys.

This year in New York we walked down the street with the ticker tape and the millions of people standing by screaming "We love you!" I mean, to know that the guys were marching down that street to all those cheers, that at last they had come home — I think I must have had a perpetual grin the entire time I was on parade.

*Now retired, Eunice Splawn lives in Sumter, South Carolina. She spends much of her time traveling. In 1986 she will be back in school, working on a counseling degree.*

# Becky Pietz

*Becky Pietz grew up in Richmond, Virginia. Her father, a pharmacist, "was what you'd call the old country gentleman. He used to go back to his home town and visit all the old ladies who taught him all the way through school." Becky's mother "made a big thing about tracing the family tree back to Robert E. Lee and, before him, to Captain John Smith. I think this is where my patriotism came from."*

*Becky attended a high school with a military corps. Afterward she went to Virginia Tech, "which is seventy-five percent military. Although I'd never had any contact with anybody in the military, I was really drawn to it. Besides, you grow up with Audie Murphy and John Wayne movies, and — even if you're a girl — you know you're going to go and be a hero somewhere."*

*In 1969 Becky joined the Red Cross. She was trained as a medical social worker and, in 1971, assigned to Vietnam, where she worked in hospitals in Qui Nhon and Danang. Five months into her tour, Becky resigned.*

AFTER I GRADUATED, I came to D.C. to look for a job. Someone, I don't remember who, said, "Why not work for the Red Cross?" Well, the only thing I knew about the Red Cross was that they gave summer swimming lessons. So, when I walked into their headquarters in 1969, I thought I would be applying for a camp counselor position.

When they told me about their Service to the Military program, I knew I wanted to sign. The program offered worldwide mobility. It offered the advantage of working in a military setting. And it also offered the opportunity to work in hospitals, which I thought sounded interesting.

I trained in Ohio, at Wright-Patterson Air Force Base. There was a whole group, about a dozen women all going to hospitals in Southeast Asia. Some of us were Red Cross and some of us were Air Force — so I immediately became familiar with the military. Also, we had, as patients, a lot of Vietnam returnees. Plus on the base there were all the Air Force personnel.

When I told my father I was going to Vietnam, he said, "Well, if I had a son I'd expect him to go." My mother didn't say anything — she absolutely refused to discuss it. My grandmother, I remember, got drunk, and my younger sister got angry. My friends had very mixed feelings. Some of them were antiwar — I lost a few of them.

It's hard to describe, but although mentally I realized I was going to a war, I didn't realize it emotionally. I remember I felt invincible. I just knew that everything was going to be fine, that it was going to end up like all the war movies I'd ever seen. Everybody was supposed to go home and live happily ever after.

It has not been that way at all.

OK, we land in Saigon. The plane is descending. I'm sitting there looking down, saying to myself, "If we can only get to the ground, then everything will be all right." You know, since Vietnam, I will not get on planes; I sometimes wonder if that has to do with what I felt when we were landing in Saigon. "If we can just get down, then everything will be all right. . . ." Funny, I'm just now remembering that that was going through my head.

I won't go over bridges anymore, either.

So it was four in the morning and still dark out. You could see the lights on the runway, I remember that. And I remember it was hot, humid, sticky, and strangely quiet. The fighting had stopped, but you didn't know what would happen.

After a few days in Saigon I was sent to Qui Nhon, which was over on the coast. As a medical social worker, I provided emergency communication between the servicemen and home. I handed out comfort kits: comb, razor, soap, toothpaste, toothbrush, all in a little box. I was also supposed to provide informal counseling services. But unlike the patients in Ohio, the patients in Vietnam were either sick or dying, or sick and transferring out, or well and going back to their units. You really didn't talk much to the patients in Vietnam.

The trouble with ending up in a hospital in Vietnam was that it gave you time to think. You thought about where you were and what had happened to you. This is why we ended up with a lot of servicemen just hanging around the hospital — they wouldn't want to go back to their units because all of a sudden they were afraid. As long as they were in the field and busy, they were OK.

But put them in the hospital, give them time to think, and every-thing just sort of shuts down.

There were also the patients who never made it home. The one I remember most vividly was Paul Nolan. When he first came in, he couldn't talk because of his wounds. I don't know what had happened to him, but his whole body was like someone had taken a cigarette or maybe a hot ice cream scoop and just burned every other half-inch. After a week or so he was able to talk and I helped him write a letter home. And then Paul Nolan died. He's the only one whose name I remember.

I was in Qui Nhon a month when they called me up and said, "We need you in Danang." So I packed everything and went. Danang was sort of exciting. The hospital was on a peninsula where the only road back to the main base was always getting cut off. I don't remember being afraid, though. Like I said, I felt invincible. I think a lot of the civilians felt that. We were young, we were idealistic, and, as compared to the military, we had more reason to be optimistic. There was even a joke at the Ninety-fifth Evac that if it ever got shelled, the first shell would bring all of us out with our cameras.

Like, I remember getting into an argument with a nurse one night. A grenade had come over the fence, but I was in the middle of doing something and had taken my own sweet time getting from the compound to the bunker, because I just didn't feel that a grenade was very significant. But this nurse was real angry. Maybe it was the difference in our ages or the difference in our back-grounds, or maybe it was just because I was civilian and she was military. But it just didn't seem to matter. It wasn't that important to me.

I remember this other nurse at Danang. She'd lined her room with comforters. She must have ordered a dozen comforters from Sears or Montgomery Ward and then she'd covered the walls of her room with them. At the time I didn't think about it, but now I know she was looking for a place of peace and calm, a place where she could escape what was going on around her.

After Danang I went back to Qui Nhon. And then I decided I'd had it. I resigned after my fourth or fifth month. It wasn't as if I had an opinion on the war as to whether we should be there or we shouldn't. It was just that I couldn't cope with any more dead burnt bodies.

I remember my supervisor was surprised when I handed in my

resignation. She said she had no idea I was having any trouble at all. But I was. I was looking at all those wounded young soldiers and not talking to anybody and thinking what a waste it was.

That's how the Wall [the Vietnam Veterans' Memorial in Washington] makes me feel. I look at those names and think, "What a waste." I don't see the Wall as a tribute; I see it as a magnification of all the waste the war caused. That's why I don't like the Wall, and that's what being in Southeast Asia made me feel — that everything was a waste.

When I got home I wanted to talk to my mother. But she just flat out said, "I don't want to hear about it." "I've got to tell you," I said. "I've got to tell you about Paul Nolan —" "I don't want to hear about it. I don't want to hear any sad stories —"

After that I just sort of totally withdrew. I was embarrassed even to say I'd been there. And that's how it was for a lot of years.

I didn't even talk about Vietnam with the man I married. He was a vet. We'd met in Danang. It was midnight and he'd flown in by chopper because he'd heard they served real waffles at midnight chow in Danang. I was out wandering around — it was too hot to sleep — so we went to breakfast together. When I came back to the States I ended up marrying him.

He was Army and crazy. Absolutely crazy. Did you see that HBO special about the Vietnam veterans living up in the wilds of Oregon? Well, that's him. He lived up there for a lot of years. Now's he hiding out in Korea. Just hiding — doesn't want to see anyone, doesn't want to talk to anyone.

I think he and I got maried because we were in the same place emotionally. We were both just really not able to cope. I don't know what we thought we were doing, though, whether we thought we were helping each other or not. But he turned out to be a very violent person and I ended up leaving him because of that. I remember being afraid to sleep in the same house with him. When I left him, I hadn't slept in six months.

In 1975, after my marriage broke up, I had a lot of problems with Vietnam. That April, just after North Vietnam invaded South Vietnam, I ended up in the hospital for a — quote unquote — rest. I remember lying in the hospital listening to the news and cringing, knowing Vietnam was part of the problem yet being unable to tell anybody. I mean, it sounded so dumb, just thinking about it — "Hey, don't you hear that news report?" — and having that be significant.

106

What had happened was, I was just totally unable to cope. My marriage had broken up, I had a young child I was trying to raise, money was very tight — and North Vietnam was invading South Vietnam.

Everything was crashing down around me.

After about ten years I sort of said, "OK, you have to get a hold on your life." What I came to realize was that my experience in Vietnam had more control over me than I had over it. I didn't want to be a victim of that experience any longer. So I decided I was going to do something, and I did it. It was pretty much, you know, mind over matter. Like if you're an alcoholic you have to admit you have a problem and then you make up your mind you're not going to have the problem anymore.

But I think there will always be something very dark and sinister about the Vietnam vet. And we, the civilians who served there, will always be sort of floating. Think about it too hard and you get kind of desolate: no direction, no purpose, no reason to get up in the morning. That's how I get when I'm really wrapped up in thinking about it. I feel very desolate. I feel a big, black hole and I don't know what's inside it and I don't even know how to tell anybody why. All I know is I want it to go away, only I don't know how. I'm feeling that big, black hole right now. I feel like I'm just kind of floating.

I felt like this after seeing *Apocalypse Now*. Somebody told me it wasn't really a movie about Vietnam, that it was just another war story. So I went to see it, and boy, was I a basket case for ten days afterward. But even though that movie upset me, I think it was very well done. I liked *Coming Home*, too. *The Deer Hunter* I did not like. I don't think I ever understood what was happening — it didn't make sense to me.

Sometimes I read about Vietnam, sometimes I don't. Sometimes I watch shows on TV. And sometimes, watching TV, the strangest things will hit me.

Like I was watching one show of a Vietnam vet returning and he was relating an experience about coming in from the field and some back-lying commander yelled at him that his boots were muddy. Well, the same thing happened to me. I had been in Danang and it was raining and now I was on a C-130 [transport plane] going to Saigon. The C-130s had no seats; you sat on the floor and got filthy dirty. And, unlike the nurses, who wore boots and fatigues, we wore these powderblue skirts and white shoes. Well, I get to Saigon and my shoes are a mess and this supervisor gets real upset about it.

So I was watching the show and remembering what it felt like to get yelled at for dirty shoes. Now that may have seemed silly and trivial to a lot of people watching the show, but it really hit home to me. I mean, it was like what that soldier was saying was exactly what happened to me. I remember I kept asking myself, "How did they know that?"

And once on that new show, *Call to Glory*, they showed some scenes that were supposed to be Tan Son Nhut. Tan Son Nhut looked like when you walk into the storage bins in the basement here — a bunch of chicken wire all hung together with two-by-fours or something, or maybe a bunch of cages in a warehouse. The whole inside of the airport was like that. So I was watching this show and feeling just like I was back in Tan Son Nhut. Then they showed what was supposed to be the Continental Palace in downtown Saigon — you could get real strawberries with real cream there — they showed that on the show. And I just couldn't believe it was a movie set. For days I went around thinking that it just had to be Vietnam.

Speaking of Tan Son Nhut, I remember sitting in airports forever and ever. Once I was sitting in this airport smoking cigarettes for, I don't know, about five hours, when this GI came over and said, "You look like you're in bad trouble." Because I used to shake a lot. Smoke cigarettes and shake. Since then I've learned I have a thyroid problem. It could, of course, have been caused by a lot of things, but it started in Vietnam.

They say Agent Orange was all over the place. And I know thyroid problems are symptomatic of having been exposed to Agent Orange. But my biggest fear about Agent Orange is what is yet to come. I sort of think it's going to be like all those men in the forties who were exposed to the atomic testing. Now it's forty years later and they're developing all sorts of horrible types of cancers. I think Agent Orange is going to manifest itself in that way.

I guess you think it gets easier the more you talk about Vietnam. But I don't think it gets any easier at all. In certain respects, it gets kind of almost scary. Because maybe it gets harder instead of getting easier, so you start wondering why it isn't getting any easier.

After this interview I'm not going to be in control of the aftermath. The aftermath is going to be in control of me. But I think the story needs to be told. And if it's going to be told, I want to be part of the telling, because I was there and I know what happened because it happened to me.

*Becky Pietz is currently a senior programmer/analyst for Claritas, responsible for creating and maintaining demographic data. She lives with her son in northern Virginia.*

# Linda Hiebert

*Linda Hiebert grew up in Milwaukee, Wisconsin, where her father was a pastor in a Nazarene church. Although her parents "weren't militaristic, they were certainly very patriotic. My father felt very strongly about supporting the government — the whole idea of government being questioned was just not a part of my life at all. The first time I voted, when I was eighteen, I voted for Nixon."*

*In 1969 Linda transferred from a Nazarene college in Illinois to Goshen College in Indiana. "Goshen just happened to be Mennonite. And, ultimately, that was what changed my life." After graduating with a degree in nursing, Linda went to Vietnam under the auspices of the Mennonite Central Committee. From 1973 until 1975 she was an instructor at a nursing school in Nha Trang.*

AT THE VERY END of my college experience, I met my husband, Murray. He's an active religious Mennonite. He was also a Canadian and very political, while I, at that time, was very nonpolitical. So it was an interesting but difficult time for me. Everything was new. Everything was changing. Because, through Murray, I was becoming politicized.

One aspect of the Mennonite faith is a belief in helping people of other cultures. The church encourages young people, especially, to do service overseas. So Murray and I asked to go to Latin America — the one place I did not want to go was Vietnam. In part this was because of the war. But also I felt that Asia was so very mysterious, that the Asian people would be hard to understand.

As it turned out, Vietnam was the only place the church had openings. So, finally, Murray persuaded me to go.

Nha Trang is on the coast, about halfway between Saigon and what was then the DMZ. At that time, it was almost untouched by the war. Nha Trang had a military academy, and occasionally you'd hear rocket fire, and once in a while the airport would be hit by guerrillas — but even so, it was almost a fishing-village atmosphere, very quiet in comparison to the rest of Vietnam. Unlike Qui Nhon or Danang or Saigon, Nha Trang didn't have many refugees. So, even though we were right in the middle of Vietnam, we weren't always feeling the war.

I was teaching nursing and Murray was working as a generalist, which meant doing administration work for the hospital compound. Although the Mennonites provided personnel and money to help support the hospitals, both the hospital and school were under the auspices of the Vietnam Protestant Church, which was itself connected to the Christian Missionary Alliance Church. The Christian Missionary Alliance Church supplied missionaries to the Bible school that was in Nha Trang. So we were not by any means the only Westerners in the city.

In addition to working as a nursing instructor, I began translating information about generic drugs from English into Vietnamese. I also, in the fall of seventy-four, began working in the women's prison. The women's prison was in the very center of Nha Trang. It had high walls and a big gate, and when you walked in, you had the feeling you were entering another world.

The prisoners were not only women who had been arrested for thievery or prostitution but also women who had been arrested for political reasons. How many women there were in all, I never knew for sure, but I'd say there were between two and three times as many women as should have been. The conditions were very crowded. I remember the first time I saw the sleeping rooms: women with their children were lying on mats on slabs of cement. Venereal disease was rampant, as were a variety of other problems. Dysentery. Parasites. So once a week I'd go in and examine the women and give them what little I had in drugs.

I felt very strongly about helping these women. But it was hard, and it was frustrating, because when you go into a situation this bad, you suddenly realize "I'm not equipped to handle this." Basically all I could do was put Band-Aids on serious problems. I wished I could have done more — those women and their children were really suffering, and they had no access to medical attention except what I could provide.

I don't know, maybe I could have done more. But in late seventy-four Murray developed cancer and we had to go to Manila for radiation treatments. When we finally got back to Vietnam, in the beginning of March of 1975, the situation had started to unravel. But more on that after a while.

One of the other things I did was take the nursing students out into a resettlement village for ethnic minorities — a "strategic hamlet," in American military jargon. It was a little camp not too far outside the city. Some of my students, I remember, were quite shocked — they'd only been to the countryside for picnics, so they'd never seen how peasants really lived.

The basic problems in the resettlement villages were much like those in the women's prison: dysentery, dirty water. Very basic health problems, like a mother would lose her ability to breastfeed and start feeding her child sweetened condensed milk diluted with unclean water. Then the child would get diarrhea and a whole system of problems. Again, I quickly realized how unprepared I was. I'd been trained in a highly technical atmosphere. And here I am dropped down in the middle of a culture with very basic problems, in addition to a concept of medicine that was totally different from anything I understood.

One day one of my nursing students fell into a catatonic state. You see, there was a lot of pressure on my students — education was extremely important to the whole family, and if they didn't do well, they were severely reprimanded. So this student was failing and psychologically just could not cope. My first response, when we found her in a catatonic position, was to give her Valium, put her in a quiet setting, and then get psychiatric care for her. But the Vietnamese — even the Vietnamese nursing instructors, who'd been trained in Western medicine — reacted like Asians. They started rubbing her with Tiger Balm. Then they started coining — using a coin to rub her — and pinching her forehead. This was supposed to bring the bad blood to the surface of the skin. Well, in their culture, this was the remedy they'd found to be the most effective. It was shocking to me. I said, "What are you doing to this child?" Then I had to go away and think. And what I realized was that Western medicine and my culture don't have all the answers.

For the most part, my husband and I were not afraid for our personal safety. We felt very strongly about separating ourselves from the U.S. military presence, and the Vietnamese seemed to understand this. But a couple of times some, well, bizarre things happened. Once my students and I had gone out into a village and come across a woman who was dying from what seemed to be hepatitis. We took her and her small child in a minibus back to the hospital, where, during the night, she died. So the next morning we had to take her body back to the village to her husband. When we got there, the villagers told us the husband was up in the mountains collecting firewood. "Go up that road," they said and pointed to this dirt track. So we left the body in the hut and the child with a neighbor and started along this track in the van to look for the husband.

We went about ten kilometers into the mountains but never found him, and so we had to return. When we got back near the dead woman's village, a man stopped us. "What are you doing here?" he said. We told him we were looking for the husband of this woman who had just died, that we wanted to talk to him and help him. "Wow. I haven't been up that road in ten years. It's controlled by the Communist forces."

We didn't spend any more time on the road than we had to.

But, you know, it was interesting. You go off on a road and suddenly you're not in areas controlled by the South Vietnamese government anymore. So that was one of the times I was afraid for my personal safety.

Remember I told you we got back from Manila in March of 1975? By then most of the staff had been evacuated to Saigon. Toward the end of the month Murray and I started trying to figure out what to do. We were concerned about not abandoning the Vietnamese we'd been working with at the hospital — many had already gone, but some were still in Nha Trang. Well, the director of our organization came up from Saigon to see about our leaving. Everyone knew, of course, that Nha Trang was going to go very soon.

So we stayed, this small group of us, trying to decide what to do. Murray felt that he wanted to stay in Nha Trang for the change, but I felt we shouldn't, since he'd just come through radiation therapy and really was not very strong physically. Anyhow, one day toward the very end while we were trying to decide, we went into town in our van to the bank — the hospital itself was outside of town, right on the ocean — to withdraw the money from the Mennonite Central Committee account. Going into town, we suddenly realized that the area was full of ARVN soldiers, who had come out of the mountains. They were ragged, tattered, shoeless, hungry. They had rifles but no money, and they were angry at their commanders for deserting them, angry because they'd had to walk out of the highlands to the coast. And of course they were afraid — they had no idea what was going to happen to them, or what would happen to their families once the PRG [Provisional Revolutionary Government] took over. They had heard so many rumors.

The closer we got to town, the more we began to hear stories about the refugees coming out of the mountains. So we went to one camp that was a couple kilometers from Nha Trang. And what we saw were hundreds of people milling around the camp. All these stunned people. . . . They were trying, you know, to get to the coast, and from the coast to Saigon. Just masses of people. Only there was no food, no water, no gas. We heard stories from them about cars and trucks that would run out of gas along the mountain road, and these desperate masses would rush up and push the truck over the mountainside with the people still inside them. Everything was just total chaos — you can't imagine the panic, the absolute panic. People had no idea what was going to happen to them. They all wanted to get out. Soldiers would see a car and decide they wanted it, shoot the driver, haul his body out, throw it over the mountainside. Anyone with a gun was extremely dangerous. And there were lots of guns and all this panic.

Our boss, Murray, and I got into Nha Trang and to the bank. We were coming out with the MCC money, and there were all these ragged soldiers milling around the street. Just as we were coming out we heard a shot. A soldier had seen an old woman leaving the bank ahead of us and had killed her and taken her money. It could just as easily have been us.

I don't think our being American had anything to do with our not being shot, because the soldiers, at that point, were so desperate and angry. I really think it was just by chance we escaped harm. Still, we stuck around till the thirty-first of March; we knew pretty well when the PRG soldiers were coming. Finally, on the morning of the thirty-first, the American consulate in Nha Trang said, "It's now or never — this is the last flight out." So we took it.

There were people who did not. Americans.

I remember, at the airport, seeing a couple of people I'd never seen in Nha Trang. One of them was black. He had a Vietnamese wife and children, and he put them on the plane. Whether or not he was former military, I don't know — my guess is he probably was. But I remember watching this black man say goodbye to his Vietnamese family. And then the plane took off.

I've always wondered about that man, why he would have stayed.

Just before Murray and I left Saigon we went with some Vietnamese friends to a restaurant on the Saigon River. It was a tiny place, really a little shack. I remember we were sitting there with the city on our left and the rice paddies stretching out in front of us — just sitting there, talking. Then we notice this airplane take off and come back. It started coming in lower and lower. "It's not going to make the airport," our friends said. "Sure they are," I said. To me, it looked like they were coming in for a landing. There weren't any signs of trouble — no doors open or anything. "They're going to make it," I said again. "Oh, no," our friends said. "The airport is not over there." And the plane slowly came down and went below what we could see — below the rice-paddy level — and then suddenly there was this huge ball of fire. We were shocked. Just absolutely shocked.

A few hours later, we went into the city and found out it was the orphans' plane. I can't remember the exact count, the number of children that were killed.

Murray and I went to Bangkok and after that to Laos. We were sent by MCC to check it out and see if maybe we could help work on resettlement of refugees for a while, but we ended up staying three years. When we got back to the U.S. after five years in Southeast Asia, we were, well, overwhelmed. Even though, intellectually, we understood the differences in the cultures, we found ourselves enraged by all the money people were spending in the U.S. and also all the waste. We were defensive with everyone, including our families.

Of course, after a while that subsides and you go on with your life. But both of our lives are still intertwined with Southeast Asia.

*Linda and Murray Hiebert are on the staff of the Indochina Project in Washington. They have been back to Vietnam ten times.*

# Ann Powlas*

*Ann Powlas was born and raised in Concord, North Carolina. Her father taught in a state school for boys; her mother worked in a hosiery mill. Because her mother worked evenings, Ann "came home from school and cooked supper for my father and brothers, took care of the dishes and things. I also, in high school, played some basketball."*

*Ann "always wanted to be a Navy nurse. I think I'd seen literature about Navy nurses at the county fair when I was young. So me and this other girl talked about it all through high school. But I didn't do anything about it until my junior year in nursing school, when I started thinking, "Well, I'm not getting married and don't want to stay here, so what am I going to do when I get out?"*

*After graduating from a three-year nursing program in Concord in 1970, Ann joined the Army. From June of 1971 until April of 1972 she was stationed at the Third Field Hospital on the edge of Saigon, where she worked on the tropical diseases ward.*

THE DAY I DECIDED TO JOIN I was in OB, watching these women go through labor, and I was really kind of bored. I remember looking out the window and all of a sudden it hits me: why not join the Army's nursing program?

When we got out of class that afternoon, I called the Army recruiter. I think then I wrote them a letter and — my gracious — the next day they were calling back. Now this was sixty-nine, and nurses were really in demand. So they took me out to dinner and really put on the charm, and boy, I was all for joining. My mom and dad had to sign for me, though, because I was just nineteen.

It took a long time to get them to sign, because in my mom and dad's day, during World War II, women in the service were considered to be bad people. They just knew I was going to come out

---

* Three or four paragraphs of this interview were taken from a letter, dated June 26, 1985.

a whore. But they finally signed and I was finally considered a PFC, so I got my check every month to pay for the last part of nursing school.

In June of seventy I graduated and went to Raleigh to take my state boards. While I was up there I was sworn into the Army Nurse Corps. During the student nurse program you're considered a WAC. Then you're discharged and enter again as an officer in the Army Nurse Corps. So, anyhow, in June of seventy, me and this other girl went to [Fort Sam Houston in] San Antonio for basic training.

Basic was not too hard. We didn't have any real physical exercise or anything, not what you're thinking of these days as basic training. One of the main things I remember from being at Fort Sam, though, is walking to the PX on a Saturday morning — it was just I and another girl — when a group of young civilians drove through the post. They leaned out the window and yelled "Pigs!" Just because we were military. So after that we didn't dare wear our uniforms off post.

My first assignment was in Virginia, at Fort Belvoir. I worked there, in pediatrics, until April of 1971, when I got my orders for Nam.

I wanted to go to Nam, but just when I was going to put in for it, another girl — she lived overhead from us and had just gotten back from Nam — told me, "Oh, don't put in for it. If you put in for it, you won't get it." So I didn't. And it was starting to look like I wasn't going anywhere, like I'd just be in pediatrics forever. Then one day the assistant chief nurse came down and said, "I'd like to talk to you in private." I thought, "Well, what did I do?" She took me in the treatment room and sat me down and said, "You've got orders to Nam." I said, "You're kidding." Because, you know, I was excited. And she said, "You want to go? Oh, sometimes I tell people they're going and they cry and cry." I told her that when I came in the Army I knew what was going on, and that I wanted to see it, because Vietnam was what was happening.

So after a month's leave I flew from Charlotte to Atlanta to San Francisco. On the plane I met a major. He was in the Rangers and this was going to be his third tour in Nam. I guess he took one look at me and saw this scared second lieutenant. That's probably why he took me under his wing — because the closer we got to Nam, the more scared I got.

You know, when we first took off from Charlotte, I never really thought about it. But then I looked back down and said, "I may never see this place again." So the farther from home I got, the more it was starting to hit me.

On the flight to Tan Son Nhut there were about a hundred guys and me. Except for the stewardesses. I don't know what it was, if they were jealous or what, but those stewardesses would not give me any service at all. If I wanted something, one of the guys I was with would have to ask for it.

Anyway, we land in Tan Son Nhut. It's about ten o'clock, and it's dark. When the plane comes down, it just drops — it's not like a long, gradual descent. You're just down. The reason, they told us, was to keep from getting shot down. I remember saying to the major, "Well, that's interesting."

There were no lights on the plane. I stepped off and almost fell. And I remember it was humid — you know, it's hot and humid in North Carolina, but it's nothing compared to what it was there. I broke out in a sweat, was wet in no time flat.

Well, I went inside and was the only female. No one, none of the Army personnel, knew what to do with me. Finally this major found somebody that said, "Well, we can put her at Camp Davis." There was a little room there, so I spent the night in it.

The next morning at breakfast I met another nurse. She was leaving for R and R, and she really gave me the lowdown — the GIs, the weather, the hospitals — she really told me a lot. After breakfast I went and caught a bus over to Long Binh to the Ninetieth Replacement. It was a much more primitive setting. At the Ninetieth there were Quonset huts and a little outdoor john. It was a small compound with a large fence around it. The first night, I heard small weapons firing and there were geckos running up and down the wall. I pulled my mosquito netting a little tighter and didn't sleep a wink that night. I spent two or three days at the Ninetieth, in the officers' club, mostly. Everybody there was getting ready to go someplace else, so there was nothing to do but drink and listen to the horror stories of people leaving Nam. I especially remember the chopper pilots — they could really lay a line on you.

I was scared. You know, there were so many stories, you just didn't know what to expect. And of course the things you'd seen on TV back in the States, it was all coming back to you. So you sat there expecting horror for twenty-four hours a day.

So anyway, I went over to see Colonel Lane, who was the chief nurse in Vietnam. She wanted me to go to Third Field. The next day I took another bus back to Tan Son Nhut and then got a ride to Third Field. I remember, on the way to Long Binh, seeing all the rice paddies, also the Vietnamese working in the fields. And I remember being shocked when this Vietnamese riding a bicycle got off and just urinated right there on the side of the road — you know, like it was the most natural thing in the world.

At the hospital they were so happy to get me, because they were really short of help. Colonel Lane assigned me to Third Field to work peds [pediatrics], but when I got there I was assigned to tropical medicine. They were in bad need of staff. We worked twelve-hour days, six days a week, and lot of times we worked overtime. The usual shift was seven to seven. But when you worked days, you often didn't get off till nine or ten o'clock.

It was a fifty-two-bed ward. A lot of times we just had one R.N. and two corpsmen, so you really worked nonstop. The corpsmen were fantastic. Those guys knew their job. They had to; most of the guys who came in were very, very sick. They had fevers of a hundred three, a hundred four. And they were in the hospital for things like malaria, hepatitis, typhoid, even TB. We also had typhus cases and one suspected case of leprosy who was sent back to the World for diagnosis and treatment.

One patient I got really close to. He had rabies, and I felt awfully bad when he died. I hated it when we lost anybody, but it was even worse with him, because I got to know him so well. When this guy came in sick, he'd told us he'd been bitten by a dog a few weeks earlier, but that he'd brought the dog in and had it tested. Well, he was getting to where he couldn't stand to drink water, couldn't stand the sight of it, and he thought he was going mental — you know, cracking up. We weren't very busy at this time, so I used to talk to the guy a lot. And then one night — it was a Tuesday — I came in and saw he was starting to get dehydrated, so we started an IV on him. When I cleared the IV tubing of air — you have to run the air out of the tube to prevent it from getting in the bloodstream — a few spots of the fluid came out. And the guy had a pharyngeal spasm. It was just the sight of the water that caused the spasm. That's why they call it hydrophobia.

By this time the guy was really getting scared. I spent most of the night and the next day talking to him. On Friday I was off. I went over to the ward that day to pick up my mail — it was about lunchtime, I remember — and the guy was convulsing again. Only this time he was foaming at the mouth: he had large amounts of bloody mucus, requiring almost constant suctioning. It was classical, really classical, rabies. That afternoon he died.

I had never seen rabies before I went to Vietnam. I had never seen malaria, either. That was one thing about the Army — in basic at Fort Sam they took us to a make-believe Vietnamese village, they showed what to do in an ambush, they taught us how to set up a field hospital, but they didn't prepare us for the diseases that we saw over there.

They didn't really prepare me for other things, either. Like the personality disorders. Or the drug addiction. We had guys come in who were just troublemakers and could not fit into the Army way of doing things. We had guys come in that tried to fake mental illness, so they could get shipped back to the States — lots of times we shipped them right back to the field. I remember one guy, this young medic who had had malaria and was going to be shipped back to the field. He did not want to go; you know, he was just real scared. Well, one night — I was working nights again, I must have worked an awful lot of nights — when most of the patients were asleep I was sitting at the desk doing some paperwork. This young medic — he couldn't sleep — came up and sat down to talk. All of a sudden he pretended to pass out on the floor, and when I got down to see what I could do for him, he grabbed me. Thank goodness, one of the corpsmen came and got him off me. I don't really know what the guy's problem was, except that he was scared and wanted to stay out of the field. I couldn't blame him for that.

Of course, we had some real fatigue, guys who just were exhausted mentally and physically. On them we used sleep therapy. We'd clean them up, sedate them, get them something to eat, take them to the bathroom, then sedate them again. We used to keep them sedated for maybe three or four days. Anyhow, after they were rested and had something good to eat, most of the time they went back out to the field. I have wondered if they had any mental problems later.

The last six months I was there, the Army set up this amnesty program for guys that, if you wanted to turn yourself in voluntarily for drugs, you could, with no marks against you. So a lot of guys would come in and say, "I'm a drug addict." There got to be so many that we had one of the open bays just cleared for the drug patients.

Marijuana wasn't considered one of the problems. The problem was heroin. Most of the guys were shooting it. In fact, we had a lot of guys develop infections. One guy — he was not on our ward, but I knew about him — developed such a severe spinal infection that he became a quadriplegic.

The guys who were really sick were always very appreciative of everything you did for them. But it was very hard to talk to the drug cases. I myself was never involved in taking drugs. But I do understand it: there was a lot of peer pressure on new guys in Nam. You know, shoot a little of this and you won't be scared. That kind of thing. And they felt sorry for themselves, you know — people back in the World are having a good time, and here I am in Nam. It was hard working with those guys, though. Like, someone would have friends that would come by with heroin, or Vietnamese mama-sans and papa-sans would sell it to them. We ended up having to close off this part of the ward — had to have an MP standing guard, so that only staff went in.

Occasionally the nurses had to give urine specimens for drug detection. We called these "golden flow tests." They were unannounced and we had to provide a specimen while another female officer observed. That was to keep us from cheating. It was humiliating. We had to do this also to get out of the country. I remember on the way home stopping in Japan and getting checked by drug-sniffing dogs. So that, even after I got home, I was always careful about even carrying any type of medication.

You know, I was shocked when I was in Nam by all the drug problems and disease. I'd thought before I went over that, well, all the casualties would come from being shot at. But, where I was, that was not the way it was at all. Also, there were fewer combat casualties in the seventies than there were in the late sixties; we had fewer troops by then and ARVN were doing more of the fighting.

As far as coping goes — the long hours and the frustration — there was really nothing to do but drink. So we drank. But really, at Third Field, the morale was not all that bad. Everybody got along, and close friendships developed. We didn't talk about the war much — we laughed about it some, and we cussed it. There was not that much sitting around feeling sorry for yourself. We just wanted to go home.

Of course, there were times when we got pretty emotional. The patients were so young, and it was hard to see them die. I remember right before Christmas this young door gunner — he was nineteen — came through the hospital. He'd been on his last flight and the chopper was shot down. Well, here it was a few days before Christmas and this young kid finishing his year was supposed to be going home. We couldn't help but think about his family — they were getting ready for Christmas, you thought, but now they'd be getting ready for a funeral. Yeah, when the patients died, you couldn't help but think about their families back home.

You couldn't help but think, too, of the demonstrators. That was hard — thinking of them waving VC flags and hoping for a VC victory. I wonder if the demonstrators back home ever thought that this was also wishing for American defeat. I thought the American flag flying over the compound was a beautiful sight; it was a little piece of home.

I understand some Americans even donated blood and medication for the enemy. Well, our young men needed that blood. I think it's fine to express your opinion for or against the war, but what those people did was an act of treason. They certainly couldn't express themselves like that in Vietnam after the communists took over. I'm sure you've seen film of Jane Fonda sitting on an anti-aircraft gun in North Vietnam, with NVA troops all around her? Well, this gun was used to shoot down our pilots, and there she is laughing. If it had been any other war, Jane Fonda would have been placed on trial as a traitor. Instead, the vets come home and are treated as dirt, while she continues to make huge sums of money. I never see any of her movies.

As far as race problems go, race was not an issue among the nurses and medical people. Our chief nurse was black, but she wasn't the type of person who, when you talked to her, made you think of race. In fact, when you worked with her, you didn't even think of her as black. She was very well educated, very understanding. And being from South, you notice race. But you just did not think of her as black.

Now the Vietnamese were different. There was a lot of tension between the Vietnamese and the Americans. The Vietnamese hated us — but they didn't hate our money. They would steal anything, so we had to be very careful with what we had. Mama-san knew what each of us owned, and when I left to come home she took the few things I'd left behind for my roommate. Because the Vietnamese thought we were all rich, and we were, compared to them. I did meet some very nice Vietnamese and went to the home of one lady who worked for us at Tan Son Nhut. But I'm afraid most Americans felt superior to the Vietnamese.

It could all have been due to their government — the Vietnamese people were dirt-poor, and their government was corrupt. And my God, there were Buddhas everywhere — Thailand was even worse, they had gold Buddhas there — but Buddha sure wasn't doing them much good, was he?

Our government — when it decided to turn Vietnam over to the Vietnamese, it just went hog-wild. They even air-conditioned our hospital for the Vietnamese — we never had air-conditioning! And the kidney machine — we had the only renal unit in Vietnam. We had a renal specialist and a nurse that were going to teach the Vietnamese how to operate the kidney machine, but I don't know if they ever did. Of course, we knew that after we were gone the Vietnamese were going to bust it up and sell all the parts. So trying to teach them was useless.

My roommate, Sandy — she was from Nebraska — worked on the Vietnamese ward and hated it. I don't believe I could have tolerated working on that ward. I felt I was there to take care of GIs, not Vietnamese.

Though of course we would go out to the villages on MEDCAPs, and the kids would just love it when we came. There was this orphanage on the other side of Tan Son Nhut with about a hundred and fifty kids in it. A groups of nuns was taking care of them. We went over there sometimes with some MPs — I knew a lot of the MPs who had sort of adopted these kids and would do things for them. So a couple times we went over and took medicine and gave them what we could — we didn't have much to spare — and boy, the kids just loved it. They would take you around and say, "Hey, here's my pal." They were all so malnourished and covered with scratches and cuts. One little boy — he was really cute, was like our pet — I remember because he was about three years old and had the biggest, brownest eyes. Only one day he fell and got a nail in his eye, and the eye was protruding. There was just me and this other nurse. We tried to talk to him. We bandaged the eye and then tried to see if we could get the nuns to bring him in to Third Field, but he never did show up, because a lot of the Vietnamese thought hospitals were places where you just went to die.

The orphanage was a small compound: two buildings, one of which was just a great big open one. The babies, I remember, were just laying there in their own feces and urine. And the flies — I mean, the nuns tried, but there were just so many kids. And they all had these big, swollen bellies. I'm sure most of them died. So it was very sad.

Our compound, while I was there, was never hit. But Tan Son Nhut was right across the road from us, and of course they were hit. I understand that during Tet of sixty-eight, the Third Field was completely surrounded by VC. At one time — we were only about thirty-five miles from the Cambodian border — there was intelligence that four divisions of NVA were coming down from the border. And later I saw maps of all these tunnels that were under Saigon and Tan Son Nhut, which would have meant that we had a tunnel very close to where we were. But the odd thing is, after the first few weeks, you're just not afraid anymore. I don't know whether you deny it or what, but you just don't think about dying. Because if you thought about it, you'd just drive yourself wild. Plus your age. At that age you're always thinking, "Well, nothing can happen to me!" Nowadays, you know, I'd be scared to death.

I left Nam about two months early. I had gotten an R and R to Hawaii in February, only when I got to Hawaii things didn't feel right. You know, I was so eager to get to Hawaii — Hawaii is a dream — but the whole time I was almost eager to get back to Nam. I don't know — it was something. Something just didn't feel right.

So I went back to Nam, and when I got there, they told me Nixon was announcing a troop withdrawal and that people who had been there longest were getting to leave. So I got home the first of April, 1972. I was excited about getting home, but like with Hawaii . . . I don't know. Because I didn't really know if I wanted to come home. You know, for months you talk about getting back to the World — you keep a short-timer's calendar, you mark off each day, you keep it beside your cot at night, and when you get down to the last day, well, there's a picture of Snoopy — but I don't know. I wasn't that thrilled that I came home. I just felt that, somehow, I did not fit in, and I felt numb — which is why my fiancé and I eventually broke up.

I was supposed to have gotten out of the Army in June of seventy-two — my time would have been up then — but they went ahead and discharged me in April. For a few days I had to wait for paperwork, just sitting in California, and this was the week before Easter — you remember the Easter offense? Well, the VC and NVA attack began, and all of us waiting for paperwork just sat around and watched TV. So it was a very boring time — I am trying to think of the right words to use.

Because here you are watching some stupid advertisement on TV, thinking that you've dreamed and dreamed about getting back to the World, but also remembering that over in Nam you'd been working these long hours. . . . And so you never really fit in again. Because so much had been going on for so long. And then here you are back in the World and nobody wants to hear about it. All your friends are still in Nam.

One night after I got home I went to see a girl I'd been good friends with in nursing school. Her baby was six or seven months old, and she and I just had nothing in common. I remember I talked to her husband more than I talked to her — he'd been in the Navy, and I felt we had more in common, even though this girl and I had had some real good times in nursing school. So times like that make you think. And what you think is: I'm all alone.

A couple years after I got back I decided to join the Legion. I had been very depressed for a long time, had hardly talked to anyone about Vietnam. Well, as you probably know, there's some conflict between World War Two veterans and Vietnam veterans, especially women, so I have had some run-ins with the Legion. I never go to any of the meetings, but I've kept my membership for ten years. Lately, though, I have been thinking of getting out — sometimes when I show my card to get into a Legion ball game, they have things to say. You know, "Are you a veteran?" — things like that. A few weeks ago at a ball game one of them even asked me if I was using my husband's card. I said, "It says 'Ann Powlas' — how can that possibly be my husband?" And he said, "You're a member of our post?" And I said, "Yes, for ten years." That made me so mad I sat down and wrote the Legion the letter I'd been wanting to write for ten years. I told them that not only was I a lifetime member of the VVA, but that the VVA welcomes women into their organization. And that it was time the Legion stopped acting like they were a little boys' clubhouse — you know, no girls allowed.

I mailed the letter on like a Friday afternoon — one copy to the state headquarters and one to the editor of the Legion magazine — so the guy at state headquarters, who wrote me back, couldn't have gotten it until Monday. But on Wednesday morning I had a letter waiting for me at the post office. This guy who wrote back was a Vietnam veteran himself. He said that he was very sad, but not surprised, that this had happened to me.

The Legion magazine didn't print my letter. So, after all this, I'm not going to renew my membership.

The Legion just does not believe women Vietnam veterans are really veterans — the older vets have no respect for any women vets. What they don't understand about Vietnam, though, is that there was no rear — the VC was everywhere, even in the hospitals. But a lot of people feel like, well, if you weren't out in the bush fighting, you're not a real veteran. And, for a long time, that was how I felt about myself.

Like last week at work a World War Two vet was telling about World War Two and someone — not me! — mentioned that I was a Nam vet. This guy said, "Well, if I was a Nam vet, I wouldn't tell anyone." Nam vets aren't respected because people feel it was a bad war, so automatically that makes us unworthy of any respect. Well, his saying that hurt, but I didn't say anything. Because it's still hard, sometimes, for me to think of myself as a vet and take pride in my service.

The activities in New York [the celebration in honor of the New York memorial in May, 1985] helped, but now I have to get back to reality. I appreciate the New Yorkers for giving us pride in ourselves again — after the parade I could finally tell myself, "You're really a Vietnam vet!" In New York I talked, laughed, and cried about Nam, but that was with other vets.

Here in Salisbury it's the same as it was before the parade in New York — I've had one person who really wanted to know what happened in New York and how I felt.

You know, sometimes I'm just busting at the seams to talk about Nam, but I know better. I usually regret it when I talk, so I'm trying to keep my mouth shut. Only sometimes things just slip out.

*Ann Powlas and her husband, Barry, live in Salisbury, North Carolina. Ann is a nurse at the Veterans' Administration hospital there.*

# Judy Jenkins

*Judy Jenkins grew up in Appleton, Wisconsin. Her family is Episcopalian. Her mother worked in the home; her father, an engineer, owned a small business. As an adolescent, Judy worked as a camp counselor and city playground leader. At the University of Wisconsin, which she entered in 1963, Judy majored in social work.*

*"What really changed my life is one of my professors. She recognized my flair for recreation work — at the time, I was doing recreation for delinquent teenagers at a state reformatory. Anyhow, this professor had been with Army Special Services in Korea, and she urged me to join. I thought that sounded wonderful — I'd get out of Wisconsin, see the world. So I signed up for Germany.*

*"Just before graduation, I was accepted into the program. But they said they were sending me to Vietnam."*

*Judy was in Vietnam from 1967 to 1970. Her work with the Army took her all over the country.*

WELL, I HAD MY DOUBTS. So I went to Miss Lee, my professor, and said, "Do I really want to go to Vietnam?" And she said, "Oh, yes, it will be just like Korea." So, armed with her encouragement, I accepted the assignment. And on graduation day, I dropped the bombshell on my parents. My mother absolutely fainted. She nearly had a heart attack.

But I was determined, so that was it.

Three months later I went.

One other woman and myself went over on a regular airline that was for the soldiers. For thirty-six hours we were stared at by all these guys — that was something to get used to! Plus the sea of green. Because, at the time, I was not too familiar with the military.

It was twilight when we landed in Saigon. I remember looking down and seeing all these little cooking fires. Tiny little curls of smoke were coming up at us as we landed. And when we got off the plane, the heat hit us like an oven. I was in my girdle and nylons and everything — I just totally was not dressed for the heat and humidity.

We were put in a caged truck. It was very disconcerting. Then, as we're going through downtown Saigon with all the sights and smells and noises, we have to divert around the presidential palace because a Buddhist monk is immolating himself. I could see him as we passed a corner. He was just sitting there crosslegged, on fire.

To me, that was unbelievable.

And then we arrive at the hotel. As we're walking in, there's a soldier with his hand on the butt of his gun. All of a sudden it hits me — that this is not like watching the war on television. I can get killed here. There are real bullets. Up in the room there's wide tape across the windows. The tape, they tell us, is to protect us from shattering glass when we have rocket attacks. Well, by this time, the other girl and I were clinging to each other in sheer terror. I didn't know why I'd gotten myself into this. Because it wasn't the way Miss Lee had said it would be at all.

The war was right on our doorstep.

Later that evening we went out to see Saigon with some soldiers we had met. I remember sitting in a restaurant sipping a cocktail and looking out at the flares. And, mellow with a drink or two, I was thinking that there was nothing I could do about my situation. That kind of philosophy — it's what you see on "M*A*S*H" — is what saved me through the whole thing. Because you cannot stay in a state of terror all the time. Sometimes you say, "What the hell."

My first post was with the First Infantry Division, not far from Saigon. The guys would sometimes come in straight from the field. They would be filthy, stinking like you wouldn't believe, but they'd come in for a cup of coffee. I remember their hands shaking, and the haunted look in their eyes, and I remember they'd start telling these stories. So the war began to encroach on me. I began to realize what these guys were going through, and, more than ever, the war started to seem real.

About a month before Tet, I was transferred up north to Qui Nhon. I was with the Eighth Transportation group — they carried all the supplies from the docks to Pleiku and the Central Highlands, so it was a very critical route. OK, we're in a valley outside the city — that's where they stored the trucks. We're very vulnerable, because we don't have a lot of firepower. And suddenly it's Tet, and all hell is breaking loose.

For ten days we're under siege. The VC are broadcasting from the radio station in Qui Nhon, and we're hearing through radio contacts what's going on around us. Reportedly, a North Vietnamese battalion is coming down the two valleys, right toward the V where we're located, and there's a possibility we'll be overrun. So for days we live believing that all of us are going to die.

I saw people cracking around me. You know, we're holed up in bunkers. We're shooting at snipers. We're having sapper attacks. There was this commander who didn't help things, either. He kept saying, "I'm not worried about being overrun. I've got trading material. I'll give them my females in exchange for our safety." Well, of course it was a joke. But it was terrifying, because the thought of being captured was terrifying.

I had read about what happened to white women in Asia. Graphic, historical accounts — like the missionaries in China at the time of the Boxer Rebellion, what happened to the women. All that kind of thing. And I decided that, if we were overrun, I'd grab a gun and kill myself. Because I believed I'd be raped and tortured if I managed to survive.

On the back of my ID was a paragraph saying that, according to the Geneva Convention, I was to be given the status of second lieutenant if captured. What bullshit! I mean, the Vietnamese weren't going to be able to read that. And even if they could have, what would they have cared? So, during the ten days we were under siege, I thought about things like that.

I think the thing that kept me in Vietnam as long as I was — and what got me through those ten days — is that I was so busy being a caretaker I wasn't aware of my own needs. I was there to make things better for the guys, to be mother, sister, the girl next door — to take their minds off the war and listen to their problems. I didn't have time to grieve — especially not for myself — because there were so many guys I saw myself as taking care of.

Well, somehow we never got the major attack. Maybe they heard we'd been warned or something; I don't really know. The worst we actually had were sapper attacks. That's when they'd break through the perimeter and throw in some grenades and probably, you know, all get killed. Then, in the morning light, you could see the bodies impaled on the barbed wire fence.

Our barber — the guy who cut my hair just a week before Tet —

turned out to be a Viet Cong. So were two very young fellows who swept the floor at the rec center. And that was very, very unnerving. I mean, imagine the shock of knowing that people who'd been on your post, right there among you, were really trying to kill you.

This kind of insidious threat — the knowledge that there were no front lines, that everywhere was a combat zone — was a hard thing to live with. Day in and day out. The war was with you all the time. For instance, I remember feeling the little tinkle of dog tags around my neck and reminding myself I could go home in a body bag. Because dog tags were in case you were so disfigured they couldn't tell who you were. Yeah, Vietnam had a way of playing on your mind. And it wasn't just the guys in the jungle who felt it. Everyone felt it. I know I felt it, too.

Well, back to Qui Nhon. Part of my job was to go to town on errands, and I always had to go by jeep. I remember being in those jeeps and feeling like a sitting duck in a carnival shooting gallery. Because you knew there were snipers out there, just waiting to pick you off.

One time this other girl and I were invited to a promotion party. So we got all dressed up in silk and heels and hairpieces — you know, the whole thing. In the middle of the party an intelligence report came in. It was rumored that there was trouble and all groups should disperse. So when the police chief of the district — he was American and some sort of colonel — offered to drive me back to the compound, I said, "Fine. I'll go with you." I put a flak jacket on over my silk dress and a steel helmet on over my hairpiece, and we started back toward the valley. It was twenty miles and we were in a jeep.

All of a sudden, as we pass the ammo dump, we're fired on. I flatten myself against the floor — silk dress, the hell with it! — and the driver floors it and takes off. We made it just in time, but the jeep behind us got its tires shot and had to stay behind and shoot it out.

The whole time the police chief was firing back — I was lying there on the floor of his jeep — he kept saying, "What's going to happen to my career if a woman gets killed in my vehicle? What's going to happen to my career?" Later we managed to laugh about it. And he gave me this as a memento: it's an ashtray made of machine-gun bullets.

On another occasion I found a huge piece of shrapnel not far from where my bed was. We'd just had a rocket attack. And I remember thinking that this horrible piece of metal could have landed right in my body. Still, you couldn't go around in terror all the time. You had to get sort of fatalistic — if my number's up, it's going to be up. You had to think like that or you wouldn't make it. But you still went to the bunkers.

Another time I remember we were fired on in a helicopter. I couldn't hear the firing because of the noise of the chopper blades, but all of a sudden one of the door gunners pointed and I looked out and saw the tracers. Well, then the helicopter goes sideways and we start skimming the trees to get out of range. I remember I was terrified. Absolutely. I also remember, afterward, the anger that I felt.

We women, you know, were noncombatants in a place where we could have gotten killed just as easily as the men. Only we couldn't shoot back. We never had the chance. So what do you do with all your fear and anger? You internalize it. You just absorb it. Because you have a job to do, and that job involves taking care of people.

We couldn't let ourselves feel fear and anger. Just like we couldn't let ourselves feel hurt.

For instance, once I got a letter from my great-aunt. She was in her eighties, and we were very close. Well, my great-aunt had a parakeet who was her only friend, because all her friends had died. Anyhow, I got a letter from her telling me her parakeet had died, too. It made me cry. I was sitting there at my desk, crying. And I was supposed to be out calling Bingo for the guys.

Well, I knew it was a silly thing, but on the other hand it wasn't. This parakeet was very important to my great-aunt. So I'm sitting there crying and the woman I'm working with comes up to me. "Look," she says. "I don't care what you just read in that letter. You go out there and you call Bingo. Those guys deserve a respite from the war. That's your job. That's your mission — to make things better for them. Now get the hell out there!" And she grabbed me by the scruff of my neck and sort of scared me. So I went out and called Bingo.

It was hard to let yourself cry.

I remember the time, though, I really cried my eyes out. I was in the hospital, being treated for some sort of intestinal bacteria.

I liked to go into the villages and eat with the Vietnamese. I had a lot of Vietnamese friends, because I was really big on learning about the culture. So I ended up in the hospital with intestinal problems a lot.

Anyhow, I was in the hospital. Instead of being in bed, I was going around to the different wards, talking with the guys, taking them gum and cigarettes and candy. Somehow I ended up in triage, where they were bringing in patients from a helicopter crash. There was one guy — I will never forget this — who was burned over ninety percent of his body. You couldn't tell whether he was black or white. He was just a lump, like a burned marshmallow, and there was a tube at one end and this rasping breathing — "Aaaah!" — like that. And I looked and I said, "How can this horror justify a war? This was once a human being." They said he'd die within a couple of days. That infection would set in, that there was just nothing to work with. And it was just one of the most grotesque things I've ever seen — a body burned to a crisp that was still rasping for breath.

It was so shocking. It was just surrealistic. That's the only word to describe it: surrealistic. After that I purposely avoided going by triage.

But, you know, trying to make happiness in the middle of a war — that was sort of surrealistic itself.

Like once, at Christmas, I climbed up the guard towers in a Santa Claus suit. I'd been thinking about the poor guys on guard duty, how they'd be all alone on Christmas Eve, while the rest of us were having parties. So after our party I dressed up like Santa Claus and took little stockings filled with gum and candy and cigarettes to the guys who were on the towers. I had somebody drive me around in a jeep — I climbed every guard tower on the post.

The commander of the post was horrified. The next day he called me in and read me the riot act. "Do you realize what a prime target you were, climbing those towers with white fur on? That was the stupidest thing I've ever heard of — the stupidest thing you've ever done!"

I'd been so wrapped up in Christmas I'd forgotten about the war. And I felt those guys needed me. They needed me to make things better.

I think feeling needed was what kept me in Vietnam so long. Originally I'd signed up for one year. But when I learned there was no one to replace me I stayed another two months.

Back in the States I felt I'd aged twenty years. I felt I'd crunched twenty years of life into those fourteen months, kind of like a fast forward on a tape. I didn't fit in. I didn't know what to do with myself.

For a while I went to the University of Wisconsin. This was sixty-nine. The antiwar demonstrations were in full force. I remember walking to visit a professor and getting hit with tear gas; there was a demonstration going on and the police popped some tear gas, and the wind just blew it in my direction. I thought that was a little ironic: I've just been through the war and now I'm getting tear-gassed.

Well, I didn't know what I was going to do with my life, so I decided I'd just go back for another year. Army Special Services was short of personnel. And I think I missed the special sense of power I had in Vietnam. When it came to bartering and getting things done, I was one of the best. I knew all about the supply system. Because, you see, none of the official supply channels worked. If your rec center needed paint or plywood or something, you had to find a place with a surplus, get friends to fly you there, and figure out what you could trade for what you needed. That gave you a great sense of power. And you always felt justified in using the power you had, because you were using it to do things for other people. I also think I missed the respect I got in Vietnam. Because if you worked hard, the guys all respected you.

So I signed up again. This time, I thought, I'd know what I was in for. And this time I'd be able to steel myself.

I've often thought that if I had a daughter I wouldn't want her to go through what I went through. I'd want her to be challenged by life, but I wouldn't want her to be destroyed. Vietnam had the capacity to destroy. It's a wonder I survived. I'm not saying I survived without emotional scars, though I think I came back stronger despite them. Scarred but stronger. Still, I wouldn't want my daughter to go through what I went through, because it was, well, just too harsh a test. As a woman, you had status and power if you understood the networks of supply and communication, if you worked hard, if you kept down what you felt. But you also lived in a glass house. You were always stared at. You always felt vulnerable. And of course all the just plain horror... There were things I loved about Vietnam. There was also much that I hated. It was a schizophrenic existence: that's the best word to describe it.

After my second tour, I spent six months traveling in Asia all by myself. I went tiger hunting. I went to Nepal. I went to Afghanistan, way up to the Russian border. When I got back to the States, a terrible boredom set in. But I knew I wanted to build a life here. I knew I didn't want to be an adventurer forever. I also knew that sometimes it takes more courage to deal with routines than to deal with anything else.

It was hard at first. For a long time it was hard. There were a couple of broken engagements — one of them right before the wedding — and months of sleep disturbances and nightmares, when the horrors were coming back. Working with vets, with guys, has helped me learn to live with my own experiences. I'll never forget, but at least I can put the memories in perspective and get on with my life.

Sometimes, though, I remember the tape across the window of that hotel room, the tape that was supposed to protect me from shattering glass. Little things like that made me realize how innocent I was when I first got to Vietnam, and how fast the war became a reality in my life.

*Judy Jenkins and her husband live in Summit, New Jersey. Judy is finishing a master's degree in social work; she is a counselor for Vietnam veterans.*

# Jill Mishkel

*Jill Mishkel grew up in Brooklyn, New York. Her father is a jeweler; her mother was a factory worker. Although Jill comes from a family of nurses — "I had nine aunts and uncles who were nurses" — nursing was "just the last thing I wanted to do. But I didn't want to be a teacher and I didn't want to be a secretary, and back in those days that was pretty much the choice. In high school I didn't go to my prom or anything like that. I was tall and skinny and had a bad complexion. I wore flared skirts when everybody else was wearing straight skirts. Also, I was very shy."*

*Jill graduated from nursing school at nineteen. A year later she joined the Army, requesting assignment to Vietnam. From July, 1970, to July, 1971, she was stationed at the 24th Evacuation Hospital at Long Binh, where she worked on the neurosurgery intensive care unit.*

WHEN I JOINED the service I was living with my parents, working in a small community hospital taking care of drunks who got in car accidents in the middle of the night. I was a hippie. Smoked pot. Hated Nixon. Thought the war was wrong. But I knew they were still drafting people and I thought I should be doing something. Partly I was bored. Partly it was the Florence Nightingale syndrome — you know, go over there and take care of the guys who are getting blown to bits. But I don't think I ever perceived myself as going off to fight a war.

I tried to join the Air Force first. I wanted to be a flight nurse. But it seems you had to be pretty to get in the Air Force — they came to my house and took full-length pictures and half-length pictures and side profiles. I had to go out and buy a dark-colored dress with a belt — I didn't own a dark-colored dress with a belt; I had to go out and buy one. It was like being in a beauty contest or something. Well, I didn't get in the Air Force, which is just as good because the guy who was trying to get me to join, the recruiter, told me I could be a flight nurse. I could never have been a flight nurse — my eyes are bad. The guy was obviously lying or something.

After that I went to talk to the Navy, but I didn't really care about water or anything like that, so I figured I'd join the Army. The Army was suitable. My father was very patriotic; my mother had always wanted me to join the service. But then when I was in basic training I got my orders changed to go to Vietnam — my original orders were to Fort Ord for six months because I wasn't twenty-one — and when I called to tell my parents, my mother went crazy on the phone. She cried a lot. You see, my mother wanted me to join the service, but she wanted me to go to Germany and meet a doctor. And she was exactly right: I should have gone to Germany. I should never have gone to Nam.

I had a lot of fun in basic training. There were some helicopter pilots at Fort Sam [Fort Sam Houston, San Antonio, Texas] getting four weeks' worth of medical training, and that's really who I hung around with. Me and this other nurse, we dated them. They were crazy. Out of their minds. Used to fly stoned or tripping. They were good guys, though.

I went over as a second lieutenant who would soon be promoted to first. I did not much care where I was stationed — told them I just wanted to be with my friend Sue, who I'd met in basic training. So when they sent us to Long Binh, about five miles up the road from Tan Son Nhut, Sue was pissed as hell. She wanted to go up into the boonies and thought it was my fault that she got stationed at Long Binh.

Long Binh was a very, very large Army post. It's where MACV was, where our financial office was, and it had two hospitals. Originally it had been a village, but by the time it became command headquarters, there was no village left. It was all Army, and it was really humongous.

The staff I worked with consisted of five nurses, eight corpsmen, and two doctors. On the neurosurgery intensive care unit, there were nineteen beds. I worked with three of the nurses and maybe four or five corpsmen. It was hard work — the first few weeks, especially, were just hell. All our patients were either unconscious or awake but basically retarded. Vegetables, really. We called them gorks — gorks because they'd lost part of their brain. There were also spinal cord injuries, paraplegics, and quadriplegics.

It was all traumatic head and back injuries. Basically, what we were doing was cleaning them out and trying to keep them alive. Yeah, traumatic injuries — gunshot wounds, grenades, shrapnel, injuries from walking into helicopter blades — we had a few of them, you know — blast injuries, mines, all that kind of stuff. I'll show you some pictures later. I have some nice horrifying pictures.

Some of our patients recovered, though I don't remember very many who did. No, I don't remember very many of them getting better. They must have — I mean, they couldn't all have died — but now that I think about it I only remember one getting better. For a long time he was what we call stuporous, meaning he was thrashing. He really was not with it, though he wasn't quiet, either, and he was funny because he'd lie in bed on his stomach with his knees curled up in like a fetal position, but on his knees and elbows, and you'd go up to take his temperature and you'd stick the thermometer in his ass and he'd start cursing. He wouldn't move and he wouldn't pull it out, he'd just start a string of curse words, which would stop when you pulled the thermometer out. But he woke up. He woke up and was fine, was perfect. He was a nice, quiet, shy young man, and when we told him about all the cursing and screaming and punching — I mean, you'd go up to touch him and he'd hit you — he just couldn't believe it. Because he wasn't that type. Didn't curse or anything, especially in front of women — anyhow, I don't remember anyone but him getting better.

It was weird, you know. I can remember people saying to me — even in Vietnam — "How can you work there? Even regular intensive care with burn patients — even that — is better than working with all those gorks." Last November when I was in Washington I met a nurse who had been stationed at my hospital working on the neurosurgical ward for a while, only she got transferred to another hospital. I finally asked her, "Well, how did you do that?" She told me she couldn't take working with vegetables, so she asked for a transfer. She went to another hospital.

There were some things you did not do. Like you did not ask yourself questions like, "Why are you doing this when all these guys are going to die anyway?" If you did, you'd just despair. Yeah, you'd just have to kill yourself if you started asking questions like that. So you just worked. You had to work, you couldn't *not* work, because if you didn't do it, somebody else would have to. Anyhow, you've got to try. Because who's to say who's going to die and who's going to recover? The brain has miraculous recovery capacities. We had one little boy, a little nine-year-old boy, who had a frontal lobotomy and afterward was perfectly normal — the rest of his brain could function perfectly, could take over for the missing part. Of course, he had this big dent in his head because he didn't have a bone there, and he didn't have a frontal lobe, but we made a plate to fit in there for him. It was a metal plate with a flap of skin over it. I have pictures of him, too. He was a real cute little kid.

At one point we had lots of kids. There was one we called Lee Ann. She was hydrocephalic. A garbage-can baby. Because what's a Vietnamese woman going to do with a hydrocephalic baby? Throw him away. That's the way it was. Anyhow, a GI found Lee Ann, brought her in, and we did a shunt on her — you shunt the fluid from the brain to the kidneys. She got better. We thought we'd cured her. And then she came back and died. Well, she would have died anyway, because you've got to keep on replacing the shunt as the kid grows, and the Vietnamese weren't capable of doing that kind of surgery. The Americans leave, the kid dies. It would have happened anyhow. We had another kid who was a battered child. Typical battered child syndrome — Vietnamese mother, GI father — the father was the one who was battering his kid. I don't know if you've ever seen a battered kid, but they're like autistic kids; they just don't focus on anybody. They're withdrawn. Real withdrawn. He was there at Christmas-time.

Among the other medical procedures we performed pretty routinely were brain irrigations. Yeah, we did that a lot. You put a catheter in one side and a catheter in the other and you squish fluid with antibiotics in it and it comes out the other side. And we had a lot of patients who had trachs for breathing because they had such severe brain damage they couldn't breathe on their own. So we'd put a trach in. We had these IPPB [intermittent positive pressure breathing] machines. They were supposed to be used to assist alert patients, make them take added breath. We used them as respirators. And you'd have to suction them and they'd be dry because there would be no humidity in the machine — and you'd squirt saline down into their trach and they'd cough and the phlegm would come out in big clumps. We had goober contests, they were called goobers. It's like who could hit the wall farthest. The patients were unconscious, they didn't know what was going on.

I know it sounds weird or cruel, but this kind of joking around was part of our way of coping. When you have seven people lined up in beds and they're all the same — I mean, when all you can do for them is suction them, give them their intravenous, empty their Foleys [catheters]. . . . Maybe flip this one or stuff some pillows behind his back so he'll stay there, and flip the next one, back and forth. We had guys on Stryker frames, guys with spinal cord injuries. I remember one time we must have had five of them.

You know, sometimes it was hard talking to the other nurses, the ones who worked on other wards. Because on our ward you didn't write letters home for the guys. You didn't get to know them, talk to them. You couldn't. They were just gorks. I mean, they were either unconscious or very stupid and retarded. Like this one guy, a helicopter pilot who had walked into the tail rotor. Like that kid I told you about; he lost his frontal lobe — it was what the corpsmen used to call the "give a shit" lobe because in an adult if you took out the frontal lobe, they didn't give a shit about anything. Anyhow, he was still awake and healthy, but he was very retarded. I remember he dictated a letter to one of the nurses to send to his wife and two kids. It was just like a five-year-old's: "Dear honey, I did this very stupid thing, I walked into a tail rotor," and all you can think is that this guy is going to go home and his wife is going to have three kids to take care of. Because this guy was not going to be with it ever again.

Like this other guy, this Navy guy, who also lost his frontal lobe. He claimed he had fifteen wives or something. His name was Louie — it's just about the only name I remember — and he was real jolly, a funny guy, telling jokes all the time. Louie was incontinent, meaning he didn't have bladder control. We used to get him out of bed and sit him in a chair, just to move him around a bit. And we gave him a bell — tried to teach him to ask for the urinal, made a game out of it. "Hey, ring the bell the next time you have to go to the bathroom, Louie." So he rings the bell, we get excited and all go running over, and there's Louie, sitting in the chair soaking wet. So we say, "Hey, Louie, why didn't you ring your bell first?" "I had to pee first," he says. And then he starts to laugh.

We had one patient who came in walking and was sent to Japan to die. The doctors knew he was going to die, didn't want him to die on the floor — what we thought was a minor concussion was really a skull fracture. He was in for three days, and the day he was supposed to be discharged he came up to me — he was packing his stuff — and said, "Hey, what's this?" And he was leaking cerebrospinal fluid through his ear, so I said, "Oh, shit, let me go get the doctor." He ended up with an infection, brain malfunction, kidney malfunction. He just went down. From bad to worse. To, well, irretrievable. It was right at Christmas.

Sometimes the doctors would make decisions to let patients die. You know, they'd say things like, "I don't want to see this guy when I come back tomorrow morning." It seems like a cold attitude, but it was necessary, because there were too many patients and we only had so much time. So you wouldn't suction them and you wouldn't turn them and they'd die.

The nurses weren't supposed to make that kind of decision. But I remember one time I did.

It was a Vietnamese man, an old man. He'd been there a long time. He just got worse and worse and worse, and we were real busy and he was deteriorating rapidly and one of the corpsmen came up to me and said, "I'm not going to work on that guy tonight; there's too much else to do." I said, "OK." He was going to die anyway. And he died that night, from just not being cared for. I don't feel good about that. It wasn't my place to make that decision.

I don't know, it was weird sometimes. Like they used to blow up the ammunition dumps and the mirrors would fall off the walls. And my mother used to send me ceramics — she was into ceramics — stuff to hang on the walls. "Mom," I'd tell her, "you know that Cancer plaque you sent me? Well, it broke." And she'd send me a new one. Make a new one and send it to me, and I'd put it in the drawer so it wouldn't get smashed.

Yeah, she was always sending me ceramics. And food. These great CARE packages. I mean, once a month I'd get a box this high and that big, and it would be stuffed with potato pancake mix, Aunt Jemima's, cookie mix, pizza mix, breading for chicken. . . . It's amazing what you can do in a little electric frying pan. We used to take a gurney and put a sheet over it and turn that into a table. Right there in the ward. We'd fry chicken, make potato pancakes. The guys didn't know the difference. Sometimes we'd do crazy things — throw buckets of water, have fights with syringes. On New Year's Eve we had this great party in one of the hootches, which moved to the ward at midnight. People were milling around. Drinking. We had all these balloons, only they weren't balloons, they were condoms we'd blown up. They were hanging all over the place. And all these gorks. All these patients. You know, just . . . you know. And all these people just partying all over the ward.

One of the good things about being over there was that you had more boyfriends than you could possibly ever want. You had your pick, basically. And you could get anything, anything you wanted. If you wanted a ride to Saigon, you could go hang out at the helicopter pad and somebody would give you a ride. Or steaks; the doctors were always good at getting steaks. Booze you could get real easily. There wasn't really all that much you wanted, though, that you couldn't get at the PX or in Saigon.

Saigon — I remember at Christmastime I was in Saigon with one of the other nurses. We were shopping. I had all my money in my shirt pocket, and these little kids came up and, you know — just "Gimmee, gimmee, gimmee!" They were grabbing at us. We finally managed to push them away. Then we were walking down the street again and I noticed the flap of my shirt pocket was open and all my money was gone. Well, this other nurse and I walked back and saw two of the little kids that had robbed me standing on the corner. I grabbed the one kid and said, "You've got my money! Give me my money!" The cop across the way, of course, totally ignored me, and the kid was screaming, "No money!" Just then four black GIs came up and grabbed ahold of the kid and said, "Hey, what's going on?" I said, "The kid just robbed me. It's probably in that big black patent leather pocketbook she's carrying." That's when one of the guys says, "Man, she's not a sister!" — meaning me — and let the little kid go. They all started walking away then, and I went bullshit. I screamed, "What do you mean I'm not a sister! I'm an American! I'm a nurse! The next time one of you people come onto my ward I'm not gonna suction you, I'm gonna let you drown in your own secretions —" I was screaming and hollering. They just ignored me and walked away.

There was other racial stuff. The black guys kept to themselves. They were arrogant, and they were always doing the dap — it was some kind of secret code, when they'd clap their hands and do all sorts of things. Yeah, they'd stand in the middle of the hall, in everybody's way, and dap. You always had to walk around them.

I didn't know any black corpsmen. I think there must have been some, but most of the blacks I saw were supply people and auxiliary personnel. Of course, I know there were a lot of black grunts, and of course we had black patients and black guys visiting their buddies, but we never associated. My feelings about blacks were really not good over in Nam. That was real upsetting to me, because I'd always thought of myself as this liberal. And all of a sudden I hate the Vietnamese and I didn't like the blacks — I had black friends in nursing school, so it wasn't like I was prejudiced to begin with, and I don't consider myself prejudiced now — and I didn't know what was happening to me.

I had a friend who had a friend, a black helicopter pilot, who got fragged [injured by his own men]. This guy wouldn't get into the whole blackness thing, he used to hang around with white guys. Well, there were four or five guys assigned to a helicopter and they were all working on it one evening, and they got fragged by blacks. I remember one guy lost an eye. The guy they were after, my friend's friend, was lucky — he got some shrapnel in his ass or something, but he wasn't really hurt.

Like everybody else, I thought going home was going to be wonderful. I thought it was going to be just . . . I don't know, maybe I didn't really think. I know I wanted a ham sandwich, bakery white bread, lots of lettuce and mayonnaise, and a big glass of real milk. And corn on the cob. Everyone had a meal. Most people wanted Big Macs, but what I wanted was for my mother to make me a ham sandwich.

It was weird. My last two weeks were really a daze. All I could think was "Nobody can ever make me come to this place again."

I got home and was just freaked out. The first, maybe the second, night back, I went out to a bar with my girlfriends. I told them not to tell anybody that I'd just come back from Nam, so of course they went around and told everyone in the bar. People came up to me, screamed stupid things like "Medic!" Asked stupid questions, like "Did you kill anyone over there?" What they didn't know is I could have killed them right then. So everyone was having a wonderful time getting drunk and I stayed about half an hour. On the way home I threw away my birth control pills, because I figured I'd never sleep with another man again, that they were all assholes. But, you know, I went back a week later.

I also remember going shopping with my two sisters and being really freaked out. It was summertime and everybody was in short shorts and halter tops. Bright colors. Everybody laughing and having fun and shopping and buying things. And I'm thinking, "God, I'm more at home in Vietnam." Yeah, I was in Sears, I was buying underwear. My two sisters said something like "We'll be right back" and I'm handing this woman money for underwear and I start crying. They didn't know why I was crying, didn't know what was going on. I didn't either. All I knew was, guys were fighting a war over there and here everybody was having a great time at this mall, buying things they didn't need.

So I was home for thirty days and then I went to Fitzsimmons in Denver. That was easier for me, because I got to go back to an environment where I felt at home. At Fitzsimmons I worked on what was called the lower extremity ward. Amputees. Guys who had been in Nam.

After I got out of the Army I only told a few people I was a veteran. At Hartford Hospital I worked in the intensive care unit, but I wasn't friends with the people I worked with. I remember people thinking I was really weird. When I told people, they just looked at me and walked away. Or they asked, "Why did you go? Why did you want to do something like that?" Or they'd be talking about the war and not want to hear anything I had to say about it. Finally I stopped telling people. I think that happened when one woman told me to just forget about it and it would go away. I started screaming, "I don't want to forget about it! It's a year of my life, what do you mean forget about it!" But I did. I buried it really deeply. Got involved in the Women's Movement and became a radical feminist. The women in my rap groups all knew I'd been in Vietnam, but we never talked about it — we were too busy talking about the terrible things our mothers did to us when we were three.

One night — this was early in seventy-three — I went to a VVAW [Vietnam Veterans Against the War] party. That was weird; I really felt at home. There weren't any women vets there except me, and I think I only told a few people I was a vet, but it was nice because it was just like being back in Nam. The music was up too loud, people were smoking pot, nobody was dancing to the music but everybody was vibrating, kind of jumping or going in circles. I met two men that night: one of them was Clifford, who I lived with for about six years.

Clifford and I got involved very quickly. I felt comfortable with all his friends, comfortable with him, though we never really talked about Vietnam. Oh, he had his stories, and I had my stories, but they were all very superficial. I remember we went to see *Coming Home* and afterward I cried for three weeks, but Clifford and I didn't talk about it. I think I might have said that the ward in the movie looked like the ward I worked on in Denver, but we didn't really talk.

We didn't get married because he said he didn't feel stable enough to make a commitment, and I didn't want to make a commitment until the relationship started falling apart. I had been in counseling, and I went back, and then the two of us started seeing a counselor, but Clifford just wouldn't talk. I would talk and he would sit there and just not say anything. One day, I remember, the counselor said, "Okay, Jill. Don't talk today. Today is devoted to Clifford." And he sat there for an hour in silence, sat there with the chair backward, glaring. He was a great glarer, Clifford was, one of these people who can look at you and you feel just like you're dying.

I'm still hung up about Clifford. He's married and lives in Florida now, but I went for years expecting him to come back. I have only one pattern to base my life on, and that's my parents: they're in their sixties and happily married. So I just never thought Clifford and I would break up.

The year he left, 1980, was a real bad year. I drank too much. Stayed alone. Or I'd do the bar scene, you know, go to a bar and pick up some guy. Then one day I decided to go down to the Vet Center. I was thinking about Clifford and what I thought were all his problems, and I went in to see this woman counselor and told her how I wanted to help all these suffering war veterans. That's when she started asking me questions and I started to cry. She got me into a rap group after that, a veterans' rap group. I spent about four months there, crying. It was good, but some of the guys had trouble with me. I got into screaming arguments because they just didn't think I'd been in combat.

I was active with vets' groups for a while. Lately I haven't been; it feels like I'm just rehashing all the same crap I hashed out once. And I don't like going to the meetings because everybody makes a big deal out of me and wants to cry on my shoulder. "Oh, a woman vet," they all say. "Oh, how wonderful!" When all I did was go to work every day. And when it was stupid to have gone to Nam in the first place.

Yeah, I really wish I had not gone. Because I do think I still have a lot of problems with it, basically. A lot has to do with the patients I cared for, the amount of people I've seen die. Thousands, it seems like. I'm back in counseling now, have been since November, but, you know, a lot of times I get real pissed — Nam never goes away; I don't know what to do with it, I still have nightmares and things like that. So I don't know where I'm going to end up. Sometimes I just want to bury it all over again and not deal with any of it.

Yet, somehow, I keep on. I deal with it. I said "Yeah" to you when you called, and now I've been sitting here for however many hours we've been talking, feeling really weird. But I know there's a way out of it. There has to be.

One last thing: it's the best thing, probably, that's happened to me in a long time. Last year I heard from Diane, the woman who was my chief nurse in Nam. In New York last May [at the memorial celebration] we met up again. Talking to Diane made me sure that all of it was real — that it's not just my dreams, my nightmares, that are real.

It's been hard for me to trust my memories. But knowing Diane is having the same problems makes it easier. I'm not alone with my craziness now. And that's important. It means a lot.

*Jill Mishkel is a nurse practitioner at Planned Parenthood in Hartford, Connecticut. Once again active in veterans' affairs, Jill is currently working on a women veterans' task force.*

# Marjorie Nelson

*Marjorie Nelson grew up in a Quaker family in Kokomo, Indiana. Both of her parents were teachers; her father later became a foreman at the Chrysler heat-treating plant in Kokomo.*

*By the time Marjorie was fifteen, she knew she wanted to study medicine. She also knew she wanted to work in East Africa. "We had had both East Africans and African Quakers visit at our monthly [Quaker] meetings. Those people had frequently stayed in our home, so I felt I knew parts of Kenya almost as well as I knew where, say, my grandparents lived." After graduating from medical school at Indiana State University, Marjorie became a resident in general medicine at Pennsylvania Hospital. As part of her residency she spent two months off the coast of Africa on the hospital ship* Hope. *"But by 1967 I knew that Vietnam was where I was really supposed to be."*

*From the fall of 1967 until Tet of 1968, Marjorie worked at the American Friends Service Committee rehabilitation center in Quang Ngai, where she treated Vietnamese civilians. During Tet Marjorie was captured by the North Vietnamese Army and held in a POW camp for two months. She later resumed work at the center in Quang Ngai.*

WHY DID I GO to Vietnam? A lot of people asked me that question. I think there are two fundamental reasons. One was to try and find an adequate response, as a Christian and a Quaker, to people who were suffering and in need: to do something personally. That was the immediate practical reason why I went. On a theoretical level, I had been raised as a Quaker, had been exposed to pacifism as one of the fundamental testimonies of Quaker faith. But I realized that that position was only theoretical with me. Would it hold water in a war situation? Well, I felt I had to find out. I didn't want to be an armchair quarterback — talking about the way things ought to be, but doing nothing, is too easy. That was a very important issue for me.

And then, on a spiritual and religious level, I really did feel I was called. Vietnam was where my vocation was at this point in time: there was work to be done and I was the one to do it.

I was recruited with the understanding that we were going to be establishing a rehabilitation center. This was somewhat of a departure for the American Friends Service Committee; they had never gone into such high-tech operations in the past. In the past they had tended to operate more on a relief basis — you know, feeding, clothing, building shelters, that type of thing. But to be providing fairly sophisticated medical care, and to be training foreigners in that, was something new. So they just recruited an excellent team of people, plunked us down in Quang Ngai, and said, "Do it!"

I landed in Hong Kong first. Hong Kong struck me as utterly and totally alien. There was just nothing familiar there. It felt very different. I loved it, I was fascinated — but it seemed totally alien. And then I went straight to Vietnam, which was even more so. Saigon was hot, dirty, noisy, chaotic. I spent a few days there getting over jet lag and then flew on to Quang Ngai, where I was immediately pulled into the activity of the team.

I felt very strongly that one must be able to speak the local language in a situation like that. So every morning I would spend a couple hours with a tutor and then another couple hours by myself, studying. It was not till after lunch that I'd go to the center. Then, after two months, I backed off and only did two hours of language study a day and the rest of the day I spent at work. By the time I'd been in the country about six months I didn't need an interpreter to talk to patients. I couldn't read a book, and I couldn't hold a political discussion in Vietnamese, but I could talk to my patients. And that was very important to me.

Fifty-eight percent of our patients were amputees. Most were leg amputees — there were a tremendous number of injuries from mines, shrapnel, grenades, booby traps, all sorts of things. Actually, because of the American evacuation system, Vietnam produced more amputees than any previous war. People who would have died in earlier wars survived, thanks to the American military evacuation system — survived with terrible injuries.

We also had a whole ward full of burn patients at Quang Ngai. When I first arrived, I decided I was going to make rounds on all the wards with the doctors who were in charge of each. And so I toured the burn ward.

I had had a little bit of experience working with burn patients before going to Vietnam. I don't know if you know anything about rehabilitation for burn patients, but it's an extremely drawn-out process, even with the best of facilities. The United States, right now, has the capacity to handle about two thousand severely burned patients at a time. I'm talking about the entire U.S. — right now, that's our capacity.

In Vietnam we saw domestic burns — burns from cooking fires, spilled pots, and so forth. We also saw napalm burns, although napalm victims frequently did not survive. And there were phosphorus burns — that's the substance that burns all the way through the flesh because it just keeps on going, even after the fire itself is out. There were also burns from general explosives. Maybe, during a firefight, the thatch of a house would ignite — we didn't call them firefights for nothing, I guess. So we saw all kinds of burns.

In addition to being extremely drawn-out, the rehabilitation of burn victims is extremely painful. And there are complicated problems even after the patient survives the burns, especially in a hospital with totally inadequate facilities. Essentially, our patients just lay in bed and if they healed on their own, fine. If they didn't they died in the hospital.

In short, it was a very depressing situation. I finally realized I was not going to be able to function if I continued to go into that burn ward, I could not help all of those people. I found the suffering so overwhelming that I was simply immobilized. So I quit going. I had to.

We could not afford to treat all those burn victims. If we had, we would have done nothing but burn therapy. Ten burn patients would have taken all of our resources. On the other hand, with those same resources, we could treat fifty or seventy-five amputees or orthopedic cases. Get them well and get them home. The burn patients just had to stay on the ward and either get better on their own or die. So there you see one of the differences between working in a Vietnamese civilian setting and an American military setting, where you had incredible resources at your disposal.

There was no running water on the wards at the hospital — there was running water on the grounds, but not on each ward. At the time I left, in 1969, the emergency room still didn't have running water. Electricity: sometimes we had it and sometimes we didn't. If you were lucky and the city electricity was running at full power, you might get a decent chest X ray, and you could get pictures of bones to determine whether they were broken or not. But that was about the extent of our X-ray capacity.

So you had to practice a different kind of medicine than you'd learned to practice in the States; American physicians coming into that setting either adapted quickly or gave up. Those were the two categories they seemed to fall into. It's possible to do everything, even surgery, without electricity and fancy equipment, but you have to accept different standards. And some of our people did amazing feats of surgery.

The other aspect of our job there involved training local people to do what we were doing so that when we left, we'd leave behind a functioning facility. And so we recruited local nurses. We also trained people as limb makers, as physical therapists, as physical therapy aides. We wrote textbooks and translated them into Vietnamese. We held classes and supervised and certified local people. By the time we finished we had, except for a physician, a fully trained staff of Vietnamese. Many of those people are still working in a rehabilitation center in central Vietnam. From time to time we hear news of their continuing work — so we did accomplish our goals. We trained people who are still serving the people of Vietnam with the skills that they learned from us.

I'd been in the country four months when the Tet offensive began. Tet is the Chinese lunar New Year and the biggest holiday of the year in Vietnam — it's kind of like Christmas, New Year's and the Fourth of July all rolled up in one. It was clear to us at the hospital that anybody who was possibly well enough to go home was going to go. And they did; the hospital virtually emptied out. So I accepted an invitation from a Vietnamese woman who was working with us. Her home was in Hue, which is the ancient imperial capital and which had more or less been set aside as off limits to the American military. I was very interested in visiting this woman's family, also in seeing some of the cultural aspects of this country that I was getting to know.

Certainly nobody I talked to knew there was going to be a Tet offensive. There had been talk of a truce, a Tet cease-fire. So I went on to Hue, thinking there was going to be at least a bit of a lull.

Before my friend had left Quang Ngai for the holidays — she'd left a few days earlier so she could go home and get ready — she'd told me that the outskirts of Hue, where she lived, were sometimes insecure. She thought it would be better if I stayed in town and came out during the day to visit her. So she'd arranged for me to stay with an American English teacher named Sandy Johnson who was working for IVS [International Voluntary Services].

The first day of Tet was very quiet. I spent the day with Sandy — the first day of Tet is the family day, so I couldn't visit my Vietnamese friend until later. Sandy and I walked around town, along the canals, looking at all the people who were all dressed up. It was really lovely; I enjoyed seeing everything. And then, that night, the offensive started.

Sandy and I spent a day and two nights in an improvised bomb shelter — the dining room table with sandbags piled around it — while the battle of Hue was going on. It was really scary: all the bombing, the shelling, the strafing. We didn't know if we'd survive. At some point somebody came and knocked on the door. We were petrified. We didn't answer. So the guy or guys said something and threw what I presume was a grenade at the front of the house — there was a horrendous explosion and fragments of metal came through the shutters and embedded themselves in the opposite wall. Then, a day or so later, the men came back.

They were NVA and extremely well organized: they had clipboards and they had names and they knew exactly where all the foreigners lived in Hue. Sandy and two other IVS workers were on the list to be picked up. I was an accident — I was picked up mainly because I was visiting Sandy. The only foreigners who were not rounded up were the Mennonites. Like the Quakers, they had made their neutral position very explicit: they were supporters of neither American intervention nor the other side's fighting. So the Mennonites were left alone. Their house just wasn't approached — their pacifism was respected.

Of course, we didn't know anything when the knock came. We were just there under the dining room table, terrified. This time, when we didn't answer, they went around to the kitchen and broke in. We could hear them rummaging in there.

The door between the dining room and the kitchen was bolted. When they found that out they began to shoot the bolt off the door. I knew when that door swung open they were going to be looking straight into the entrance of our bomb shelter, so I said, "Sandy, I've got to talk to them." Then, in Vietnamese, I asked them what they wanted. They stopped shooting and said, "Open the door!" I said, "Well, what do you want?" Again they said, "Open the door!" Now I don't know how long we would have gone back and forth — I wasn't going to open the door until I found out what they were up to — but at some point Sandy crawled out and opened it.

There were four of them — an older man and three very young men, all looking as uncertain as I'm sure we must have looked. Well, they came in and took us out on the porch and started asking us questions. They spoke no English, only Vietnamese, and Sandy's Vietnamese was even shakier than mine was. So they were asking questions and they kept asking us this one question, "Do you have any . . . something —" and I kept saying, "I'm sorry, I don't know what you mean by that." Finally the guy smiled and patted his gun. At that point I started to laugh — what an absurd question! So I told him no, we didn't have any weapons — I'd just learned a new word! — and they said they were going to look through the house and see. They also told us they were not thieves, that they didn't intend to take anything. And they didn't.

So after they search the place, they say, "We want to use your house as an observation post." I say, "Yeah, guys — help yourselves!" Because we weren't about to argue with them.

And then, about that time, we heard a rocket coming. Sandy and I turned and dived for the bomb shelter just as the rocket hit the roof, while the soldiers all just stood there. Sandy, I remember, was absolutely mortified. She felt we'd behaved — in the eyes of the Vietnamese — in a most undignified manner! I, however, was much too frightened to worry about my dignity.

Well, they couldn't use the house as an observation post because the roof was gone. So they left us alone there for another day. Then they came back and took us into custody. We were processed and registered and everything and then taken to the mountains west of Hue.

They put us in these little houses built out of bamboo, saplings, and a particular kind of jungle leaf. This leaf was sort of like a fern, and it was water-repellent. The leaves were woven together to make panels, like clapboard on the side of a house. Then there were more panels on the roof, kind of overlapping like our shingles. So that's where we lived.

Sandy and I were together the whole two months — they didn't separate us. Part of the time we were in the same camp with American men who had been captured in the battle of Hue; some were military, some were civilian. Although we were housed in a separate part of the camp, we took our meals with the men and were allowed to talk with them quite freely. The men were ultimately taken to Hanoi; Sandy and I remained in the camp two months.

The first few nights there was a guard posted outside the door of our little hut. Then, one night, he wasn't there anymore. I remember we were very concerned about that, we really had felt much more secure when the guard was out there. Because once, on one of the days when we were walking through the mountains, I suddenly came around a curve and saw Sandy just looking at the lead guard. "He heard a tiger," she said to me. So I was not in the least upset to have a guard with a gun outside the door. There were beasts in that jungle: tigers and who knew what else.

In a situation like that you worry initially about getting raped. But after a few days, when we had gotten to know these people, there was never any question in my mind. Once you get past the point of thinking of people as ciphers or impersonal enemies, you're past the point where you might get raped. And they really did want to get to know us. They were very curious — and so were we.

It was interesting to watch the soldiers' reactions to us. I remember, when our guard was still outside the door, how these groups of soldiers would come along and stop to talk to the guard. Sandy and I would sit very quietly, listening — after a while we knew exactly what the script was going to be. First they'd say, "Well, I understand you have some American women here." And the guard would say, "Yes, that's true." Then the soldiers would say, "We hear they speak Vietnamese." And the guard would say, "Yes, that's true." "Oh, come on," the soldiers would say. "They don't really speak Vietnamese!" "Yes, they do." "We don't believe that!" "Well, ask them yourself!" And then these heads would appear in the doorway and one of the soldiers would get up the courage to ask us something in Vietnamese. Usually it was "What's your name?" Or "How old are you?" And when they realized we could speak at least some Vietnamese, their reaction tended to be hostile — now they could really tell an American what they thought!

Now they could ask why we were in their country bombing their villages, raping their women, killing their children.

I very quickly developed a little stock paragraph. I would explain — I had learned the word for pacifist — that I was Quaker and a pacifist and that I had come to Vietnam because I did not believe in the war. I told them I had come to help people suffering because of the war and that I wished all the soldiers, on all the sides, could go home. Well, the astonishing thing was that they believed me. They never argued.

What I came to realize, as I talked with more and more Vietnamese, was that their propaganda machine told them they were fighting against the American government, not against the American people. So they believed the American people were on their side. And as soon as they could pigeonhole me as American people rather than American government, everything was fine. I wasn't their enemy.

But I also came to feel the need to be faithful to the Quaker testimony about truth speaking. I felt I had to set the record straight and tell them that what they believed really wasn't true. So I told them that, although I didn't support my government, a great many American people did. And occasionally a soldier would ask me, "Well, why is that? How can that be true?" And so I constantly had to explore just how far I could go in talking with people. I did learn a lot of vocabulary in those two months!

Anyhow, I would explain as well as I could. "Well, now," I would say, "if your government tells you something, you believe it, don't you?" And they would say, "Oh, sure." So I'd say, "Well, our government tells our people that the Vietnamese people have asked them to come and help them, and our people believe our government." Which, you know — given the simple language I had available — was a pretty reasonable explanation of the real situation. It sure gave Sandy and me some interesting opportunities to talk with people.

Several of the men stayed around long enough that we got a chance to hear about their personal lives. One man — he kind of took responsibility for us — had fought at Dien Bien Phu. He was in his mid-forties and was one of the two or three soldiers we met who spoke English. This man had been in the Army for over twenty years and he had endless tales to tell. Some people, believe it or not, even gave us their addresses.

So we were never mistreated. But we did think we were going to be kept there for years, and that was very sobering. When we were first captured we were told we were going to be taken to the mountains to study communism and that we wouldn't be released until the war was over. Of course what went through our minds was brainwashing in Korea. Nothing like that ever happened, though.

They kept asking us if we had any requests. I always told them I had three. One, I wanted to write letters to my family to let them know I was safe. Two, I wanted them to make it possible for me to continue studying Vietnamese. And three, I wanted them to find a way to assign me to a civilian setting where I could continue my work. I explained that I wasn't willing to work in the military but that I was willing to work in Communist Vietnam if I could work in a civilian setting. They did let me write letters to my family. They did help me study Vietnamese. Their answer to my third request was always "We would never ask you to live under such difficult circumstances. We appreciate your offer, but we don't need your help."

At the time I didn't believe that was their real motive for turning down my third request. I thought it was, instead, a polite way of refusing an offer that was politically unacceptable, that they did not want to admit they needed help. Now, I'm not so sure — since then I've learned that many of the Americans they kept in captivity eventually wanted to collaborate with them and that they'd had some very bad experiences trying to keep these Americans alive. Americans just didn't survive very well under jungle conditions. They got malaria, they needed more calories than a Vietnamese, their resistance was very low. So now I'm inclined to give them the benefit of the doubt: it may have been that they'd just discovered that Americans were a poor bargain.

After two months the decision was made to release us. I remember Sandy and I were taken down into the camp bomb shelter, where the commander, who spoke English, told us that they were going to have a good-bye party for us. There were about ten or twelve soldiers in the camp at the time, and they all came down into the bomb shelter and said, "We're here to tell you good-bye." One of the guys brought a dishpan full of peanut brittle and a couple of canteens of tea, so we sat and ate peanut brittle and drank tea and talked about life in America, because the commander had told the men they could ask us any questions they wanted — and what they wanted to know about was life in America.

I think the first question they asked was "Do Americans cook with wood or coal?" They also wanted to know things like "What kind of animals do you raise?" "What kind of crops do you grow?" Just very common, ordinary things, things they could relate to. Finally the camp commander asked me whether, if Robert Kennedy was elected, he would end the war. I had to think about that one for a minute. Finally I said, "Yes, I think he'll end the war if he's elected, but he'll end it for the wrong reason." "What do you mean?" the commander asked. "Well, let me tell you what I mean. I think he will end the war not because he thinks America is wrong, that we shouldn't be in Vietnam, but because he thinks the war is costing too much. The American people are not willing to pay the cost — you know, the casualties and the money both are beginning to wear on people. There is also a lot of moral uncertainty about our role in Vietnam. Still, my main perception is that people are simply not willing to pay for a war they don't understand, a war whose roots and motivations are unclear to them. And that is why Kennedy, if he is elected, will end the war."

The commander listened. He understood exactly what I was saying. "Well, that makes sense," he said. Then he told us he hoped we would not use the term *prisoner,* that he hoped we'd consider ourselves to have been their guests.

I believe we were let go for a number of reasons. First, the hand of God. Second, the fact that the Quakers had established a good relationship with the Vietnamese — we had always been assured that no harm would come to members of the Quaker team. Third, my brother flew to Phnom Penh and talked with the Vietnamese officials at the embassy there, and several approaches were made in other places. Another explanation might be that the local people who got to know me sent a report up and said they thought it would be in the best interest of North Vietnam to let us go.

Before we were released, they did ask me if I would promise to go home. And I said yes, I'd promise them that. Only they never asked me to promise not to come back to Vietnam, and I didn't promise that. I went home and brushed up on rehabilitation techniques. Then I went back to Quang Ngai and finished out my two-year term.

When I finally left again, in 1969, I was going home to get

married. It was a very difficult decision, but I knew I had to go. I also knew I was leaving a part of myself in Vietnam and that I would find a way to go back there.

*Marjorie Nelson is an assistant professor of family medicine at Ohio University College of Osteopathic Medicine, where she also heads the section of Preventive Medicine and Public Health. She has been back to Vietnam twice.*

# Lieutenant Colonel
# Marsha Jordan

*Marsha Jordan was born in Sydney, Nova Scotia, and grew up in a small town across the harbor. When she was sixteen her family moved to Boston, where her father worked as a shipper and receiver. "We came to Boston by bus. I remember crossing the Mystic River Bridge and seeing all those lights and thinking, 'Lord, what are we getting into? How are we ever going to find our way around in this huge city?' "*

*While she was in high school, Marsha worked part-time as a nurse's aide in nursing homes around Boston. In 1964, at eighteen, she entered nursing school. Three years later she became an American citizen and, hoping to be trained as a flight nurse, joined the Air Force.*

*Marsha flew in and out of Vietnam with the 56th Air Evacuation Squadron from August of 1969 to August of 1971.*

**B**ACK IN NOVA SCOTIA, if you were a woman and took on any education at all, you did three things: you were a teacher, you were a nurse, or you were a secretary. I said, "I can't sit behind a desk typing all day and there is no way I could get up in front of people and teach any type kids, so I guess I'll have to try being a nurse because it's the only other thing left." And I did. I had always enjoyed being with people and after two years of working in a nursing home, I was sold on going into nursing.

Recruiters came to our school of nursing from the Army, the Navy, and the Air Force and talked to us about the programs available in the different services. I decided to try the Air Force. They had good educational opportunities. You would travel. Also, I wanted to be a flight nurse. I thought that would be very challenging. So after I lost twenty pounds they said that they would accept me.

Like probably most people, I was hearing some of the things about Vietnam. You know, the casualties. So I knew the war was going on, but for some reason, I never paid much attention to it. At that point, it just wasn't something that I was listening to. Even when I was coming in the military, it just didn't hit home, not until I came to Sheppard Air Force Base in Wichita Falls, Texas, where we did three weeks of indoctrination. As part of our training we had — among other things — a simulated aircraft accident where we had several casualties and had to triage and take care of them. It was at that point, with all the lectures we were receiving, that I started to realize how involved we were in Vietnam. I started watching things more closely then, seeing how things were going over there. Finally I said, "I want to go over. I want to go over but I want to be a flight nurse."

I wanted to be a flight nurse because I liked the challenge of being away from the hospital, the challenge of doing it by yourself. On all our flights, we only had two flight nurses and three medical technicians — they were like corpsmen — and once you close those doors, and that plane takes off, then you are responsible for the entire load of patients. So it was the challenge of the work. Also, I wanted to see what was going on in Vietnam.

Flight school, which was at Brooks Air Force Base in San Antonio, was a very long and involved six weeks. They start the program off with altitude physiology. We learned how the changes in the atmosphere affect the body and affect not only a healthy person, which it does at all times, but also how it impacts on your ill patients. For instance, at altitude, it's like going to Denver. You're going up $x$ number of feet; the air gets lighter and you don't have quite as much oxygen. Anybody who has a low hemoglobin due to loss of blood or other things, then they're going to need additional oxygen. So, in flight school, they concentrated on how changes in the atmosphere affect your ill patient, and not only the patient but also the equipment. We also did a condensed, concentrated review of all systems of the body and what can go wrong with them and how you manage those changes in the air. Then we did training flights, with some simulated casualties. We'd either be a crew member or we'd be a simulated patient and we'd have to care for them and learn how to unload your patients — put them on board the aircraft safely — and how to arrange them inside the aircraft so that you could care for them. Then we learned how to get them off the aircraft safely and put them onto the ambus, which is just a large bus equipped to carry litters as well as ambulatory patients. So we learned all that, and then they sent us to survival — we went out in the field and learned how to survive with basically what we would have from an airplane if we ever crashed, either in the woods or on water. The aircraft that we were using at that time was a 131 on the stateside and a C-141 for your long, overseas flights. So that was the aircraft I was going to be flying in, the C-141 Starlifter — that's it [a model] up there on top of the TV.

The training, I thought, was very, very realistic. You know, just simple things like IVs. At the time, all of our IVs were glass bottles. Now we have plastic bags that, as the fluid comes out, the plastic bag collapses, where with the glass bottles, there was a rod going up through the neck of the bottle that allowed air to go in as the solution came out. So as we did changes in the altitude, you had to learn how to properly vent them to prevent the air from expanding in the bottle. There was a way to vent them so that they would work a little more the way we wanted them, but you still had to, after takeoff and reaching altitude, go around and check all your IVs to make sure they were dripping the right way. Once you landed, you had to go back around and make sure they were dripping all at the correct rate, because the flow rate changed every time you went up in the air, also when you came down again.

So let me tell you about our routing system. We had two main C-141 squadrons over in the Far East that were responsible for bringing the patients from Vietnam. One was at Clark Air Force Base in the Philippines and the other one was my squadron, the Fifty-sixth, at Yokota, Japan. We interflew missions. By that I mean, even though I was assigned to the Fifty-sixth, I might fly with somebody that was assigned to the Fifty-seventh; it just depended on who was on the ground and who was available.

What we would do, we had some main routes. From Japan we would go to the Philippines, and from the Philippines, we would go into Vietnam. One of our flights did what we call a turnaround. It would pick up patients from Vietnam and take them to the Philippines. Then the other flights that we had would pick the patients up in Vietnam and take them to Yokota. From there, they went to either the Air Force hospital at Tachikawa Air Base or to the Army or Navy hospitals in the area. Some of them, if they were stable enough, would stay on that plane when we brought them from Vietnam into Yokota. There another medical crew would take over, and then they could go in one of two directions, either into Travis Air Force Base in Fairfield, California, or into Elmendorf Air Force Base up in Anchorage, Alaska. From there another crew would take over. Some of the same patients would still be on the plane. Anyway, we would go from either one of those bases and if the patients were coming through Elmendorf, we'd take them across the northern route, stopping at major medical facilities along the northern part of the United States and terminating on the East Coast, usually at McGuire Air Force Base in New Jersey. The ones coming in from Travis would stop along the southern routes at our main points and they would either terminate at McGuire or at Charleston Air Force Base in South Carolina.

It's a long, long flight and very long for the guys who were on those planes. You have to visualize them — some are sitting, and those who could not sit, we carried on a litter. Inside the aircraft, as you walk in — you're coming in the back end — there would be stacks of litters. I don't know if you've ever seen pictures of it, but there'd be poles going right down the middle of the aircraft. Visualize a commercial plane with no seats in it, poles all the way down the middle of the aircraft, and on those poles are brackets. We could put patients four high on those poles and brackets, so we would have them on either side of the aircraft. Then, along the sides of the aircraft — the bulkhead — we had more poles and brackets, so we would have patients on the bulkheads. On the C-141, our normal configuration was a capability of carrying forty litters and forty ambulatory, but it could be any combination. We've carried as many as a little over sixty litter patients, the rest being ambulatory patients. So anytime you increase the litter number, then you decrease the number of seats you have available for the ambulatory patients.

The plane itself, the 141, has three missions. It's a cargo plane, so what they'd do was to take the cargo from the States, bring it over to the Far East and on into Vietnam, and then that plane would be reconfigured. They'd put these poles down the middle to hold the litters, put the airline-type seats in, and it would then become an air evac plane. The third mission is that 141s are transporters for our paratroopers and ground troops. They can drop troops in the air from the aircraft, or they can just take a whole troop of soldiers over; then they just land and let them off the plane.

When I got to the Fifty-sixth Air Evac, we were assigned to what we call a flight nurse instructor. That was one of the more senior nurses assigned to the squadron, who had been there flying and had proven that she or he knew the system. So I was assigned to the instructor, and my first flight was back to the States. It went into Travis. What I can remember about it was when these big doors in the back end closed and the plane started to taxi, I said, "Lord, I'm here with these people all by myself!" Of course, I was fortunate in that there were experienced people with me.

Some of the ambulatory patients did not require that much care most of the time, but you still had to watch them for complications. We were seeing a lot of amputations of all extremities and a lot of fractures. Some of the biggest things were fractures caused from primarily shrapnel and bullet-type injuries. We were also seeing burns, a significant number of burns. I will tell you about the burn flight later.

We didn't carry that many burn patients on the routine flights, but we did have a few that had minor burns that didn't require a lot of specialized care during the transport. We had a lot of abdominal injuries, where they received shrapnel wounds, gunshot wounds to the abdomen, and we had lung problems, respiratory problems, due to chest wounds. That flight into Travis was the first time I'd seen these kinds of injuries.

Like I said, that first flight I truly don't remember. I was just so overwhelmed with everything. Of course, on the plane, most of the injuries are wrapped, with dressings on them, so you don't get to see the actual wound. That's one thing we seldom did, take a dressing off from a wound when the patient was inside the aircraft. It was a dirty environment and if you take the dressing off, you increase the chance of infection, and the wounds were sometimes already infected due to the type of injury from the dirty shrapnel.

But the flight that I remember as being really my first was flying from Japan and going down to the Philippines for staging into Vietnam. One of the things in the Philippines was they always had an extra crew on a standby, so that if there was an urgent need to transport any patients, whether it be from the Philippines to another medical facility or if they had an increase in casualties in Vietnam, then they would add on a special flight. So we were put on alert, which meant they could call up and say, "Be ready to go in thirty minutes." Well, that happened my first time down in the Philippines. I was put on alert and we were given thirty minutes to get to the flight line. There we were briefed that we were going in to Vietnam to pick up twenty-four burn patients, men who had been in a personnel carrier and had gone over a land mine. They were all on litters, all with significant burns. Well, we had to take all kinds of extra supplies for IV fluid, because when we take them to altitude, it's very dry. Even though most of them had dressings on a good part of the burns, the moisture is pulled from the wound and pulled out through the dressing. So we had to take several boxes of IV fluids with us and NG [nasogastric] tubes, which were tubes going from the nose into the stomach to prevent any type vomiting. The thing we were not notified of was that seven of the patients were on respirators, which meant that they had significant chest problems and swelling around the neck.

We loaded up with all the equipment and flew into Danang. When we got there, the patients were waiting for us on the flight line. They had been brought in by helicopter from where the Army had treated them, and they were already hot, already getting dehydrated from the heat. It was just unbelievable to me to see these twenty-four people lying on litters with dressings all over their arms, burns all over their chests, and faces covered with Silvadene cream and just about all of them with IVs.

In the aircraft it was difficult to configure them. We were trying to figure out which ones we could put in the top of the litter tier and those that we wanted down on the bottom so that we would have better access to care for them. It was all being done fast to get them off the flight line, get them on the plane, get them to Yokota so that they could go to the burn center — everything was moving so fast and I was feeling like, what am I doing here? I didn't really know all of what to do, but I was trying to do my best — only I didn't know if that was going to be the best or not. Also, the ones that were on the respirators had to be watched closely.

A flight from Danang to Yokota is just about four hours; it varies with your winds, but it's roughly four hours. Well, I never saw four hours in the air go by so fast. By the time you went around and made sure that the ventilators were working properly, changed the IV bottles over, put new solution up, helped them with their fluids — they all had arm injuries and so they couldn't bend their arms — by the time you made the rounds, we were almost to Yokota. At Yokota there were helicopters waiting on the flight line to take them over to the burn unit at an Army hospital. Some did not make it; I found out later that a couple had died. But the majority of them survived.

I never had a patient die on the plane. I came close several times, but we were able to take the appropriate measures to keep them alive until we got on the ground and got them to a hospital. Some did die not too long after we got them to a hospital. But the thing that I remember to this day is the camaraderie of the guys on the plane. The ones that were not as severely injured would be supporting their buddies. They'd joke and kid around and you'd get involved with that. You'd learn about their hometown and family waiting for them back home and what they were planning on doing when they got back and got better. The most frustrating part was once they left the plane, they went off to another hospital and we lost complete contact with them. We just had no idea what happened to them or where they are today. I found that very frustrating. I've wondered many times whatever happened to so-and-so, wondered what he's doing.

There was one patient that I remember to this day. I don't remember his name, but he was a Marine and had both legs and one arm amputated, and he was blind. He was going back to a girlfriend and to his family, and he couldn't wait to get back home and be with them — his spirits were so high, and his buddies were helping him. But, you know, I just can't help but wonder today, did he maintain that spirit or is he one of the ones that has had problems and was not able to cope? He was just so upbeat. I think he was just feeling lucky that he was alive. Even though he was not going to be able to walk again, even though he only had one arm and was not able to see, he was alive and some of his buddies were not. I also think a lot of it was the upbeat of his friends, them saying, "Hey, you can make it!" But like I said, once he got back here and lost a lot of that camaraderie, what is he doing today? I think about that. I often wonder, when I see some of the vets that are in the news, the ones that were injured and are not doing well — I often wonder, was I one of the ones who took care of them on their flight back?

Every time when the pilot would announce that we had landed in the United States, or even sometimes just as the wheels touched down and they knew we were on American soil, they started clapping and pillows would fly in the air. They were just so happy to be back in the United States. So they kept that upbeat going for you. It would have been very easy to get depressed, seeing all the injuries and the maiming that had been done to so many of these guys. Sure, I had days when I'd say, "Why are we here? Why are so many of our young guys being put through torture, having to come back and learn to live with such disabilities and disfigurement?"

For instance, I mentioned the burn flight. You didn't always get as much upbeat from that flight as you did from the others, because if they had a lot of injuries that involved their face, they couldn't talk with you. And so many of the burn injuries were from the waist up. Guys would take off their protective clothes because it was so hot and then they'd end up going over a land mine or something. Then, when the carrier would explode, they got burned from the waist up. Some of them did have protective clothing on, but it just wasn't enough to save their face. So they couldn't talk to us much. Also, a lot of them were in a lot of pain. They were probably the sickest ones that we had to care for. You can fracture something or you can have a large, gaping hole in an abdomen, or a large hole in your leg, but that will close over and not be as noticeable to people. However, when you have a severe burn, you have to graft, and so much of it being on the arms and the face, you know that they're going to be living with that burn for the rest of their life.

So I was always busy. I was always working. I didn't really question why we were in Vietnam. I felt we were there for a reason, and then, after spending a little bit of time on the ground and seeing their [the Vietnamese's] living conditions outside of Danang and down around Saigon, I said, "We're fighting to hopefully upgrade the way they're living." That's the way I looked at it. If we aren't there, then their living conditions are going to get worse, they're going to be under communist rule, and so we're there to try and prevent that.

I was on the ground for a total of three weeks. One of our jobs was to go into Danang, Cam Ranh Bay, Tan Son Nhut, and see all the patients before their flights. We had to evaluate what they would need for equipment, maybe augment the incoming crew, see if the patients were really stable enough to fly. We'd talk with the physicians, and see what exactly was going on with the patients. Then we'd set up what we call a load plan, which designated the location in the plane where the patients would be, as far as whether they would be closer to the bottom so we could reach them more readily. So I did see them [the Vietnamese] in their shanties, the little shacks they were living in. I saw all the sandbags around for their protection, and I saw just a lot of poverty. Their hygiene was practically nonexistent. You'd see them selling their vegetables and things like that along the street; little kids were begging for anything. As far as living conditions, it was just very depressing.

I did get a chance to go to the beach that is off of Danang, just outside of Danang Air Base, I don't remember the name of it. But I can remember being on the beach and thinking how beautiful it was. Then, just down the shoreline, you could see the gunfire and hear the noise of the bombs going off. And I remember thinking, "God, this countryside is so beautiful; why is it being destroyed? Why can't we just enjoy it?" It was gorgeous, just a gorgeous beach.

I can't say that I was ever afraid for my own life. I don't know, I've thought of it many times since then. Today when I fly and we go through thunderstorms or whatever, it scares me. But at the time, I never gave it any thought at all. I just knew we were going to land safely, I'd get the patients on the ground, and we'd be OK. Even when I was on the ground in Vietnam for those short times, and we had to go into bunkers and take cover, I just knew that the good Lord, I guess, was going to be there with me. I knew it wasn't going to happen to me — I think that's how a lot of people survived. They said it wasn't going to happen to them. I always believed I'm going to be OK.

Fortunately, I didn't know about one incident until after it was all over. We were coming into Danang. We were on final approach. Then, all of a sudden, I knew that we were making a very rapid descent. Just before that, I had heard a thud and really wasn't sure what had happened. Then we quickly started descending and when we got on the ground, they told us that we had taken some fire. So we looked. We had taken some shells that had put a few small holes in the aircraft. Everything was functional — the shells didn't penetrate deep enough to cause a rapid decompression or anything like that.

That was the only time that I was fired at that I know of. Why we were not fired on more often, I have no idea, because the plane was not identified as an air evac plane. It's a cargo plane. There are no medical markings on it whatsoever. Like today, our C-9 is used only for aero medical evacuations, and it has a big red cross painted on both sides of the tail, but the 141s do not. The Viet Cong would have had no idea whether it was coming in with cargo, with troops, or whether it was coming in to pick up patients going out on the airlift. So why we did not lose more, why we didn't have any that were shot down, I can't explain. But we did not lose any. It wasn't until we did Baby Lift with the C-5, which is a huge transport plane, like a 747, that one crashed. To this day they think it was probably a mechanical problem, but it crashed in Vietnam and we lost a flight nurse. That was the only flight nurse we lost doing air evac, which is amazing. We were lucky. There's nothing that I know of to explain it, nothing at all.

I did not talk about Vietnam for a long time afterward, not till seventy-seven or seventy-six, when the Air Force sent me back for my bachelor of science in nursing in Denver, Colorado. I was there with a group of nurses that had been in Vietnam. Not only Air Force, but Army also, and we started talking about things. But I think the most rewarding thing was going to the dedication of the Vietnam statue in November of last year. Another flight nurse and I had a chance to go to the activities the day before with a former Green Beret. We went to the Special Forces Hospitality Room, and when the guys found out that we were medevac nurses, one of the Green Berets called the room to attention and introduced us. You know, it was just all those cheers and thanks for bringing me home or thanks for bringing my buddy home, and what have you. I could not believe the number that came up to us that evening, wanting to give us a kiss, saying, "You nurses of the Air Evac, we've never seen you, we lost touch with you all, but you got so many of us home safe and sound." And so that was ten or eleven years later. It was a long wait, but I think a lot of vets were experiencing the same wait.

The reason, I think, the women had to wait longer than the men is that the news media was concentrated on the men. Not much was being said about females being over in Vietnam. Then we came back and didn't say anything about it — we just felt we'd been over there to do a job, we'd done it, and we'd come home. I can't speak for the Army, because they had certainly more people over there, but in the Air Force, once you'd get back to the States, you were not with that many women — or men, either — who had been in Vietnam. People would ask, "Well, how was it over there?" And you'd say, "Fine. It was hard work and it was challenging and it was very rewarding." But that was all we'd say. I don't know why we didn't talk more about it. We may have gotten the feeling that people really didn't want to hear, that they were just asking how was it just for the sake of asking. Many times people would ask and then you'd start to say something and they would change the conversation or do something along that line. They really didn't want to hear what it was like. I think that's how a lot of Americans were for a long time. They really did not want to know, they had no idea, they could not grasp what it was like over there, especially for the women. And when we started having the problems with so many of our guys coming back on drugs, I think Americans just wanted to shun the whole thing and not really accept what had happened and why we had been there. So, you know, sure they said, "Why were we there in the first place?"

I think if we have another conflict, like in El Salvador, we're going to have some of the same problems. People are not going to understand why we have to be there and why do we have to protect them. Like in my generation, we may see or may not see the results of Vietnam falling to the communists. But one way or the other, if there is another conflict, I will go.

Part of my job here as chief nurse is to ensure that all the nurses and technicians receive wartime training. We assign them to various treatment teams and then set up various scenarios for simulated casualties. We'll arrange to have some type of a simulated accident occur on the base, whether it be an airplane accident, a truck rolling over, or a school bus bringing kids home. Then we bring the simulated casualties into the hospital and the physicians, the technicians, and the nurses decide what would you do for this patient if they come into your hospital in this condition; they also decide which patients would be treated first, who would be treated later.

We also train for nuclear attacks. We have a team that is taught how to suit up in a decontamination suit that will protect them from the nuclear fallout. What we would do: we would all go down to the basement — we have shelter areas designated — and the decon team would be the one that would be taking care of the patients or casualties that have been contaminated by radiation. They have procedures for hosing them down and making them

168

clean and ways of checking with machines to make sure they are no longer radioactive before we would then bring them into the shelter area. So we're training for that also, plus all the day-to-day patient care.

Well, I can think of one last thing. Certainly if the book is read by civilian nurses, I would like them to know this: just today I had one of my young nurses who has been in the Air Force three years come down to talk with me. She had gone to a course at Sheppard and from the presentations there had finally realized that why we are in the military is to prepare for the time of war. Military nurses will be taking care of a large number of casualties and seeing a lot of injuries, disfigurement, and maiming of young people. So she came down and talked to me today and said, "I don't think I'm going to be able to handle that. I never really had given it any thought until now. When I came in the Air Force, I came in for the chance to travel and just to be doing nursing. But it really dawned on me that our mission is to keep our American soldiers as healthy as possible and get them back to the United States from a conflict as soon as we can and with as little medical problems as we possibly can." That was the way she put it. And for a young gal to admit that she could not handle that — well, it's like with civilian nurses. They don't really realize what our mission is. They see us as being nurses but doing the same thing that they're doing on a day-to-day basis. But our primary mission is to take care of the active-duty soldiers, airmen, and seamen, to get them back to duty as quick as we can so they can defend our country. That's what we're here for. So being a military nurse is not like being a civilian nurse. Seventy-two hours from now, I might have to leave this place and go to a conflict.

As for the young recruits, I don't think they really look at why they are coming in the Air Force, the Army, or the Navy. Right now, because we are so far removed from war, I don't think they even think of it. But that's really why we have the Air Force, Army and Navy nurse corps — so that we can take care of the casualties if and when there is another war.

*Marsha Jordan has been in the Air Force for seventeen years. She is currently stationed at Dyess Air Force Base in Abilene, Texas, where she is Chief of Nursing Services. Her next duty station will be MacDill Air Force Base in Tampa, Florida.*

# Jeanne (Bokina) Christie

*Jeanne Christie was born and raised in Madison, Wisconsin, where her father was a fireman. In the winter of 1967, after graduating from the University of Wisconsin with a degree in art education, Jeanne joined the American Red Cross SRAO [Supplemental Recreational Activity Overseas] Program. "I wanted to do something different before I became an old-maid schoolteacher. I was a real duck in those days — severe haircut, hornrimmed glasses, sleeves down to my elbows. I had male friends but not boyfriends, and I had very little self-confidence."*

*Jeanne spent five months at the Army Subcommand in Nha Trang. Then she was assigned to the First Marine Division in Danang and later to the 35th Tactical Fighter Wing in Phan Rang.*

I'D GROWN UP in a very protected family, in the Midwest, with all the Main Street values. Because I wasn't from a big city, I wasn't aware of so many facets in life. In that sense, going over to Vietnam was a break.

The Kalamazoo school system had accepted me when the Red Cross came through with their option. They called and said, "This is the Red Cross. Would you like to have a job in the Recreation Program and go to Vietnam?" I said, "Yup," and they said it again, and I said, "Yup" again. Then I called my parents and told them I was going to Vietnam. I thought it was a chance for adventure, a neat thing to do. But I had never been to a war before, and I had a lot to learn.

The ARC probably told me that I was going to a war zone, but I didn't hear a word they said. I went back to school and told the dean's office that I was sorry I couldn't make graduation because I had to report to Vietnam. Still, nothing connected. I hadn't been a big television watcher, and all the reading I had been doing was from textbooks. I really didn't even know where South Vietnam was, though I had a good idea of its general location — I knew it was in Asia — and knew it would be a long plane ride to get there.

When I left for the training in Washington, D.C., I was dressed like the American flag. Navy blue suit, red and white polka-dot blouse. The training, I remember, was mainly about how to tell the different branches of the service apart and how to tell who was an officer and who was an enlisted person. We were also told how to wear our uniforms and when we could wear civilian clothes. They did role-playing to teach us the proper ways to answer an off-color remark and how to take a drink when we were in uniform. The ARC even told us how to respond in tacky situations and when to dodge a real slippery deal.

I'm sure gals from the big cities gained a different set of skills. But I was very naive — being from Wisconsin did have its drawbacks — which may be one of the reasons the ARC accepted me.

All of the women recruited at that time had the chance to go to Vietnam or Korea. I really wanted to go to Vietnam — Korea was cold, and after the long winters in Wisconsin I had no desire to be cold again.

After our training, we were taken from D.C. to San Francisco and Travis Air Force Base. Going to Vietnam, it was a full plane, but there were only seven of us from the ARC. The flight took thirteen hours, and a thirteen-hour flight with a bunch of strange fellows is a little long, but we all tried to make the best of it.

Going over we were all still in la-di-da land. We probably said, "Isn't it great that we're going to Vietnam!" We hadn't the foggiest idea of what we were doing or what we were getting ourselves into.

The plane flew into Saigon at night. It was absolutely black. I remember as we got closer, the tension grew. Then the captain announced that the aircraft lights would have to be turned off — it's an eerie feeling, flying in nothing but blackness.

When the aircraft stopped, all the lights came on. The military started screaming at the poor fellows, and I remember them being terribly frightened. Because they knew this was it, that for many of them their lives were over. They were just peons and they stood a good chance of being blown away.

The women were held until most of the men were off, and then we were asked to go down the steps. By that point somebody was screaming at us and everyone was screaming at everyone else. They took us to a plywood billet. It had mosquito netting — it was a typical military bunk — but, best of all, it had walls and a ceiling.

That was our first night. It wasn't until dawn that I actually saw anything of Vietnam.

We spent a week in Saigon with the Red Cross honchos. Funny, I had a phone call while I was staying there. I couldn't believe I would have a call because I didn't know a soul in country! But it was a fellow from Milwaukee who had heard a girl from Wisconsin was coming through. He was with the Red Cross, too.

I don't even remember his name. He was one of those individuals who comes into your life and then disappears again, but he had a motor scooter and we went all over Saigon on it. I remember going to the zoo and thinking it was just great. I loved the architecture and the flowers; Saigon, at that point, was just a big exotic city. With all the traveling, I can't recall having any fear at all. I don't remember the hotel we stayed at. It had cold tile floors, laundry lines out the windows, bare minimum beds, and of course the first gun racks I had seen. I can recall thinking that perhaps there really was a war going on somewhere — but not in the city I had seen.

After a week in Saigon the girls were sent to the various locations, depending on how the honchos thought you could handle it. I went to the Army in Nha Trang. When I got off the plane the girls in the unit had me sit on the floor of the jeep with my helmet on — in addition to our uniforms, we were issued fatigues. I spent that first night on duty, sitting on the front steps of the hootch, with my helmet and a whistle, right next to the concertina wire. I'd been told that if anyone came through the area I was to blow my whistle. So I sat there in dire fear, hoping I wouldn't have to blow the darn thing. Of course it was done for fun, but then this was early sixty-seven and the units were still having a good time.

Nha Trang itself was beautiful, with its white beaches and turquoise sea. And it had magnificent French restaurants — though I did get dysentery and had to literally be carried to the hospital.

Our center had a cement floor and open screens so the dust could blow in all the time from the streets. Our hootch was cement with a tile floor and screened windows. At the hootch we all shared a housekeeper — her name was Bien — and I considered her a very special friend. We became really close. I saw her every day until the day I left Nha Trang. She was the one who cleaned me up when I had dysentery; she was the one I showed how to make French fries, meatballs, and milk gravy; she was the one I did shopping with. We used to sit for hours and she'd tell me stories about the people she knew and her observations of the gals in the unit. She tried to teach me Vietnamese, but I ended up teaching her more English, though at the market I got so I could ask for vegetables and fruit.

Bien got dishes for me at the market, just the everyday stuff, but I thought they were beautiful — I still have two tea containers she bought me. She was such a sweetheart. I really loved the woman. To this day I look at the refugees and wonder about Bien. But her husband was ARVN and the VC killed most of them, so she's probably dead, too.

I don't know if you know it's a great honor to be invited to a Vietnamese home. Well, one day Bien invited me. Her home was a little shack, really a shanty — they had only one bed for the five of them.

I met Bien's husband and we had tea and tried to talk. The whole time the neighbors were standing outside of the window, touching my hair, which was very blond — they had apparently never had a chance to touch blond hair. That day the neighbors also had blue eyes to look at.

Bien used to tease me about my glasses. She'd say, "Blue eyes, weak eyes. Why all Americans with blue eyes wear glasses? Dark eyes like Vietnamese, good eyes, no wear glasses."

Anyway, we shared our cups and had tea, and finally her husband was going to do his great honor and give me a ride home on his motor bike. He gets on the bike in front and I get on the back and the bike goes WHUPP! Right up in the air! The poor man was mortified. He weighed maybe ninety pounds and couldn't get the bike down in front. By now everyone had gathered around. They thought they should put me on the handlebars, but I said — appropriately — "No, thanks!" So I believe I went home in a pedicab; they were not going to let me walk home because that would be a dishonor to the family.

I went everywhere in Nha Trang in those days. Oh, there were terrorist attacks — in fact, once a little kid was trying to blow up a restaurant we were going into. I was with a Navy officer and we'd just gotten out of the pedicab and were getting ready to walk in when we saw this little kid running down the street and heard the crack of the gun. They shot the kid. That type of thing was not that uncommon, yet nobody really thought about it.

173

I was still so naive. And the people were very protective of us. We used to ride out to the White Horse ROK [Republic of Korea] Camp sitting on the back of the trucks — we were right in all the traffic, among all the Vietnamese. In our little blue uniforms with our Instamatic cameras hanging off our wrists, we could have been picked off. But we weren't.

No, in Nha Trang we didn't really see the ugly side of the war. The air base did get hit a couple of times, but we lived at the hospital compound and only heard it.

So I still hadn't been exposed to the heavy war. The casualties I had seen were ones the Army could patch up and return to duty, or they were malaria victims. I still didn't know what it looked like when people were blown up.

Maybe the worst thing I saw in Nha Trang, aside from the kid being shot, were the body bags. I remember I had to go to the hospital one day and do a program. They were pulling the green plastic garbage bags off the truck, and I heard the thud-thud-thud — it's a sound you never forget — so I asked the guys what they were doing. When they said they were throwing the bodies off, I took a deep breath and went, "OK." Then I had to go into the wards and be effervescent and program.

The body bags had bodies in them with no head or arms or feet — they weren't bodies laid out all nice and straight like you see in pictures. No, these bodies were just dead weight. They fell off the truck and went thud. Maybe seeing the body bags was when things started to register, but I'm not sure.

I used to go swimming with some of the Navy SEALs in the area. They were heavyweights in demolition, but I never asked them what they did and they never tried to explain.

I had many crazy friends from both the Army and the Navy in Nha Trang. Perhaps the one I did the craziest things with was a Navy officer who lived near the SEALs. He was always willing to do something zany. For example, I convinced him to take me into one of the local bars one night and buy me Saigon tea. I had never been in a — quote unquote — house before, but I had heard the men talking about what went on inside and I wanted to see it firsthand. Well, this fellow was known to be a fun-loving guy and very well respected by his men, and I knew by his physical size that I would be in no danger. So he finally said he'd do it, and in we went. The men that were in the bar laughed and shuffled their girls to another lap or knee, and then the fellow that I was with announced to the madam that I wanted some tea and that he was going to buy it. Needless to say, we had quite a few people checking out this scene; my presence in the bar slowed down the work! When we left — I can still visualize this — my friend's men didn't know if they should salute him or ignore him.

The stories that went with that one went on for quite a time.

Thinking about relationships with men, I can honestly say that I didn't have a problem with men coming on to me. I was so naive I never realized what they might have been saying. Or if I did, I refused to believe anyone would say something like that. I was still into just having fun. We all worked real hard doing runs and working in the centers, but it was still a good time.

Around five months into my Nha Trang assignment the unit moved off the hospital compound and into the city. It was in an area that had a lot of prostitutes, so our curfew was adjusted to protect us from what might happen. We also had an ARVN guard, who was totally useless. He used to walk through the house at night when he was supposed to have been standing guard; I remember waking up one night and seeing this man in my room with a loaded weapon. He was taking everything off my dresser — jewelry, money, cameras, anything he wanted. Only you're not going to spook him and yell "What the hell are you doing!" because he had a loaded weapon — if you moved, you were gone.

I never got vocal about him until he started beating up the housemaids during the day. When he finally beat up Bien, I lost my cool. I screamed and shouted, ranted and raved, and probably told some of the U.S. military I wanted revenge. The problem was, the ARVN guard was the best security we could get at that time.

Thinking of security, or the lack of it, brings to mind the two nurses* that were shot to death while I was in Nha Trang. One of the gals had been dating several men and had run into a guy who just couldn't share. He got mad at her and went to her quarters and shot her. Her roommate heard it and came in. Then the guy shot the roommate. Finally he turned the gun on his own brains and blew them out.

The fellow that shot the nurses was so nice-looking — tall, dark

---

* As Jeanne remarked in a letter that followed our interview, these women may or may not have been nurses. "Nurse" was a common term for American women in Vietnam; even Red Cross volunteers were mistakenly called "nurses."

hair. What a waste! I knew his friend who used to fly for Air America, a blond fellow, and he was the one who told me.

It shook me up to think that we were very expendable commodities. Also, knowing the other women as friends of a friend was getting a bit too close.

On the lighter side, there was another gal. She joined our unit after I'd been there several months. This gal was real cute and definitely a pistol. When we lived in the house in town, she used to sleep up on the roof, where it was cooler — at least she did that until the roof caved in. She would also get up early in the morning and go jogging. We all thought she was crazy to go out that early without protection, and the Vietnamese just couldn't believe it. Why would anyone run, they thought — let alone an American and a female? It was something the Vietnamese just couldn't understand.

This gal came from Georgia. I tried finding her after Vietnam, but to this day she's one of those that has become a dead end.

Nha Trang was a strange place. Perhaps the truth of the war had not set in — I could honestly write home that I had gone to a French restaurant and had the best lobster thermidor and the most magnificent onion soup of my life. But two months later those restaurants were all blown up. That's how much the war escalated.

After five months at Nha Trang I was sent to Danang, with the First Marine Division. Being with the Marines meant getting out to the field a lot, and doing the job we felt was so needed. Often we'd fly out to the LZs and at times even end up in one that was hot — the situation would change so fast. It all starts to sink in when you're sitting in a chopper and you look back at where you've been and see an air strike going in. The military was careful not to let this happen when you went out in the morning, but as I said, things changed rapidly and counting the bullet holes became a joke.

With our work, the driver would pick you up at dawn and you would chopper out to the various units. You'd try to make it to six or eight units before the day was through. You'd talk to the guys and serve them lunch if it happened to be lunchtime, or if you got there early you'd have breakfast with them.

We had some marvelous things happen with the fellows out in the field. One time they brought me chocolate-covered Turtles —

where they got them, I don't know. And why they didn't melt from the heat is beyond me. Another time there had been some unexpected changes in the schedule and we ended up sitting on the sandbags, drinking warm orange soda and watching the action in a distant area.

I can recall too easily the first time I really had to go to the bathroom out in the field. For the guys it was easy, but for us it was a different story. I had waited until I thought my eyeballs were going to float before I finally said I wanted some privacy. Out in the field the — quote unquote — privacy might be a bush. But for me, that day, it was some of the fellows holding up green canvas as a barrier. The men said they didn't hear a thing, but I was thinking, "How can I squat and make this quiet?" Then the tinkle tinkle tinkle turned to the roar of an airplane or the rush of a racehorse — the point being that when the men sensed we were embarrassed, they never made an issue of it. They were true gentlemen.

Basically, when we were out in the field the men loved anything we did. For instance, when we went into the LZs the guys would sit on the hill or whatever and watch us in total awe. Some of them would flock to you and talk as fast as they could; others couldn't say a thing. But all of them would stare. They knew every movement we made — nothing we did escaped them.

For those who couldn't talk with us, it must have seemed strange to have us drop in from the sky. For the others, it was a chance to laugh and get a bit of relief from the war. Most of the time we took audience-participation programs and Kool-Aid. The audience-participation programs were silly things: question and answer, flashcards, felt-tip pens, rubber bands. All of us had rubber bands, because they were a great ice-breaker. What we did was put a rubber band over a guy's pinky and thumb and tell them they had to get it off without using any part of their body. Eventually they'd start laughing and teasing each other, and before they knew it their minds were on something other than the war.

There were other crazy things we did to divert their attention from the war, but the program was a simple one: the morale of the troops was what was most important. Unfortunately, we were also known as the — quote unquote — fun and games girls, which does not translate well back here in the States. When my children — many years later — asked me what I did in the war, the explanation I ended up with was that some people patched others up, some people shot others, but I played games.

So it was a specific program designed to help the morale of the military we supported. As silly as this may sound, we personified the American women to the men. We were their homes, their sisters, their mothers, their wives, their girlfriends. We were reminders of what they had lost and what they had to continue on for.

I mentioned what gentlemen the fellows could be. Well, they were always looking for ways to help. When I left Nha Trang I was "Jeanne," but in Danang I lost my name tag. Of course, this would put me in an awkward position of being somewhat out of uniform in the Marines' eyes. Anyway, I was down at the flight line center and a gunny [gunnery] sergeant came in with a new name tag for me. It was "Sam." No first name, no last name. Just "Sam."

One morning when I went to work, the Public Affairs Office came in to take shots of us for the public service spots on TV. My blond hair looked great, my smile was perfect, and right on the front of my light blue uniform was my "Sam" name tag. The spots required us to say, "Hi. My name is so-and-so, from the American Red Cross at Freedom Hill." Because I couldn't say my name was Jeanne, with a Sam name tag on, I said, "Sam." It stayed "Sam" after that. I always had fun with it. It made for great conversation out in the field.

Programming was sometimes terrific and sometimes the pits. The worst part of working in the Danang area was programming in the morning at the LZs and then ending up in the hospital for the last run of the day. It would just blow your mind to see the guys laughing with you in the morning and blown to bits and in the hospital by afternoon. That tends to be a real demoralizing item when you're the one passing out the smiles.

When we went into the hospitals to program, we were not supposed to get the men too active. Our job was to look them in the eye and convince them that everything was all right. As difficult as that may have been at times, there were moments when the men were the saviors. One fellow — he had lost both his legs and was being med-evacked out — gave me a safety pin for my belt because he would no longer need it, and I would. Because I had had bad legs as a child, I wanted to — but never did — tell him what a fight lay ahead of him. Instead he turned my psyche around and gave me more than just that little pin — more than a million little pins.

Another time I tried to talk to a guy and he started to cough up blood and mucus through his larynx tubes. But I couldn't be terrorized by it and had to go back and face that fellow; I could do more damage by being offended by his limitations than by being understanding. So I talked to him and smiled and said, "It's OK. Don't talk to me. . . . I'll just stay here and talk to you." You learned to smile and cry at the same time, until you finally built up a facade and could literally look at somebody dying and smile like Miss America or whatever we personified to them.

I remember once getting into an area where I obviously should not have been. People started screaming and yelling at me. I think it was a burn ward and new casualties had just come in. I remember smelling something absolutely putrid — the smell of burned human skin is a hard one to forget. I don't know how the staff, doctors and nurses, learned to cope with so many guys in such bad shape.

The casualties of shrapnel always used to make me wonder. Some were in good shape; others weren't. They all looked like somebody had taken a giant pepper grinder to them.

There are other aspects of the experience that had to be dealt with, too. On the healthier side, the guys in the field had their trophies that they shared with us. Both sides collected trophies, and although I only heard about the VC's, I saw some of the ones our guys collected. I had fellows bring me ears to see, and I thought they were apricots. I remember being shown the scalps of the VC, and little peckers in little glass jars. Because it was a way of survival for some of the men, I tried never to let on or pass judgment on them — again, that would have done more damage than just letting it pass by. In that way I tried to protect the men I dealt with. They had become my guys, and like kids collecting frogs or birds' eggs, the guys wouldn't collect trophies forever. So it was all right.

If there's one problem that really haunted me for a long time after Vietnam, I would say it was a simple one that had to do with a kid, a young man in Danang. We had the usual Vietnamese workers at the center, plus several extras to do special jobs. One of them was this kid, and another, Hoa, was a fellow who had come down from North Vietnam. Since I had had a good relationship with the population in Nha Trang, I was given the job of being the liaison between the locals at the center and the military. The problem arose when weapons — men checked in their weapons as they came into the center — started disappearing. This obviously got the men in trouble, and I was the one who had to talk to the Vietnamese staff to try and resolve the situation. Well, I tried several things. I tried talking with Hoa and having him talk to this kid, this specific young man. Still, the guns would disappear. So I tried talking to the young man, and eventually, I begged him not to come back to work because I had a fairly good idea of what his fate would be. Also, I honestly believed he was not the person who was shifting the guns.

The next morning when I went to pick up our workers, the kid was there — I had failed to convince him, or somebody else had convinced him differently. That day, I had to take him to Marine headquarters and sign the papers on him. It was instant justice — guilty as charged.

After I signed the dotted line, the kid belonged to the Marines. He started to scream and claw at me to give him another chance. But it was too late. I had my driver drive off. Later I asked one of my Marines about what was done. His reply was the one I didn't want to hear.

I loved my Marines and could understand their position. But for many years, I could hear the kid screaming.

Most people don't realize that there were Red Cross gals who died in Nam. With all of us flying around and traveling all over, it's amazing that there weren't more problems. Most of us thought we were invincible. If we had thought about how expendable we were, or dwelled on our vulnerability, we would never have gone to some of the places we went. If we had thought about the whole thing, we probably wouldn't have gone to Nam.

The three that died in our program were in Nam after I was. One died in a jeep accident, one from a mysterious illness, and one was stabbed to death by a GI.

The problem that nobody talked about back then — having it happen to you was a fate worse than death — is being raped. Normally the men were very good, but rape did happen when they would get skunk drunk or stretched to their psychological limit and just go crazy. If a gal happened to be in the wrong place at the wrong time, it could happen.

As a woman in Nam, if you got raped you really had no recourse.

The military was very nasty about it, and naturally it was always the woman's fault. In Nam I knew of some of the options that were offered any gal who found herself in a family way. None of them were pleasant, and none of them left the gal with an ounce of self-respect. Since Nam, I've heard of many more women who had that happen to them, and they only confirmed what I knew then.

We did have guys attempt to break into our quarters. In fact, one night I heard the dog bark and yelled at this guy. I didn't have so much as a popsicle stick, yet I got him to halt and put his hands over his head until the MPs could get there. Situations like that were a total game of bluff.

There were some spooky things, too. At night I would walk out in the driveway and hear something or somebody running off in the brush. It really made you wonder if you were being watched. We also had some ARC gals' photos appear in VC pockets — they'd taken pictures and were either tracing the gals down or watching them. That was spooky!

I'm not sure what the VC were planning to do to those gals. They could just have been using the pictures as propaganda, or they could have actually been trying to pick them off. You know that there were three German nurses that were captured; only one lived to tell about it.

My last duty station was at Phan Rang Air Force Base. By then I was developing a real negative attitude. I just couldn't smile anymore. I loved the Marines, but I had started to speak up, so I wasn't any use to them.

The Air Force was very different from the Marines. The Marines were dirty and in combat a lot. The Air Force was clean and really didn't kill — only their bombs did. In Phan Rang it was clean, and we never saw any casualties. With the Marines, we'd lived under their standards, but with the Air Force we lived in air-conditioned comfort. Phan Rang was real nice, but it was boring beyond my wildest dreams. Even with the Hundred-and-first on the other side of the base and the Aussies in the middle, it was boring. And even after I was promoted to unit director, I still missed Danang.

Basically, Phan Rang was one long party. We did have some program runs, but as UD, I wanted to let my new girls go out, so I would hold down the center. With the boredom, I took to doing illegal things for excitement. I got a F-100 fighter ride before I left.

I had acquired a G-suit, combat boots, black glasses, and helmet —
I looked like Rocky the Flying Squirrel! Another time I caught a
flight up to Hue and Danang to get a case of toilet paper. As a
honcho, I could go out to the flight line and tell them I needed a
ride. The fellows would take you almost any place you wanted to
go, if they had a flight booked.

It was insane what I could do and get away with: all the little —
quote unquote — errands I had to run. At Phan Rang, I learned
to drive a car. I learned on an Air Force staff car. I used to get up
at the crack of dawn and go with my — quote unquote — teacher,
before the roads had even been cleared.

I was short by then. I both wanted to get out and to go back
and protect my Marines; I wanted to be left alone and I wanted
to be busy. It was a crazy time. I was getting fat from the lack of
exercise and started to take diet pills, which were legal then and
very easy to get. The new energy made me want to take more.
Diet pills in the day and parties at night did not do a thing for my
state of mind.

At Phan Rang we did MEDCAPing [Medical Civil Assistance
Program], in conjunction with programming, at the orphanages.
In the orphanages I saw kids that were so badly deformed and
injured that — with the flies and all the smells that went along
with it — my walls just went up. I had to isolate myself in order
to save my sanity. A lot of the gals I worked with liked the orphanages, but I went out a couple of times and said, "This is it!"
Because I'd seen enough of the maiming, the destruction, and the
hurt. So I stayed at the base most of the time, waiting for the
dinner hour, waiting to go home, waiting for the time to pass. I
just didn't care any more.

When I was finally able to DEROS, I left for Saigon. Tet had
just started, and I ended up getting stuck in Saigon with several
other gals. We had a hard time getting around, and food was not
easy to obtain. Cokes and doughnuts were our meals. It was the
only time as a — quote unquote — donut dolly that I ever saw a
doughnut.

By that time I wanted out. The old story of being put in a pine
box even began to sound good. Eventually I ran into a colonel I'd
known at a previous duty station and convinced him that if I could
get back to Cam Ranh, I could hop a flight out. He volunteered
to fly me back to Phan Rang, which was close, and I accepted.
That evening he flew me out in a small bird-dog spotter plane. I'll

always remember the fires around the area; it was an unbelievable sight.

I got to Cam Ranh the next day and was all set to hop a flight out when they discovered that my passport had not been stamped. I had to go back to Saigon, then back to Cam Ranh. Naturally I missed the flight. So I ended up putting on my flight suit and going up to any aircraft on the flight line that was manifested to leave for anyplace. Finally I talked my way onto a flight that was going to Okinawa, and that, unconventional as it was, was how I got out of Nam.

Back in the States I found I was in such a different world. In Vietnam I'd been taken away from the world I'd known, and yet, when I got back home, I wasn't sure where I should have been. I found myself in limbo, in a dream world. Things didn't make any sense. Trying to find a job was a hassle. I either had all this experience and/or no experience. Life didn't function the way it had before. In Vietnam I'd had responsibility, power, ability. At home I felt I was a totally inept boob. It was weird. And worst of all, it made me very angry.

Eventually the Red Cross gave me a job at Great Lakes Naval Hospital. I caused all sorts of problems for them while I was there. All the sweet ladies who volunteered, and the older staff, thought of me as a monster. And I was. I was the first woman they had run into who had been to Vietnam, and they got the full brunt of my storm.

The saving grace at the hospital were the men up on the wards. I could go up on the wards and get the men to do almost anything. I would sometimes just go up to the wards to talk and shoot the breeze. I treated them like human beings. We all spoke the same language, because we had all been to Nam.

My whole personality changed when I went to Vietnam. I came back to find myself doing things I never would have done before. I would test things just for the challenge — like driving a Porsche on the side of the turnpike just to see how stable it was. I even jumped on beds to see how long till they would break. I cried a lot then, too. I didn't know why, and I didn't want to answer the unanswered questions in my head. All I knew was that I hurt and wanted to be back in Nam. I wondered why I wasn't married like all the other girls at home — why I wasn't raising a family, why I didn't fit in anywhere.

Finally I packed my bags at Great Lakes and moved on to

Oxford, Ohio. At Miami of Ohio, I got my master's in education supervision. While I was at Miami, I sealed off Vietnam. I didn't watch TV when Vietnam would come on, and I refused to follow it in the papers. I simply let it fade out of my frame of reference.

When I graduated, I decided not to stay in the States, so I found a job on Guam as the associate director of the USO. It was on Guam that I met my husband. He had not been to Nam, but he was in the Navy.

Ten or twelve years went by and I still didn't really talk about anything that really dealt with Vietnam. One evening when we were at a friend's house for dinner, the subject came into the conversation. One of the husbands had been in the Navy as an interpreter and the other two men had been in Vietnam. We decided to all get together and look at each other's slides from Vietnam. That was when the feelings and emotions started creeping back.

For me, my behavior was totally out of character. Some friends said I was crazy; I said I wasn't. I just didn't know or understand what was happening. Through it all, my friend Peter, also a Nam vet, stuck with me. Another vet, a guy I met in Boston, finally asked me what I was seeing. But my mind was going wild, and I was unable to verbalize what was happening in my private war.

I spent several pretty rough days at that point. One day I tried to keep busy by making cookies and ended up walking around the house with a measuring cup, trying to get the sugar from the pantry. I just couldn't function in a normal manner. My poor husband didn't know what to do or how to act. Things were going through my head so fast . . . like the kid I had signed the papers on. He had come back to haunt me. My own children would run up to me wanting a hug, and I would just lose it. Little things didn't make sense and, in turn, my whole life didn't make sense. I couldn't put my memories and values in order. I would make calls to friends and then be totally unable to talk, so I'd hang up. I knew people who had been to Nam were the ones who could begin to understand, yet I felt that it wasn't right to burden them with my problems.

Finally, one really traumatic thing happened. Peter and I had finally decided that we would go to a vet center and sit in on a rap session — you know, join forces with other vets. To build our courage up we stopped at a bar and had a stiff one, and then went to the center. We were late, didn't know they didn't allow vets in who had been drinking. So we opened the door and started to walk in. The team members who were on duty that night got up and started towards us. They pointed at Peter and said, "He can come in but she can't!" I was gone — totally demolished. They had leveled me right there. Fortunately, Peter said, "What do you mean? She was there. She was in Nam." For several minutes they argued. To me it seemed like forever. But after a few minutes the team members and the rap group decided to let us stay.

It wasn't till it all came back and hit them on the head that they said, "Yeah, there were women in Vietnam."

After that I decided there must be other women facing the same concerns and frustrations. Eventually I began to work on the issues. And I started coming out of the spiral.

*Jeanne Christie is a designer for a New York textile firm, a free-lance faux bois painter, and a part-time teacher. In addition, much of her time is given to organizing women Vietnam veterans, both civilian and military. Jeanne, her husband, and their two children live in Milford, Connecticut.*

# Anne Allen

*Anne Allen grew up in a large Italian family in Hartford, Connecticut. She moved to New York and worked her way through Columbia, graduating in 1962 with a history degree. Shortly afterward, Anne began freelancing as a journalist.*

*In 1967 her husband, George, also a journalist, was asked to go to Vietnam for ABC News. "George said he would go, provided he could take his wife. I have to tell you that my mother was absolutely outraged, because now she had three things to be mad about: I didn't stay home and marry the guy next door, I went off and got myself a college education, and now — for God's sake! — I was going off to a war. I mean, what kind of crazy daughter is that? People avoid wars. They don't go to them, not when they have a choice.*

*"A lot of my friends felt the same way. 'He has to go,' they said, 'but you don't.' And I said, 'You've got to be crazy — this is an exciting chance. I'm going to do it — I want to go!' So I went."*

*Anne and George were in Vietnam from June of 1967 to December of 1968. While George worked for ABC, Anne free-lanced for the North American Newspaper Alliance and other organizations. They also, during that time, adopted their first son, Billy; two years after their return they adopted Sammy. Both Billy and Sammy were orphaned in Vietnam.*

WHEN GEORGE AND I first got to Vietnam, we made a deal. The deal was that I would stay out of trouble spots. As a correspondent working under deadline, he had to go where the shooting war was. But since I was doing features and didn't have to worry about the time element, I didn't have to put myself in the middle of the shooting: for instance, I didn't have to be at Khe Sanh. But it didn't take long to understand that every spot was a potential trouble spot.

Of course, over here all of us watched the war on television. Over there, we did, too. A couple times a week we saw the rushes — the film that had been shot — but among the things film doesn't show, or can't show, is the stink. Also the heat. When I got off the airplane at Tan Son Nhut, the heat was so tremendous — I'll never forget it. It was as if you were walking into a steam bath.

OK, you go to MACV [Military Assistance Command, Vietnam] and present your credentials. Then you get an ID card, which, among other things, allows you to travel. Then, what you do is, you start looking around. I was interested in doing family and children stories, stories on Vietnamese family life.

I want to tell you that what I saw — as journalist but also just as a human being — was a great deal of suffering. I had never seen death before, not firsthand. I remember as a child going to Italian funerals, going to the funeral home. But that's all very nice and clean and tidy. And I remember, of course, visiting many friends in the hospital, but I had never seen death firsthand. In Vietnam I saw death firsthand. I had never seen open, gaping wounds firsthand, and I saw that. No, I had never seen people suffer the way I saw it in Vietnam. There were women who lived on the streets, and children living in cardboard boxes — there were children wandering everywhere, living on whatever they could. When I first took Billy out of the orphanage, one of the first things he did was pick up a cigar butt. We were walking along Cong Ly — it was a major thoroughfare, a lot of American soldiers walked along Cong Ly — and Billy started smoking this butt. I was horrified. He kept saying, "Good. Good." He had a nicotine habit at seven.

So those were the kinds of stories I most wanted to do — stories on the Vietnamese, on families and children. Now understand that, in Vietnam, it wasn't easy to do things. Here, if we want to go somewhere, we jump in a car. If we want to talk to someone, we pick up the phone. But in Vietnam if you wanted to talk to someone, chances were they didn't have a phone. So you had to get in a cyclo or borrow a Honda or borrow a car. Then you had to try to find the person. Also, the language barrier made things very difficult. Vietnamese is a tonal language — it's constructed on five tones — and not at all like any European language. If we had stayed another eighteen months, I would have made an effort to learn the language. It's very hard to interview someone when you don't have a language in common.

The other thing is, the Vietnamese often told you what they thought you wanted to hear or know, and that, of course, is not it at all when you're interviewing somebody and you want to find a story. But they're very polite. They would try to give you what they thought you wanted.

Often what you would do was hire an interpreter. If you were lucky, you had a good interpreter and they did an absolutely outstanding job. Sometimes the interpreters weren't that good, and you had trouble: you wouldn't really get the information you needed.

So I was doing stories on families, children, refugees. Because I was free-lance, because I didn't have a specific assignment, I had to rely on my own resourcefulness. You heard things — word of mouth. People told you and you went. Other reporters would let you know what was going on, and you would let them know when you came across a story you couldn't use. People were very helpful, very kind. I heard many stories I couldn't use because, once people got to like you and trust you, they told you things. Then you passed it on. There was an enormous sense of sharing among the correspondents based in Saigon — Saigon, of course, was the focal point, because that's where MACV was. You were based at the Continental or the Caravelle, and you moved outward from there; we were at the Caravelle until after we adopted Billy, when we moved into an apartment.

Let me give you an example of how I worked. One day, quite casually, I met a nun on the street in Saigon. I just said, "Hello, Sister. How are you?" They're aren't too many Western women there so, you know, you tend to be polite and stop. Then I asked what she's doing there, and she tells me they're working with refugees, also teaching school. They're way out on the outskirts of Saigon — during the day they could work there, but at night they had to come back because that was Viet Cong territory. So I said, "I'm interested. I'd love to do a story on your work."

I don't remember Sister's name anymore. I knew it for years, but anyway, I'll just call her "Sister." So I went out to the outskirts of Saigon. They had a building that they'd put up, and they were feeding refugees and teaching and all that. It was a long ride out — they were all the way out in the boonies — and it was a long ride back. But I got a good story out of it.

Now, at that point, we still had our suite at the Caravelle — two rooms. We also had something that was very important: hot water. So I said to Sister — to two sisters — "Why don't you come back with me to my hotel? I've got hot water. I've got some whisky. We'll have a drink and you can take a bath." They thought that was great. So they came back and had their baths and I poured them some Johnny Walker — this is what I mean about sharing; you shared everything in Vietnam — and was passing them a second when George, who was raised by Irish nuns, walked in the door. He just couldn't believe it: two Maryknoll nuns in our suite, drinking Johnny Walker! But anyway, after a drink or two, Sister said to me, "You know, where we're living, there's an American girl. She's Senator Jacob Javits's secretary, and she comes to Vietnam every year on her vacation and works in this orphanage called An Lac. That would make a wonderful story."

This is how it worked in Vietnam. You got stories by people telling you things.

So the next morning I borrowed a car. I went out early, because it gets hot so quickly. I found the orphanage. It had a locked gate, a big iron gate. I banged and banged on the gate, but nobody came. I just kept banging; in Vietnam, you don't give up. Finally a little kid arrived, a tiny kid — a kid who would eventually turn out to be my adopted son — and just stood there and scowled at me from the other side of the gate. I said, in French, "Open the gate, please. Let me in." He didn't understand French. So I kept banging and he kept getting mad. He stood there, determined not to let me in. Finally I said the magic name. I said, "Betty." He said, "Oh" — I could see that he knew what I wanted.

He ran away and came back in a little while with the American woman, Betty Moul. I said, "Betty, my name is Anne Allen and I'd like to do a story on you." She was very rude — very rude. She said, "*Parade* magazine is going to do a story on me and I promised them the exclusive story, and I really haven't got the time to talk to you." Now, in the United States, if someone says that to you, you say "OK. Forget it." But, remember, this is Vietnam. And remember what I told you about how hot it is and how impossible things are, also how tired you are. So I said to her, "OK, Betty, fine. I respect that. If you've given someone exclusivity, okay. But maybe there's some angle to what you're doing here that they're not going to do." She said, "Well, I really don't have the time. I've got so much to do." I said, "Betty, I understand that. I understand you're only here for a month and you've got a lot to do, but how about my coming back and picking you up and taking you to a nice, air-conditioned restaurant?" She said, "Oh, Anne, I'd love it. I'm so exhausted — "

Now remember what I told you. The heat. Also, she'd flown

twenty-four hours, she had jet lag. All the kids are hungry; they haven't had anything to eat. Two hundred kids are crying — and I come along and want a story, OK? So she said, "Bug off and leave me alone," but I wouldn't bug off. I wouldn't leave her alone. Instead I said, "What can I do to make it easier?"

Well, to make a long story short, Betty stood there and talked to me for about twenty minutes. She told me how she was one of Tom Dooley's pals and how, when Tom Dooley died, she became very interested and took on this cause — she'd been raising money in the States to support this orphanage for many years. She was doing all she could to help these children, and to anyone who would help her, she was most grateful. Finally I said, "Let's not make it lunch — let's make it dinner. I'll be back tonight."

I realized I had an excellent story. So I went back and told George about it. I said, "I've got a hell of a story." Well, one of the problems with being married to a television journalist is that they scoop you. He said, "Hey, that's a great story for television. Little kids, American girl —" Sure enough, he did scoop me.

Anyhow, we went that night and took Betty out to a very nice restaurant. After that we took her back to our hotel. Well, Betty Moul turns out to be one of these great charismatic people, like Sister Teresa or Martin Luther King. Once you meet Betty, you can't get unstuck from her. So what happened with the story was that George got it — he went and interviewed her and the children and did a wonderful story. It appeared on ABC and Betty got a lot of contributions for the orphanage.

When I came back to the orphanage that night, I met the boy I'd seen at the gate in the morning. I have to tell you that the minute you walked into a Vietnamese orphanage, the kids would jump on you. You couldn't walk, you literally couldn't walk. They would grab your arm, grab your legs. Six, seven, eight of them would hold tight onto you — they wanted the tender loving care that was totally lacking in their lives. Well, that was the year of the miniskirt. I was wearing a sleeveless dress that was very tight on top, and below the waist it had pleats. I'll never forget it, because the kids kept flipping up the skirt to see what I was wearing underneath. I didn't care. But the boy from the gate — his name was Phuong — got very incensed with that. He kept slapping the other kids and saying something in Vietnamese like "Bug off" — he'd decided that, since he'd seen me first, he had rights to me.

190

He'd immediately grabbed my hand. And he kept pushing every-body away, like "She belongs to me and you can't go near her." By this time I was really beginning to pay attention to the kid.

So while we were having dinner that night, I said to Betty, "He's an awfully nice little boy." Betty, as I told you, is like a tar baby. Well, she said, "You know, you guys, when you've got nothing to do, why don't you come to the orphanage and work?" As if we didn't have enough to do, you know. But we said, "Sure. What do you want us to do?" She said, "Like, bring me stuff. I need soap. Why don't you go to the PX and buy some Ivory soap and bring it to me."

All right, so you go to the PX and you try to be very discreet and you buy six bars of soap and they kind of look at you. But you buy them and you take them to Betty. And she says, "You know, my kids never get out of the orphanage. Why don't you, when you have a few hours, take my kids and buy them a meal and take them to the zoo or something. Do something with my kids." Before we knew it, George and I were taking the kids to the zoo, taking them for meals. We would do this, we would do that. Whenever we took them out, they had to wear red hats so we could identify them at a distance.

We couldn't take more than six out at once. Even with that small number, we had a couple of near-disastrous experiences. Now you have to remember, at this time — at all times — there was a lot of anti-American sentiment. Once I took a bunch of kids to the zoo by myself. I had gotten a car, and all of us piled into it. When we got to the zoo, some Vietnamese started to pelt me with rocks. The kids stood up for me. They yelled, "Stop! Stop it! She's not what you think she is. She's a nice lady and we're orphans and she's helping us."

Phuong was seven then. Most of the kids were about his age. They all spoke a little bit of English, though only a little bit — most of the English they knew started with *f* and ended with *k*. They knew all kinds of dirty words. Anyhow, the Vietnamese could have hurt me very badly. But the kids got in the middle and pro-tected me.

By the way, I have to tell you about Phuong/Billy's name. Betty could never remember the kids' Vietnamese names, so she'd given them Western names; Phuong was also Billy. When we adopted him, I wanted to name him after my husband. But Billy would have none of it: "My name Billeee!" We couldn't budge him, so Billy he is.

Another time I took Billy and a bunch of kids to a special U.S. library in Saigon. The kids never had any books, so I thought it would be fun to take them to the library. But outside the library a Vietnamese guard told me to stop, not to take the kids in. I didn't pay any attention — you don't pay attention; it's a library and it's free. So the guard picked up his rifle and cocked it. He was going to shoot. Me. The kids spoke out and said, "What are you doing? She's a nice lady." And I said, "What are you going to do — shoot me for taking kids to the library?" Oh, God, you uncover some ugly stories sometimes. I don't know if you want to hear this one. Well, I'll tell you in this way —

Madame Vu Thi Ngai, the director of the orphanage, never allowed any of her children to be adopted. Now Madame Ngai spoke French and English. She was North Vietnamese, from Haiphong, where she had also had an orphanage. Tom Dooley had brought her down to Saigon. He saved her and her two hundred children, put them in this beautiful building that had once been a French officers' brothel. It was a lovely compound. Well, Madame Ngai got to like me enormously. Mostly, I think, it was because she understood when I told her my family is Italian. Also, she was very pleased that I spoke French and very pleased when I told her that in my family we spoke French and Italian. And she got to like me because I helped in the orphanage, even though, in general, she didn't trust Americans much, other than Dr. Dooley.

When I wanted to adopt Billy, Madame Ngai said, "Don't take him. He's too old. He's already formed. He's got a personality all his own. And he's a strong-willed boy — he's been here all his life. Take a baby. A baby you can form. You can do anything you want with a baby, but him — he's a man already." I said, "Madame Ngai, if I don't adopt him, what's going to happen to him?" She said, "He'll run away. They all run away. They all leave."

This is something I want you to understand about Vietnam: there was a wonderful sense of family among the Vietnamese. But there was also an enormous sense of practicality, of survival. The kids knew what the facts were. By the time they were twelve, thirteen, fourteen, they said, "Hell, I don't want to be in an orphanage anymore. There isn't enough to eat. There isn't enough action." So they'd run away and live on the streets. Many of them even younger than twelve lived on the streets — I mean, the place had two million refugees living on the streets, and Billy was going to be one of them. As it was, he was going over the fence every night in search of food, cigarette butts, whatever.

I persisted about Billy, and eventually Madame Ngai said we could adopt him. And so we said we'd like him to come to live with us immediately. That's what Billy wanted: to be adopted, to survive. But can you imagine not knowing your new parents' language? Can you imagine being with all these people who are sort of your extended family and then being plucked out of that situation and suddenly being put into the Hotel Caravelle, where you have four room boys on the floor? I mean, you could sneeze and they'd come and wipe your nose. Or you'd ring the little bell and they'd come and bring you whatever you wanted from room service. Can you imagine going from an orphanage to that? The first time Billy got on the elevator he was petrified. He squashed down on the floor like an animal who's trapped. I mean, he thought he was going to die.

OK, so you got a kid. As an American, the first thing you do with a kid is, you put him in school, right? So I said to my Vietnamese friends, "Give me a list of schools." And I went to at least a dozen schools. What happened was this: they saw my American face. Then they spoke to me in French and said, "Oh, we'd be very happy to have your child in school. What's the child's name?" But when I'd give them the Vietnamese name, they'd say, "Sorry. We don't do anything with orphans in this school." I'd say, "Why not?" They'd say, "We just don't have time for that. We don't want to be bothered."

Finally I went to the school — I forget the name — that was considered the best in Saigon. It was run by Vietnamese Catholics. I went in and I spoke to the priest who was the headmaster. I said, "I've been to so many schools and nobody will take this Vietnamese boy." He said, "I'm sorry, we can't take him either. We're very full." They always had a good excuse, like "We're full" or "We don't have teachers" or "We don't have any books. It's the war situation." Finally this priest just looked at me and said, "We can't take him." This was the last place on my list. I stood up and — I'm ashamed to tell you — I started to cry. I said, "How could it be that you, a Catholic priest, will not accept an orphan? How could it be that I, an American, am willing to make the sacrifice to care for this child and you won't make an attempt to teach him? How could that be? Where is your Christianity? Where is your love of Jesus? It doesn't matter what you are — whether you're Catholic or Protestant or Jewish — it doesn't make any difference. You've lost your basic faith in God. You're not bearing witness to what God wants you to do."

Well, believe it or not, this priest started to cry, too. He said, "You've taught me a very important lesson. You can bring him. You can bring him tomorrow. Thank you." Then he did something else. He said, "Well, if this boy is going to live with Americans, he should learn how to speak English." And he gave me the name of an English-language school. So this poor kid was going to Vietnamese school in the morning and then, in the afternoon — from four o'clock to suppertime — he'd go to English school. After a while Billy got pretty sore about this. He said, "I thought this was going to be fun — but too much school!" He had never had any schooling at all, and here he had to go to school all day long. Anyway, the long and the short of it is that I wrote about all this. It really made for a wonderful story.

I went everywhere in Vietnam. I went all over the Delta, to the Highlands, to Danang, just everywhere. As a journalist, you could do that — all you had to do was make arrangements. You had to tell the military where you wanted to go, and if they could accommodate you, they would. But the best way to get around was to go out to the airstrip and just bum a ride.

Let me tell you about the time I went to Hue. During the Tet offensive, some of the worst fighting was there, and the city that for centuries had been the imperial capital was just completely leveled. To demonstrate their sympathy for war victims, the foreign correspondents chipped in and — I forget how much money it was, but it was a good sum of money to buy supplies for the people of Hue. The problem was how to get the supplies to them. Everybody knew that — because the whole South Vietnamese government was very corrupt — if we gave the money to a Vietnamese government agency, little if any would benefit the people. So they gave the money to Germaine Loc; Germaine was a magnificent interpreter who at that time was working for Time/Life. She eventually married Time/Life photographer Dick Swanson. They moved to Washington — they live very close to us — and now she owns Germaine's, one of our best restaurants. Anyhow, Germaine said she couldn't go to Hue alone, that the job was too big. When she asked me to go with her, I said I would. We used the money to buy blankets and rice. Then, through Germaine's intelligence and charm and just plain ordinary savvy, we talked the Vietnamese Air Force into lending us a couple of airplanes to transport the supplies. That's how you negotiated in Vietnam. You know, it was just whether they liked you or not, both Americans and Vietnamese. A lot depended on that personal relationship. Anyhow, we loaded these planes with the rice and blankets and flew to Hue. Then, with the cooperation of the Boy Scouts, we distributed the food and blankets.

It was a considerably difficult job. First of all, everything was destroyed; a once-beautiful city was now a shambles. See this? It's a piece of a vase that had once been in an imperial palace. Everything was shattered. The city was just devastated.

So we started distributing the rice and blankets. We worked very long and hard for a couple of days, more than a couple of days. I was so impressed with the dignity of the people of Hue. There wasn't a riot. There wasn't pushing and shoving. There wasn't any meanness. People were very kind. They stood on line and waited for us to give them what we had. Little kids, big kids, old ladies, young ladies: all types of people. There was one woman who was so old and so starving that she couldn't even hold the rice, so some people came along and carried it for her. Nobody got much rice. Maybe, in our terms, three pounds.

Eventually we had to leave. The bridge over the Perfume River was badly damaged — it was in the water — so we had to climb the broken bridge. We had to climb up and down the bridge supports — up the bridge and down the bridge, over and over — to get across. I remember seeing these people trotting along as if they were thinking, "Well, the bridge is down. . . ." Goddammit, Americans get angry if we hit a pothole in the road! But this bridge was down! Anyhow, we sort of went along with them, as if, well, the bridge is down and it's an inconvenience, but we've got to get to the other side and we're going to do it.

So we got to the other side. Eventually we got to Phu Bai. It was Germaine, her sister — three or four Vietnamese — and me. We got to the airstrip, to the end of the runway, and I said to the pilot, "I'm looking for a ride." He said, "Sure. Where do you want to go?" I said, "Where are you going?" He said, "I'm going to

Danang. This is a hospital plane. Do you mind that?" I said, "No, I don't mind that. I've got some friends." He said, "Who are your friends?" I said, "They're my Vietnamese friends." He said, "God-dammit, I don't take gooks." So I said, "No sweat. I'll get another ride." Because I wasn't going to leave my friends.

I could understand his getting angry. He was the pilot of a hospital plane and had severely wounded men on board and felt the Vietnamese were responsible. I could understand. But this was an American base and I had a responsibility to my friends.

So I said, "No sweat" and walked away. Well, he came over to me and he said, "I'm sorry. I didn't mean to hurt your feelings. Sure, I'll take you, what the hell. If I've got the room." So I went to see the man who was loading the plane. Now, you have to understand what these hospital planes are like. They're really quite frightening.

This was a cargo plane, one of these big planes. The men were on stretchers stacked five high. They'd snapped the stretchers onto these poles. To see row on row, five men high like this, is quite . . . It hurts you. It really hurts you. Well, anyway, the pilot said to me, "Come on up front and ride with me." I said, "Thanks, I really appreciate the offer, but I'll sit back here with my friends." Only we couldn't sit together because the seats were along the skin, outside of the cargo area — the center of the plane was taken up with stretchers. Germaine and her sister were on one side, and I was over on the other.

I told you about the heat. When the plane got closed down and the engines were fired up, it kept getting hotter and hotter. The engines would roar, then they would whine. Time passed. The heat got worse. But we didn't take off.

One of the things you're always doing in Vietnam — you do it without even knowing it — is looking around. You always want to know what's happening, who's where, what's going on. You're always asking yourself, "How do I get out of this?" For instance, I would never ride in an enclosed jeep — the regular jeep is fine because you've got a way of getting out through the back — but with an enclosed jeep you can only get out through the front seat. I would never get into one of those things unless I could sit in the front. In other words, in Vietnam you were always looking for an escape route. So, in this plane, I was thinking, "God, this thing is going to explode or something. Where's the exit?" And I'm looking around. The engines are roaring and we're not going anywhere, and it's unbearably hot. One of the men who's strapped in was screaming with pain, but nobody could hear him over the engines. A medic came by and I bent him down and shouted into his ear. I said, "He's screaming. Give him something." The medic gave the guy something and then he came over to me and said, "I'm very grateful to you."

Anyway, this medic went forward and talked to the pilot. Then the pilot came back and told me he was sorry about what had happened out on the airstrip. He also told me they were having problems with the plane. To this day, I don't know what the problem was, whether we'd been shot at or what. But they were having problems with the plane, and they said, "Anything you can do to help with these men would be appreciated."

I had been to enough hospitals at this point to know that just by walking around — just by getting up and walking around — or by grabbing someone's hand, you could make a difference. So I got up. I walked around. I'd say, "Hi, my name is Anne and I live in Washington." And they'd say, "What the hell are you doing here?" Or they'd say, "My God — a round eye!" Some of the men were very, very badly wounded.

So after a while the medic came over to me. He said, "Anne, I want you to do us a special favor." By this time I'm completely wet — you have to understand it's boiling hot and you're in a tin can and the sun is beating down. And you've got men groaning, and you've got men wounded. They've just been through a battle and they've just been stabilized. They're getting them to the hospital in Danang. Anyhow, the medic said, "We've got one guy that we're very worried about. We need you to go over there." I said, "Don't make a fuss. Just point him out to me, like sort of with your finger, because we don't want him to know how serious it is." He said, "OK." Then he nodded and said, "That one."

Well, I go over. There are two guys down here and two guys up here and I'm scrunched down like this. And this poor soul is completely bandaged — he had one eye visible, but everything else was bandaged. The poor guy was in really bad shape: needles were stuck all in his arms. So I started talking to him; he couldn't talk because he had a trach tube. I was telling him who I was and what I was doing in Vietnam, also how I was looking forward to seeing him very soon in Danang. I said I was going to make a point of calling on him and all that. Finally I said, "My God, I've been talking to one blue eye. You must be one hell of a handsome guy — I wish I could say the same about myself, but unfortunately I haven't had a bath in a couple of days and my hair's a mess. At this stage, you should really be talking to a beautiful girl, and I don't qualify!"

He was a southpaw and he went like this — he wanted to write something. He pointed — I used to carry a pen in my sleeve pocket — so I took the pen and I handed him the pad — I always carried a notepad — and he wrote, "To me, you're the most beautiful girl in the world." On the flight to Danang, I held his hand. I held him very tight and said, "Come on now, you're going to make it. Promise me you're going to make it. Hold on —" He held on till Danang. Then, after we got there, I looked for him again. He didn't make it.

So that was my trip to Hue.

One thing I want to say — those medics and those nurses performed feats that I can't describe in any other way than to say they were heroic. If the war had any true heroes, they were the medics and nurses.

I got to know a lot of the nurses, did a couple of stories on them. I was especially impressed with the nurses who worked with the Vietnamese. For instance, take a hospital like Cho Ray — did you ever hear about it? It was a major hospital for Vietnamese civilians in Saigon. You had American nurses working there. Conditions were pitiful, three people in a bed, blood-soaked sheets, vomit on the floor, people cooking in the wards. Yet these American women did an incredible job, helping, working, training, trying to make them understand what to do. I mean, the Vietnamese were doing the best they could in an impossible situation. But the American nurses were really something. They were extraordinary. They worked long hours. They saw so little of the country — they really were worked to death.

I also went out to Third Field [Hospital] a couple of times and interviewed some of the Red Cross women, but I wasn't pleased with the interviews. In fact, I didn't do anything with them. I just didn't like the attitude of most of the Red Cross women. I did meet one extraordinary Red Cross woman — I did a story on her — but then she disappeared. I don't know what happened to her.

The Red Cross women in Vietnam weren't like the donut dollies of World War Two we read about — the old donut dollies were a different brand of women. I don't know, those women were a little too establishment. Vietnam was a mean, nasty place, and I'm not sure the Red Cross women understood much about what was happening.

Now let me tell you about Sammy, our other son.

One of the civilian volunteer doctors in Vietnam was an extraordinary man named Wayne McKinny. He was from Texas, I don't know where. But anyway, Wayne McKinney used to go around to the different orphanages as a volunteer. He had worked as an administrator for Dr. Tom Dooley in Laos and had been so impressed that he came back to the U.S. and went to medical school so he could follow in the footsteps of Dr. Tom. Then he went to Vietnam and worked in the orphanages.

Wayne McKinny got to know a Catholic chaplain, Father Bob, who was also quite an impressive man. He was a parachutist. Why anybody wants to jump out of a plane, I don't know. But to be a priest and to jump out of a plane — anyhow, the great thing about Father Bob was that he was very close to his men. He understood their problems and as a result he did an excellent job. Father Bob also comes from Texas, by the way.

So Father Bob arrived in Saigon and was assigned to a headquarters company. When he got on the military bus there was this little Vietnamese kid wearing tailor-made fatigues and jump boots. And this little kid stood up and said, "All right, all you guys," and started giving instructions and using all the GI expletives. Father Bob was horrified. He said if he had closed his eyes he would have heard a nineteen-year-old Southern GI instead of this three-foot-high Vietnamese kid. He was six years old and Father Bob thought he had the dirtiest mouth in Saigon.

Father Bob got off the bus and — you know how priests are, whether they're in uniform or not — went over to this little kid and said, "I want you to come to my office immediately!" Because, you know, a chaplain is a colonel or something, and even a little Vietnamese GI understands rank, so he said, "Yes, sir!" And so the little boy trots over to Father Bob, and Father Bob said, "Young man, you've got to stop using all that language." And the little boy said, "Expletive, expletive, who the hell are you?" Anyway, to make a long story short, Father Bob started saying Mass for this headquarters group who had adopted the boy as their mascot and began to really care about the boy. He wasn't really Vietnamese anymore — the Americans had turned him against his own people — but he wasn't American, either. In fact, he would only admit to being Korean when he was with other Vietnamese. But he would wear the little U.S. uniform they had made for him, with captain's bars on the shoulders. In Vietnamese "captain" is "Dai Wy," pronounced "Die We." And the GIs called him "the little Dai Wy" or just "Dai Wy," which soon became corrupted to the Western name "Dewey." And that's the name he had at this time. His Vietnamese name is Chuong.

The GIs took him with them to the bars in the red light district and had him interpret for them and bargain with the prostitutes. While they went upstairs with the girls Dewey sat at the bar drinking Cokes and talking. He says now that he found it all terribly boring and would rather have stayed in the military compound. Anyway, Dewey got for the soldiers what they always wanted.

Vietnam — the way the country operated, little boys and little girls stole things to survive, to earn a living. Also, the girls did what they had to do and the boys did what they had to do. They bought and sold what they had to buy and sell. And Dewey was no different. Father Bob found Dewey extraordinarily engaging, a very bright little boy. But the priest was horrified at the life he was living.

Father Bob had been told that there was an American doctor, Wayne McKinny, who took care of orphans and who got kids adopted in the United States. So Father Bob asked, "Where does Wayne McKinny hang out?" "Oh, he always goes to Tan Son Nhut. He's always at Third Field," they said, "begging for medicine, and they always give it to him. So if you want to find Wayne McKinny go to Third Field and hang around the pharmacy because he's always scrounging." So Father Bob said, "All right." Then what he did was, he went to Tan Son Nhut and started hanging around. When he asked about Wayne McKinny, they said, "Oh yeah, he usually comes on whatever night because that's the night when . . ."or "He usually comes at such-and-such a time. . . ." And Father Bob would hang out where he thought he would spot Wayne McKinny.

One day he was literally hiding in a sort of doorway in the shadows, and someone said, "There he comes, Wayne McKinny.

He's always in a hurry and he's going to mow you down, so you got to move fast." Sure enough, Father Bob sort of made believe he was talking to someone — you know how priests are. You know, "Well, nice to see you, nice to see you, Joe, I got to go; I got to go." And he sort of tripped Wayne McKinny, sort of backed into Wayne McKinny. Wayne said, "Excuse me, Father." Father Bob said, "No, no, not at all —"as if he didn't know who Wayne McKinny was. Then he said, "Who are you?" "I'm Dr. Wayne McKinny." They shook hands. And Father Bob said, "Well, what do you do here in Vietnam?" And Wayne replied, "Well, I sort of take care of kids." Father Bob said, "Do you? Where do you live?" "I live so-and-so and so-and-so." Father Bob said, "Fine. You look after kids. You know, I've got an awfully nice little kid, and you might want to take him on." Wayne said, "Sure, I might want to sometime. Nice to see you."

That was it. Wayne was out the door. He got his penicillin, or his aspirin, or whatever it was he wanted. And the Americans — that's another thing I want to tell you — these guys in the pharmacy were probably breaking rules and regulations. You're not supposed to give away government property, but we all did it. We all gave. Sometimes I would go to the PX and buy sanitary napkins or tampons and give them away because I knew they were needed.

Now anyway, this was a brief exchange — thirty seconds or maybe at the most a minute. Because Wayne's always running. You know, you think of Texans as slow-moving, but there's nothing slow about Wayne. So, you have to remember there's this thirty-second conversation — boom, boom — and then Wayne jumps into his jeep with his loot that he's gotten for his babies that he's saving and Father Bob finds out what he came to find out, that there is a Wayne McKinny. And now he has his address.

So Father Bob goes back to the Army post. He talks to little Dewey, tells him, "Now, I found somebody who's going to make it possible for you to be adopted." Dewey says, "Expletive, expletive, I don't believe it. Get out of my life. I don't want to go. The GIs are my family." Father Bob is saying, "No, Dewey, this man is serious. I know he's honest. Everybody talks about him. Now you got to trust me." So they pile into a jeep and Father Bob drives to Wayne McKinny's house.

Wayne McKinny is married to a magnificent woman, a great saint of this world. Her name is MinJo, another Texan. Now,

MinJo, like Wayne, is a little nuts! They're crazy, both of them. I mean, you have to understand that in the world there are a lot of these nuts who run around doing good. Wayne is the kind of guy who finds a baby who's dying — no one says this baby's ever going to survive — and Wayne takes that baby and says MinJo can make it better. So he takes the baby in a shoebox and he brings it home to MinJo. And — lo and behold! — two months later you've got a new healthy little baby that MinJo has saved. So Father Bob arrives and there's this haggard, exhausted woman and she's got thirty sick babies in the house.

I am not joking. That's a minimum. They always had a minimum of thirty babies in the house. They all had some form of malnutrition, cholera, tuberculosis. I mean these are all at-risk children who should be dead, but God forbid that anybody should die on Wayne McKinny. You can't die on Wayne McKinny. So MinJo has been in Saigon now, I don't know, any number of months. She doesn't know where the Caravelle Hotel is, or the Continental Hotel — all she knows is where all the hospitals and all the clinics are, all the doctors who can help her, and where she can scrounge medicine. That's all she knows. She's got some little bit of help. And she's running a hospital, an emergency hospital out of her house, OK?

The babies are all crying, wet, a mess! You have to understand it's hot — no air-conditioning, no refrigeration. You've got no refrigeration. Electricity goes off and that means the water goes off. You have no washing machines. So, the doorbell rings, and there are all these babies crying, heat, stench, diapers, and MinJo answers the door and there's a chaplain. You know he's a priest because they wear that cross on their collar — they don't wear the chaplain collar. This priest has a Texas accent: "Ma'am, my name's Father Bob." Then she looks down and she sees this little kid. She says, "Who are you?" "Well," Father Bob says, "I just met your husband today, and he's absolutely the finest man in the whole world, and he told me he takes care of kids and that he's interested in getting kids adopted. I have this wonderful boy here and I thought maybe you could do something for him." She says, "Oh, he didn't discuss it with me at all, and he usually tells me who he's bringing home." Father Bob says, "Well, it was sort of a quick meeting and he didn't have the time, you see. He was in a big hurry. And he said that I could bring the kid and that it would be all right." She said, "Gee, that's kind of funny, because we really don't have a bed for him and we don't have any room. I don't know what I'm going to do with him." "Oh," he said, "he said you would manage somehow." He's a real Texan, a real bullshit artist. "Well," she said, "if he said it, I'm sure he meant well and we'll do the best we can."

So there's little Dewey looking at this mess and all these howling kids. He's used to his pool tables and his beloved GIs and the Coke machine. And he's thinking, "My God, what have I got myself in for?" When Father Bob leaves he tells Dewey, "You behave yourself or I'll kill you!"

Wayne McKinny comes home eventually, nine-thirty at night or something like that. MinJo says "A priest came today and he brought this little kid and he said that you said that it was perfectly all right." Wayne said, "What? I don't know anything about a priest and a kid. What the hell's going on?" And she said, "Well, he said he met you at Tan Son Nhut." "Yeah," he said, "I met a priest today. Jesus! Did he bring that kid?" She said, "He's in there; I'll get him." They had one older kid already. That kid was Ri, the Cambodian boy George wrote the book about. So they brought Ri in and he met Dewey and then Wayne said to Dewey, "Nice to see you." Dewey said, "I don't like it here. Too many babies." Wayne said, "Well, God!" Because Dewey was puffing away on his cigarette. Wayne said, "I'm a doctor. No smoking! You're too young to smoke." After that Wayne would come home from work and count the cigarette butts that Sam would flip out in the driveway — he'd smoke and think no one would notice his butts.

Now what happened is that Dewey stayed a day or two and then he ran away. He couldn't stand it. He couldn't stand not being with his beloved GIs. And so he ran away. He ran back to Father Bob. Of course, he knew the streets, how to get around.

You have to understand that you could put either of our sons out on the streets today and they'd survive. In fact, one year Billy went with his classmates to study ecology in a jungle in Venezuela. What they didn't realize is that all the kids in the class couldn't hack it. They'd never been in a jungle, and they got frightened. But for Billy it was home. It was second nature. He would reach up and grab something and eat it because the vegetation in Venezuela is similar to that in Vietnam. Also, when it started to rain and they had to build a fire, it was Billy who didn't panic. He built the fire and cooked the food and was able to manage. And, to go one step further, one of Billy's classmates got hurt climbing and needed help. The Venezuelan guides picked Billy to lead the group. They said, "He knows the jungle." And this is the same thing — you put our sons out on the street and they'd know how to survive because they had to do it as children. So when Dewey had to work his way back to Father Bob, he knew how to do it.

A GI wanted to adopt Dewey, but it was obvious to Wayne McKinny and MinJo, who had become extraordinarily attached to Dewey, that the GI was a homosexual. So they didn't let him adopt the boy. Then another couple promised to adopt him, but they never came through. Finally we got a letter — we're back in the States by now — saying, "We've got the toughest kid in the world and we hope you'll take him. . . ." We read the letter aloud to Billy. We all read it aloud. And the letter ended with the sentence "Will you take a chance?" And it was Billy who immediately responded. He quite firmly said, " 'Course we take a chance! What Wayne McKinny think? 'Course we take him!"

Dewey got off the plane here — we were waiting for him at Baltimore-Washington Airport. Dick Swanson came with us and took pictures of his arrival. And one of the first things he does when he hits the ground is he looks up at George and me and says, "Hey, what do I call you guys?" And I said, "You call me Mom and you call him Dad." Then he turns to Billy and says, "What's your name?" So typically GI! We named him Samuel, after my brother.

In the car, I was holding him on my lap, but he kept jumping off. Then I realized this kid had never had a woman hold him on her lap. This kid has told everyone where to go, what to do. He's negotiated deals. And here I am, holding him as if he's an eight-year-old child. And he's not — I mean, he's forty-five years old! He can tell me things about the world that I don't know!

So, I'm holding him and we're on the road about ten minutes and we hit a terrific traffic jam. At this point Sammy slides off my lap — he's so irritated that anybody's holding him — and taps George on the shoulder. He says, "Dad, look, you see all that traffic up there? Why don't you make a left-hand turn right here and we cut through and then we detour and we make a right and you got it." George said he and Dick nearly fell off of their seats.

But in Vietnam, of course, Sam worked as an interpreter with American soldiers on night combat patrols — they would take him out to be their interpreter if they caught some Vietnamese. He would say, "Go here, go there, turn right." Because he knew the territory. He was all over the place.

In 1975, when Saigon fell, we found them both glued to the television set, watching that extraordinarily difficult episode. At one point we asked Billy, "Billy, what are you staring at?" And he said, "I'm trying to find my mother and father."

When I hear people saying, "Why do we need a museum for the Holocaust?" I think of my sons and what happened to them. I think of what I saw war do, not only to our soldiers but to Vietnamese mothers, fathers, children. And my response is always "Let's not only put up one museum — let's put up ten like it!" Because people keep forgetting — people always forget. Yes, let's put up ten museums for the Holocaust. And let's keep talking and writing about what we did in Vietnam.

We destroyed their economy. We turned their women into whores. We separated families, made orphans of so many children. We destroyed their beautiful cities. We destroyed the countryside — reduced triple-canopied jungles to bare red clay, left bomb craters everywhere. When you flew, you saw these enormous holes, like craters of the moon. It was as if you were looking at the moon through a telescope — there were just enormous bomb craters everywhere, many filled with water. Yes, it was almost as if you were looking at someone whose face was pockmarked, and the face just sort of stretched out for miles. And yet the Vietnamese kept on. The farmers kept plowing. The women kept working. They're incredibly resourceful, incredibly industrious people. And so much courage.

So much courage.

*Anne Allen is a founder of Washington Independent Writers and its first executive director. Her most recent book is* Sports for the Handicapped. *In addition to writing, Anne works full-time for a philanthropic foundation in Washington.*

# ❦ Lily (Lee) Adams

*Lily Adams was born and raised in New York City. Her mother, who died when Lily was eight months old, was Italian. Her father is Chinese. As a teenager, Lily wanted to be a ballet dancer. She also wanted to go to college, "but I knew college wasn't an option because I didn't have the money for it. So it was down to either being some kind of teacher or a nurse."*

*In 1966 Lily enrolled in a three-year nursing program at Mount Vernon Hospital. "One day — this was 1967 — an Army Nurse Corps recruiter came and showed us this wonderful new movie about being an Army nurse. Well, that was the answer to a lot of my needs. Financial, for one. And for another, I could fill the needs that I wanted to fill for John F. Kennedy. He really inspired me at an early age — I remember staying home on that snowy day when he was inaugurated, remember hearing him say, "Ask not what your country can do for you, ask what you can do for your country." And I thought, "My God, who is this man?"*

*So Lily joined the Army. In 1969 she received orders for Vietnam. From October of 1969 until October of 1970 she was stationed at the 12th Evacuation Hospital at Cu Chi.*

VIETNAM HAD BEEN very much a part of my life since my sophomore year in high school. I was going steady with a boy — I went with him for five years — and he and a number of other friends were really scared about getting drafted and going to Vietnam.

I wasn't involved in peace or protest movements because when I was in high school that wasn't the "in" thing to do. The peace stuff didn't get to be popular till I hit nursing school, and in nursing school I was working too hard to pay attention to what was going on on the outside. But I was always getting information from girls that were dating guys in college — information for my boyfriend, who couldn't get a job because nobody wanted to train him. The thinking was "What a waste! He'll just get drafted anyway!" So

I had to help him deal with his decisions on what he was going to do.

One day he decided he was going to join the Marine Corps. At least in the Marine Corps, he told me, they knew how to train people. So he joined. And I promised myself that if he died I'd join the Army and go to Vietnam as a nurse.

Well, he didn't die. But for a long time I thought about what it would be like to join the Army. So by the time this recruiter came, I was ripe. I also think I felt very guilty that the guys had to deal with these decisions — major decisions in their lives — and that girls didn't. Yeah, I felt very guilty that a lot of guys I knew got drafted and that girls didn't.

But still, I joined with the idea that I didn't have to go to Vietnam unless I volunteered. That was what the nurse recruiter told me. Because I didn't want to go to war. I wanted to serve my country Stateside but not warside. So when the recruiter said that women never got sent to Vietnam unless they volunteered, I believed her. That was the first — but not the last — time the Army lied to me.

Compared to nursing school, the Army was freedom. I had a wonderful time in basic training. I could come and go whenever I pleased, as long as I was in formation at seven o'clock — there wasn't any curfew or any housemother to tell me she didn't like the looks of my date. So I loved basic. But it struck me as funny that all they talked about was Vietnam. I didn't know why we had to go to a mock Vietnam village and look at punji sticks and booby traps and a lot of other stuff, so finally I asked the major in charge, "How come you keep talking about Vietnam?" And she said, "Well, my dear, you'll probably be going." "Not according to what my recruiter told me." "What did your recruiter tell you?" So I told her. And she told me my recruiter must have misunderstood.

Sure — her and a lot of other recruiters! Because I went around and asked all these women, "What did your recruiter say?" I was freaking a lot of women out. They'd been lied to by the Army, too.

Well, I was very upset. I was very angry. But I just told myself I'd deal with it when the time came.

My first duty station was Fort Ord, California. There was a shortage of nurses at Fort Ord. The whole time I was there I only saw a day shift on the weekends; you had to be a captain or above to work the day shift during the week. So I worked evenings and nights. I was on the orthopedic unit. When I worked evenings I had to cover two wards on my own. During this time I also decided to go to school. So this was really a wacko time for me.

But I took care of a lot of men that came back from Vietnam. I did a lot of counseling. I did a lot of hand-holding, too, when they'd wake up with nightmares. I dealt with a lot of men whose wives left them after they came back from Vietnam, dealt with a lot of men whose wives left them while they were in the hospital. And I loved working with them.

One of the things I learned is that the men from Vietnam had a lot of psychological problems. Today I know it's PTSD [post trauma stress disorder], but in those days nobody knew what it was. All the guys knew was that they needed somebody to listen to them. I'd listen to the gory stories and hold their hands while they cried. I remember one guy in particular that was very bitter. It was when Kenny Rogers had that hit, "Ruby" — you know, "Don't take your love to town. . . ." Every time the song came on the radio, the guys would blast it and just grieve in their own self-pity. So I got on the case of this one particular man. I said, "What are you playing that for?" He said, "That's me — my wife left me. And the medical board only gave me thirty percent [disability pension]." He was lame in one leg, but the VA said he could get a job, that it wouldn't be any problem.

As time went on, there were more stories. The guys would run in and say, "Did you hear about Lieutenant So-and-So? She got her orders for Nam!" One by one people were starting to get their orders. I felt like I was on Death Row, just waiting.

Some of my patients knew people in personnel. I don't know what they did, but I know they screwed around with my records so that my records just weren't available. "Hey, lieutenant," they told me, "we're taking care of you. You're a good guy." So I was at Fort Ord a good eight months before my orders came.

I didn't want to go to Vietnam. I verbalized that to everybody.

I also knew the lifers saw me as lifer material because I was a real good nurse and I covered myself all the time. I always had my records straight, played the military game very well. While I was at Fort Ord they wanted to train me to be a surgical nurse — all the surgical nurses were in Nam — and they said I'd get a raise and that they'd hold onto me, that they wouldn't let me go to

Vietnam. And I thought, "Sure! The recruiter lied to me already and I know they need surgical nurses in Nam. As soon as they train me, off I'm going to go." So I said, "No way; thank you very much, but no, thank you." They were disappointed. And I don't know, maybe they would have held onto me.

So I got my orders for Vietnam. My roommate and I got them at the same time. I remember her being on duty and coming home early with her boyfriend, and I remember I thought, "Gee, that's unusual." So she comes up the stairs looking real serious. "Lily," she says, "they came." "You mean my orders for Nam?" "Yes," she says.

We sat and cried. We didn't want to go.

Eventually she got out of it by marrying her corpsman boyfriend.

So when I come on duty the next morning the chief nurse says, "Lieutenant, I want to talk to you." I remember thinking she's going to tell me about my orders. So we're walking down the ward and she has her arm around me and she's telling me, "You know, I went all the way up to the Surgeon General to keep you because we really need nurses here at Ford Ord. But I was told they need nurses in Vietnam more than they need them Stateside. But I just wanted to let you know."

I believed her. I believe she really did try to keep me. She was very sincere, one of the better lifers. Yeah, she was one of the good ones.

So word got around real quick, like wildfire, that Lieutenant Lee had gotten her orders. I had men coming up to me and saying all kinds of things. Some would say, "I'm sorry — I heard about the orders." Others would say, "You know they really need you so badly over there. It's not that bad, really. It's really not that bad. And they need you a lot worse than they need you here." I kept hearing from the Vietnam vets about the need of nurses, so I decided not to fight my orders. I decided, "OK. If they need me, I'm going to go."

Anyhow, I go home to New York on a month's leave. I miss Woodstock by two days. I meet this guy that had been at Woodstock and he gave me a *Life* magazine with the pictures of Woodstock in it. "I don't need this," he said. "I've got it all in my head. But you're going to need it because you're going to Vietnam." In those days, see, it wasn't so negative about going to Vietnam. It was more sympathy than negativity.

It was on that last visit home that I realized I didn't belong there anymore. I'd outgrown it — it just wasn't my home anymore. I remember my father crying when I left. He wasn't sure I was going to make it back alive. And I wasn't either. Because it was starting to hit me that I was going to war.

At Travis Air Force Base I had a four o'clock afternoon flight to go out to Vietnam. I remember arriving about two o'clock and seeing a whole slew of women, about ten or twelve, in uniform. They were just sitting there looking really down in the dumps. I walked over and said, "Hi. All of you going to Vietnam?" "Yeah," they said, and they were groaning. "You mean none of you volunteered?" And I thought they were going to attack me — they were all angry, as angry as me about going to Vietnam.

Four o'clock started to come closer. We were all getting very shook-up. Suddenly there was this announcement that something was wrong with the plane, they didn't know how long it would take to fix it, and that they were going to put us up in a motel. So we drag all our gear onto a bus, get to the motel, check in, and just kind of lay around. "What now?" we say. So all of us go out to eat — when you're in a situation like that when there's thousands of men, the women group together.

We come back to the motel and hear there's a party going on. So we go to one party, walk in and the room is full of guys all drunk and passed out on the floor. They're barely even able to talk. I say, "This ain't no party for me — I'm getting out of here." So we leave and go back to our rooms. I put on my nightgown and am all ready to climb into bed and cry, when all of a sudden this guy walks in and my roommate, Gail, walks out. This guy says, "Hi. You going to Vietnam?" I say, "Yeah," and we have a little conversation. Then I say, "Excuse me" and go next door to look for Gail. "Gail," I say, "why did you leave me with that idiot?" "I thought you might want to do something," she says. "Gail," I say, "are you crazy?" That was when we realized the rumor that women join the military because they want to screw — or because they're lesbians — is a myth, but that we ourselves believed it.

When I went back to the room to tell the guy to get out, he was gone. But that attitude followed us.

At two in the morning the phones rang. "Get ready for a three A.M. flight. You are going to Vietnam." At nine A.M. we were in

Hawaii. I had always wanted to go to Hawaii, wanted to go to a place where there were other people like me — Eurasians, basically — so I'm thinking, "Here I am in Hawaii and look at the situation I'm in." When all of us are in the terminal bathroom combing our hair and freshening up, I say, "I could desert now." And everyone tells me to shut up — to stop giving them ideas.

On the plane again, two guys started asking around for a fourth partner for pinochle. I played pinochle and I wanted to kill time, so I said, "Well, here I am." One guy, I remember, was an Air Force guy in a jumpsuit. He tried to come on to me through the whole game. Still, I kept on playing because it was something to do. I don't know how long we played, but it was long enough for me to get tired of it. So I went and sat down and did some crying and some sleeping. We land in Guam. We land in Wake. Behind me Sue, this other woman I'd met, was crying the whole time. She was engaged to a Vietnam vet who was a paraplegic, and she didn't know how he was going to make it without her.

We arrive in Vietnam at four in the afternoon. They put us on buses that are all caged — the windows are wired, making you feel like a prisoner. And here I'd thought I was going to be welcomed with open arms by both the Vietnamese and the American military.

Anyhow, I looked out the window and what I saw out there was slums. And I thought, "Oh, they even have these things in Vietnam." The slums were worse than New York slums, though, because they were made of corrugated tin. And the children were dirty. They had real ragged clothes on. So all of a sudden I realize that this is a poor country. You've got to understand — when I went over there I didn't know anything about Vietnam.

We got to Long Binh, to the Ninetieth Replacement [Battalion]. I remember there was no air-conditioning except at the officers' club, so we would crawl — physically crawl — to the officers' club. Because it was hot. It was like one-hundred-degree weather. I was sweating all the time, having blackouts — people were telling me to line up for salt, to take salt tablets. Still, I was just constantly blacking out. It was just too damn hot for me to adjust to.

So I would make it to the officers' club and sit at a table by myself. I would be all ready to have a Coke and be miserable when I would get surrounded by five or six men, who would just sit down. "What's a nice girl like you doing in a place like this?"

"Where you from?" And then one or two would start putting the make on you. So I'd ignore the ones putting the make on me and try to have an intelligent conversation with the ones who didn't try. Then, after a while, I'd stop playing the games. I'd just think, "To hell with this" and go back to the hootch, where it was hot and the women were depressed. Or it was hot and they were sleeping and everything was boring. So then I'd go back to the officers' club, where it was cool and I could have a cold Coke or get talked into a card game. Well, I'd play cards and they'd treat me as an equal, but once the card game was over, they'd start coming on to me. So, in the five days I was at Long Binh, I learned to improvise my schedule. I'd figure out how long I could put up with the officers' club — the officers really were the worst ones, always — and then I'd leave and go someplace else.

Finally the chief nurse of Vietnam came to talk to us. I remember she was asking for volunteers for here, there, for everywhere — "Where do you want to go?" she'd say. Well, I wanted to go to Vung Tau. The guys had told me that Vung Tau had beautiful beaches. And it was safe — it didn't get bombed too much. So, OK, I ask for Vung Tau. And the chief nurse of Vietnam says, "Oh, my dear, we don't need anybody there right now, but we do need volunteers for Cu Chi. It's one of the busiest hospitals in Vietnam." So I say, "That's what I want — I want to stay busy. I don't want to have to sit around and twiddle my thumbs." So Gail, Sue, and I volunteer for Cu Chi. And then this chief nurse says, "OK, we have two places for Vung Tau." She says it right in front of me. And I think, "The Army has screwed me over a second time — they lied to me about Vietnam, and now here's this old biddy telling me another story." But I swore the Army wasn't going to lie to me again. And with that, I accepted my orders.

I had to go back to Tan Son Nhut to catch a C-130 [transport plane] to take me to Cu Chi. On the vehicle going there I met this friend of mine. His name was Captain Denny. Captain Denny wore a chemical sign for his insignia — you know, you wear nurse signs and you wear engineer signs, only he wore the round chemical flask. "What's that?" I asked. "That's the insignia for the Chemical Corps." And I said, "Chemical Corps — what does someone in the Chemical Corps do here?" And he said, "Well, I take care of this herbicide. My mission is to spray and kill the jungle." And I said, "What for?" And he said, "So Charlie can't hide — you know, so it's safer for the troops." And I said, "Oh, my God, how awful to get sent here just to be an exterminator. I mean, if you're going to come to Nam, you ought to come as infantry and kill some enemy. But, I mean, to come and kill weeds — " I felt really bad for him. I told him that, too, and he said, "Yeah. But it's my job." Then we discovered we were both going to Cu Chi. I thought that was wonderful — at least I'd know some people there.

So he helps me with my bags and we get on the C-130. On the C-130, instead of sitting like on a normal plane, you sit face-to-face. So there's a whole line on this side and a whole line on that side. And it's netting — you sit on netting. Also, it's loud, very loud. You have to yell at each other through the whole trip. So we're yelling at each other and then, about ten minutes out of Cu Chi, everybody hits the floor. "What's going on here?" I say. Captain Denny grabs onto me. "We're OK," he says. "Well, what happened?" I say. "We got attacked — the plane just got hit. But I can tell the plane is OK. So breathe deep and don't worry about it." The guys all get off the floor then. And at that moment I realized that these men were trained to survive in a war zone but that I was not — that I could get killed. And that if I died it was going to be the Army's fault. The Army never taught me anything — I mean anything. Nothing. Everything I learned about surviving I learned from the men.

I might as well tell you the rest of Captain Denny's story now. Two months before I was due to go home, there was a guy that came in with a patient and he had the chemical insignia on. I said, "You wouldn't know Captain Denny by any chance?" And the guy said, "Yeah, I knew him." "You knew him?" "Yeah," the guy said, "he died." I'm in the middle of trying to take care of a patient but am so well disciplined I don't bat an eye. "Well, I knew that would happen," I said.

Captain Denny and I made a pact, see. We were going to meet up again and go home on the same plane. And, you know, his is the only name I remember on the Wall; every time I go to the Wall I visit his name.

At Cu Chi they asked us where we'd like to work, and I said ICU [intensive care unit], because I had dabbled in it at Ford Ord and had really enjoyed it. They told me I didn't know what I was getting myself into. They also explained that they were going to orient us in various wards first; they wanted us to know all the traumatic areas in case we had mass cals [massive casualties] and they had to call in people from nontraumatic areas. Well, Gail said she didn't care where she worked, and Sue said she didn't care, but I still wanted ICU. So after we got our assignments we went to the officers' club.

Of course we got surrounded. There were all men. It was about then that I decided, "No more Cokes for me" and ordered white wine. And this guy comes back with a whole bottle of Mateus. "My God," I said. "Don't worry," he said. "It's not expensive — drinks are fifty cents and a bottle of Mateus is just two dollars." And I said, "Oh, my God, you can really get polluted here."

Then some other guy came up and asked how many days I had in country. I told him and he just laughed — that's when I got up and walked out. I cried all the way to my hootch — I cried; I was just devastated. I felt very alone and very out of it. So I was standing by the fence where the nurses' hootches joined the barbed wire, when these guys in a truck yelled, "How you doing? Hey, isn't it a beautiful night!" I started to feel better then. I felt like, yeah, you could keep your spirits up. But I still couldn't understand why people laughed in Vietnam. I mean, a war was a war. People were dying. But all of this was part of my introduction to the war zone.

I had been assigned to triage for the first three days, recovery for the second three days, and ICU after that. In that time period we were having mini-mass cals. Mini-mass cals are where they are not coming in all day long, five at a time every five minutes — instead it's five at a time for maybe two or three loads, and that's it. So my first day we have a mini-mass cal. A group of wounded comes in and I just stand there, frozen. What I see is a typical patient: a double amp [amputee]. No legs, the bones and muscles and everything showing, like a piece of meat in a butcher shop. So I watch. Ten people are doing ten thousand things I can't keep up with — really, they were doing too many things too fast for me to understand. Basically, they were cutting the uniform off, looking to see where the wounds were, making the assessment, getting the IV in, trying to find out if the guy is allergic to tetanus so they can give him a shot right away, and also asking him to give his name, rank, and serial number in case he goes unconscious. The majority of men did not wear dog tags because they made noise. Sometimes they'd wear them in their boots — only if you get your leg blown off, you ain't going to have a boot. And most of the time they didn't come in with the parts. They just came in with what was left over.

So I'm on the other side of the triage room, trying to compose myself so I don't have a shocked look on my face. And I'm thinking "This is crazy. They didn't tell me it would be like this." Then I started thinking "I want my mother. Why did I join? This is a goddamned war zone." So the second batch comes in and I'm feeling awful because I'm not doing anything. I'm frozen. Paralyzed.

So the third group comes in. Now as each group comes in you lose more and more staff, because more doctors and nurses are going to the OR [operating room], to pre-op, to X-ray, and so on. When we're down to about a skeleton staff, one doctor yells, "I need someone to hold this guy's head!" I think, "Hold head . . . Hold head . . . I can do that; I can hold a head —" So I run over and hold the guy's head while they stick a tube down his throat. Finally the doctor says, "Good," and after that I'm able to get the idea of what needed to be done.

It was overwhelming. I was overwhelmed by the sights, smells, yelling, moaning. . . . It was like a zoo. After I realized I could function, though, I was better.

In the recovery room, my first assignment was a POW. When this male nurse told me, I told him to shove it — I was not going to take care of any North Vietnamese. But this nurse said, "Let me tell you some things. First, I know how you feel — none of us wants to take care of the enemy. Second, these people have a lot of information. We know they're upper rank. You may end up saving one hundred GIs — so just think of it that way." And I said, "OK — you're on."

So I take care of this guy for a number of hours. And I find myself wanting to treat him like a regular patient. A few times I caught myself holding his hand and squeezing it, trying to get him to concentrate — you know, when you work with badly injured people you try eye contact, you verbalize stuff that they're OK, because that's what keeps them going. You've got to push them on so they don't give up and die. And doing this involves a lot of touch and a lot of energy.

So I was feeling very ambivalent. I was thinking, "Do I want to keep this guy alive to save one hundred GIs? Or do I want him to die because he's a goddamned gook and he's killed one hundred

GIs?" Then I find myself giving my regular good nursing care. And eventually I come to feel like this guy is really a human being and my patient — I'm happy when his blood pressure is good, worried when it starts going down.

Well, when MI [Military Intelligence] comes to interrogate him, I get very protective. I stand in front of my patient and say, "What are you going to do?" I had thoughts of them slapping him around and doing all kinds of things. The guy laughs and says, "We're just going to ask him a few questions." I go, "OK — but I'm staying here." So I stay and they ask him questions and he readily gives answers. When it's over, I ask the guy, "Hey, do you really believe all that stuff?" The guy says, "He knows he's got a buddy on the other side of the room. He knows that if he lies, we're going to know. We already got the other information — we told him already."

So I say, "Can I ask him some questions?" And MI says, "Sure. What do you want to know?" "Well, how old is he?" "He's nineteen." "Well, what does he think about the war, I want to know that. Only tell him he doesn't have to answer me if he doesn't want to." I was afraid the POW would think that, if he said anything negative, I may not treat him well. But he says something to the interpreter and the interpreter comes back to me: "The patient said that if he could demonstrate in Hanoi like you're demonstrating in Washington, he would be doing it." And I thought, "Oh, shit — this really is a human being. He's no different than my guys —"

After that I didn't have a terrible time with my POW. I was still ambivalent about him being a human being who had killed a lot of my people, but I didn't have any trouble taking good care of him. He survived. And I mean, really — after that answer I got, everything had to be different.

From the recovery room I went to the regular ICU, where there were a lot of belly wounds and it smelled awful. There were maggots all over the place — to this day I have a passion against flies, I really do. In Vietnam I had my own body counts — during quiet times, I'd go for flies. Once I got twenty-three, one right after another. The corpsmen used to tease me about my body counts, but I thought of it as saving lives. Also, it was an enemy that I could kill. I didn't have an M-16 out in the jungle, but I could kill flies. I still hate them.

The ICU I ended up in had just been opened. It was half amputations with complications and half severe burns. We had a lot of Vietnamese. I remember one Vietnamese woman who had ninety percent of her body burned — she had set herself on fire because her GI boyfriend had decided he was going home without her. And this was not an unusual story, either.

I saw things in that unit that you will never see in the United States. Like phosphorus burns that continue to burn through the body if you don't put neutralizing solvents on them. The smell of flesh burning — it's an awful smell. I remember two Vietnamese children who were so badly burned their kidneys shut down and their urine turned to wine-color. Yeah, a lot of things that here in the States you will never see.

We also had some POWs that had some MPs guarding them. Supposedly the MPs were there to keep the POWs from escaping — only when you've got an enemy without legs, there ain't no way he's going to escape. So one day I ask the MPs what they think they're doing. They tell me basically they're there to keep the GIs off the POWs — to keep the GIs from killing the POWs.

The POWs were really scared. My Eurasian face didn't make any difference, either — they were just as scared of me as they were of everybody else. I mean, they were terrified, so terrified they'd hide underneath the sheets. But you know, I never once saw a GI try to harm a POW. What I saw was "Hey, lieutenant, come here quick — the gook over there is in a lot of pain; would you give him a shot?" Or "Here — why don't you give the gook a couple of cigarettes." I'm talking about guys with no legs asking me to do these things. Times like that you couldn't help but wonder what we were in a goddamned war for. I mean, what was it all about? Yeah, the guys made it more confusing for me. But then I guess I made it more confusing for them at times.

On that ward we had a nasty doctor, a real jerk. His belief was that when you had amputees, you scrubbed their wounds with Betadine — an antiseptic soap — very vigorously. Now I don't disagree with his belief, I just don't like how he did it, and I especially did not like how he did it to the POWs. Well, I used to ask this doctor to warn me so I could get the drugs going — you give them IV Demerol or IV morphine, and that will hold them for about fifteen to twenty minutes. You'd give it to them ahead of time so by the time he started to scrub, they'd be so superstoned that, even if it hurt, they were not quite with the program. Well, when this jerk did the POWs, he wouldn't give them anything. While he was doing the process I'd be running for the narcotics, trying to get the drug going and running back and yelling at him for not telling me ahead of time. And he would have this grin on his face — "Oh, come on, lieutenant, he's just a gook —" And he would try to belittle me and there I would be pushing in the morphine and really angry. And the Vietnamese would be stoic. They would show nothing. Absolutely nothing. You can't tell me they weren't in pain, either — I knew they were in terrible pain. So when the doctor would leave I would shoot them up regularly. And the GIs would say, "What kind of animal is that doctor?"

It wasn't just that doctor. A lot of the nurses loved it when the POWs were in pain. But I'd feel guilty — it's my nature.

So I was on that ward four months. Four months and I said, "Get me the hell off this ward." I think the thing that took the cake was a black guy with no legs and a chest wound, who had, I think, pneumonia. He was going to go home in two days, when he went into respiratory distress and died. I called the doctor when he went into cardiac arrest. We did CPR [cardiopulmonary resuscitation] and we worked hard on the guy and then the doctor starts yelling at me, "What did you do to him?" Well, the doctor is yelling at me and I'm yelling back and Sue, my friend, is taking care of the guy's effects. Finally Sue comes back and says, "Here — this is it."

The guy had gotten a "Dear John" letter that evening — I remembered the Red Cross volunteer giving him a letter. "I'm going to kill her," I said to Sue. "I am really going to kill her. Goddammit — she should have read the letter first." Then I just stopped in my tracks and thought, "Right — you're going to censor letters!" So I realized it wasn't the Red Cross volunteer's fault and put my anger onto the girlfriend.

Yeah, I became very angry at the girls at home who would do such a thing, even if they did not know their boyfriends were in the hospital. I mean, when my boyfriend went to Vietnam I wrote him every day of the week. Sure I started growing away from him — started dating other boys — but I never wrote him a "Dear John" letter. Never. My letters started to get less romantic because I didn't want him to come home thinking I was lying all that time, and of course he knew what was happening. When he came home he said, "I knew it." But he also said, "You kept me alive. You saved my life by not writing me a 'Dear John' letter. Even though I knew I was losing you, I was getting your letters, and that kept me alive."

Yeah, I was really angry at the women back home that they would destroy the guys like that. Like my corpsman — they destroyed my corpsman. One day he came in hysterical. I said, "What's the matter?" He said, "I just got a 'Dear John' letter from my wife, and oh my God, what am I going to do?" So I had guys crying on my shoulder, destroying me with their pain. And I blamed it on the women back home.

I tried to make sense of it. I was forced to try to make sense of it, because I wanted to help the women back home understand what was going on. But I was always getting caught in all these different roles. With each tragedy that happened, I was caught up in it. I went around angry a lot of the time.

So I'd had it with that ward. I wanted to go someplace where I didn't have to know all the stories. I just could not take one more story about a guy who was supposed to get married when he got home in May, only he had no legs, and he couldn't tell his girlfriend. No, I could not deal with any more of that. So I put in for a transfer. I told them, "Get me out of here — get me to triage." And they said, "Great. Get her to triage — she's stupid enough to volunteer." What I didn't know till I got to triage was that you could nurse somebody for five minutes and still get very attached.

I was in triage for a longer period of time. I liked triage. We got all kinds of stuff — Lambretta accidents, babies from the orphanages, GIs coming in drunk — the light stuff as well as the heavy. But the mass-cals were heavy. Setting aside the guys that weren't going to make it to the OR — well, I had some very heavy experiences. I remember one guy who knew he was dying and kept thinking I was his wife. He was saying, "Mary, Mary — hold my hand!" So I held his hand. "Mary, Mary — I just want to let you know I love you!" At the time I did not know much about dealing with dying people except what I knew by instinct — I have since done some work with Elisabeth Kübler-Ross — but my instincts told me it would not be right to say, "Hey, you're dying in muddy fatigues and this is a war zone and I am not your wife." I mean, it was his last time on earth and I did not want to screw up his fantasy, even though I felt guilty that, in a way, I was lying to him. Well, my response was "You're going to be OK," meaning either way — you're going to live or you're going to die, but you're going to be OK.

Another guy, I remember, lay there and told me he was dying for nothing. I was just about to talk about the domino theory and try to make him feel better, but something told me, "He doesn't want to listen to that shit." So I said, "Yeah, you're right." And he died peacefully. They all died peacefully. I always thought guys in a war zone would die like in an Edgar Allan Poe story. But they always died so peacefully that it gave me a sense of peace.

The ones that would come in that were OR material — they'd come in and say things like "Oh, shit." And then they'd go, "Oh, I'm sorry, ma'am, I didn't mean to curse in front of you." And I'd say, "You can curse any way you want." For some reason I always ended up getting stuck with the Southern boys — I think we got more Southern boys in Vietnam than we got Northerners. Because I was always running into the Southern accent and the "Yes, ma'am, no, ma'am" shit. I'm used to it now, but in those days I always felt like an old lady when those guys said "ma'am" to me.

So after they cursed and apologized they always said, "You smell so good." I mean, I've got guys in shock, wide awake, telling me how good I smell. So I wrote home . . . and said, "Send me bottles and bottles of perfume." I wore Chantilly. And you know, I'm still wearing it — I'm wearing it because I'm hoping to run into my patients, hoping that even if they don't recognize my face they'll recognize my smell. For the longest time I didn't wear it, though, because it reminded me of Vietnam.

Of course, I have yet for a vet to come up to me and say, "Hey, you smell familiar." But wearing Chantilly now is just something I have to do.

A lot of the nurses, too, would wear ribbons in their hair. They'd write home to Mama and say, "Send me some colored ribbons." Because the guys loved it. They also loved pigtails — a lot of girls wore pigtails. "Oh, you look so cute in those pigtails," the patients would say. Or they'd look you straight in the eye and say, "You look so beautiful. You look so soft. You smell so good. You've got such nice eyes" — all this kind of stuff. Only it wasn't a come-on or a put-on. They were just so happy to see American women.

Our chief nurse was a real lifer, though. She used to come around and say, "You're not in uniform, lieutenant. Take that ribbon off. Take those earrings out" — or whatever. And the guys would be there in agony, just loving us.

I mean, if those guys could have gotten down off the stretchers and kissed our feet, they probably would have done it. They really worshipped us when they first came in. I know the kind of care I gave, and I still hear men today telling me about their nurses, their particular nurses, when they were in Vietnam. Yeah, they all have their special nurse, and that nurse could have been me — I mean, when vets talk about their nurse, they talk about the things I did. How I held their hand, gave them a hug. How their nurse kept them alive, supported them. How we cursed along with the men, how funny we were, how we hated the war just like they did, how antimilitary we were, and all the little things we did. Sometimes I can't believe it when I hear nurse stories from the vets — I think, "That's me." Or "That nurse and I must have been twins."

If the guys asked you to stand on your head, you would have stood on your head for them. But they would never even have dreamed of talking about sex or any of that. Their buddies that came to visit would give us some lighthearted stuff — nothing insulting, nothing to make you angry, just the same old stuff, you know — but our patients would never say anything. Or if they did, it would be "Excuse me, ma'am, I didn't mean to say that in front of you." They would apologize just for saying "damn" or "shit" — when I was going around all the time cursing myself!

Yeah, I miss the devotion. I miss the respect I got as a nurse in Vietnam. One day, I remember, there was this infantry captain who came through my triage. He says to me, "Ma'am, I have all the respect in the world for you." I say, "What for?" He says, "Ma'am, I couldn't do what you are doing. I'd rather be out in the boonies ducking from Charlie than be in here doing your job." I heard that over and over in Vietnam. I didn't have to ask for respect over there — I got it.

As far as the issue about my looking Asian, when I was in civilian clothes and walking around the compound with a guy, the other guys would just assume I was a whore. The Army used to truck in whores all the time. Guys would say all kinds of things to me — interesting things — that only whores get to hear. That used to bother me. I used to feel like telling them, "You guys don't even know that if you came into my hospital I'd be taking care of you —

giving you everything I have just to keep you alive." It made me angry. It made me very angry. Only it wasn't a personal thing; I was more angry because I was thinking, "So that's how you treat Vietnamese women." It wasn't that they'd mistaken me for one, because I could understand that. Although I would get angry when I'd go into the PX in uniform, with my ID card, and be the only one stopped by a Vietnamese soldier wanting to check out my ID. I'd think, "I'm an American — and I've got a National asking me for my ID! If he tries to prevent me from going into the PX —" You know, I'd get angry at stuff like that.

When Vietnamese people came into my triage, they'd head straight for me. I'd say, "*No bic! No bic!*" which means "I don't understand." The old ladies would get mad and shake their fingers at me. The interpreters would say to me, "They think you're Vietnamese from Saigon and that you're just snobby," because Cu Chi was out in the country. So the old ladies would get angry, thinking I was a snooty city Vietnamese.

I did have Vietnamese interpreters talk to me about how much they hated Americans. They'd tell me we were destroying their country and that we weren't doing what we were supposed to be doing. And I understood that. I really understood that.

Another time I was in triage and an old lady came in. She had gotten shrapnel in her buttocks. Well, the doctor yells at her to pull her pants down, and in my mind he was talking to a grandma — that was the day I really think I came out of the racist trance. I yell back at the doctor, "How can you do that to an old lady? If you were a woman, you wouldn't pull your pants down in front of all these men!" Yeah, from that day on I stopped being a gook-hater and started to appreciate the Vietnamese. I started wanting to learn more about them and their culture. And the more open I was, the more I asked questions, the more information I got back. It was a give-and-take thing. And you know, if you had their kids in ICU, the mama-sans would sit there and they'd watch, and then eventually they would start taking out the garbage, doing things that they knew they could do to help us out. We never asked them to do anything, but mama-san would just do it. It's their belief system: you do something for them, it's only proper that they do something for you. So it got very hard for me to put up with the racism the more I started to learn about and appreciate the Vietnamese and their culture. After a while I came to hate the word *gook.* And I hated *slant-eyed* and *slope-eyed* and *yellow skin.* I hated hearing Americans say, "Look how they sit" and "They're only subhuman" and all that other stuff. Because, for me, you were talking about real people.

The majority of the people that I learned about the Vietnamese from were the infantry men. The ones that had been out in the field — yeah, a lot of them had respect for the Vietnamese. I also worked with a corpsman who was a Quaker and wouldn't put up with anything — he got sent out of the field because he would call in med-evacs for POWs, and I mean foot soldiers, nobody important. The thinking was that POWs were a waste of your time and energy, unless they were the good ones: the ones with information. But this Quaker would not put up with that shit, so I learned I could gain strength through him.

I didn't realize my own strength back then — I was real proud that I could resist the racism all around me, but I didn't know my own strength as a nonconformist. It is easy to be racist, even for Asians to be racist against Asians. No, you don't have to be Ku Klux Klan to be racist.

My last two weeks in Cu Chi I was put on the surgical ward. They wanted to keep me out of trouble. Because I was hysterical — it's called short-timer's syndrome. You know, you're feeling guilty at leaving because now you're so highly skilled you can do everything blindfolded with your hands tied behind your back. New people coming in means that they are not as skilled, because the new people learn as they go. And there's a lot of ambivalence. You want to stay so you can devote yourself to the guys, but you want to leave because you want to live. You get bitchy. You get irritable. You get hysterical because there's one less IV bottle hanging up — I was freaking people out, saying "What if we have a mass-cal?" Yeah, I was freaking them out. So the new head nurse goes, "Well, Lily, I really think you need a break before you go home." "I don't need no break," I told her. But she shipped me over to surgical, where there was really nothing heavy, just surgical stuff. So that was my last two weeks at Cu Chi. Rather than being with my staff, I was in surgical. But in a way I wanted to be in surgical; I didn't really think I could handle more mass-cals.

I remember being in my room, saying good-bye to it. My room was my sanctuary. I was lucky enough to have ceilings over our area, lucky enough to have a door. And even if the walls were so thin I could hear arguments across the hall and people could hear me cry, my room was my haven. I had a black light and I had Day-Glo posters. It was my place to be — it was not a war zone.

It was hard for me to say good-bye to my sanctuary. I remember hoping the next person that came in would find as much comfort in it as me. And I remember giving away my posters and my black light and feeling really ambivalent about leaving.

OK, I am going home. I have my class As on — some guys went home in fatigues, but I always went along with the Army unless they stepped on my toes — and I'm wearing my unit citation. Yeah, we got a unit citation; it was a busy year, we were the busiest hospital in Vietnam in those days. Anyhow, a couple of my corpsmen are on the same plane as me. We joke around a lot. Then I find myself wanting to separate myself from them because it's too hard to think about saying good-bye.

We get off at Travis, in Oakland. There are about two or three staff people there, and they applaud us. Just airmen, but I felt real good. It was more of a welcome home than a lot of people got.

I had to spend the night at the air base because they weren't going to out-process officers that day. I remember I couldn't sleep. I kept looking out the window at the real world, thinking about going back to work, putting Vietnam behind me and leading a normal life again.

The Army gave me two hundred dollars back pay and said good-bye. They didn't give me transportation home — I think they gave me transportation money, but you know, in my head it was "They're not even going to call me a cab!" Well, I didn't know how to cross streets. I knew what the traffic light was for but I didn't pay attention to it. Instead I just stood there on the sidewalk trying to figure out how to cross the street. I was very confused. I didn't know what to do or where to go.

I had a friend from Fort Ord who lived in Monterey. So I called and was invited to stay in Monterey until I got my act together. I also got linked up with a band that was going down there — on the phone, the band manager said to take the bus in from Oakland and they'd meet me at the terminal in San Francisco and give me a ride. "Fine," I say. Then I start to describe myself. I tell the guy I'm in uniform. "Listen," the guy says, "you better get that uniform off when you get to the bus terminal." "Why?" I ask. "Because they're beating people up." "Why?" I say again. "I don't know," the guy says, "but as soon as you get to the terminal, change into civilian clothes."

I get on the bus. Everyone is staring at me. I mean, they're looking at me like I just killed somebody. I'm sitting there thinking something must be wrong with my uniform, that they're critical of me because I'm not shipshape — I really did not have any idea what it was all about. So I get off the bus. People are giving me dirty looks all over the place. Still, I can't figure it out. I had heard in Vietnam from letters back that people in the World were negative about us, only it didn't make any sense to me. Why would they be negative about us when we're saving lives backward and forward? Anyhow, I go inside, change into my jeans, and go down to my friend's house. When I get there I take my uniform out of my bag, throw it on the floor and say, "Burn it!" "You sure you don't want to save this? Just look at all the medals! What did you get the medals for?" "I don't want to talk about it — just burn it!"

So I moved into an apartment in San Francisco, on the edge of Chinatown. I lived alone and was very angry and very hostile, only I didn't know what I was angry and hostile about. I didn't know if I was angry at the country for being angry at me. I didn't know if I was angry because all that work in Vietnam was for nothing — I mean, I was very, very confused. That's why I ended up going to bars looking for Vietnam vets. When I'd be in the bar I'd start thinking, "Well, how am I going to know one man from another?" So I'd start talking to anybody that looked like a Vietnam vet — anybody that looked like a, you know, typical nineteen-year-old kid. And I'd sit and talk to various people, tell them I'd been an Army nurse in Vietnam. And I usually didn't get any farther than "Oh yeah, oh wow — that must have been hard."

During Chinese New Year I secluded myself and stayed in bed. I pulled the covers over my head to keep out the noise because I kept on thinking we were getting attacked — no matter how often I told myself it was Chinese New Year and that we were not getting attacked, I kept on thinking we were.

I didn't really know what I was supposed to do or how I was supposed to do it. I thought, "Well, maybe if I get a job —" I got a job and lasted a month. I couldn't handle the incompetency — in Vietnam nobody put up with incompetency because you were working on GIs and you didn't make mistakes with them. Yeah,

I was so used to working with devoted, talented people that I forgot what the real world was like. I mean, in Vietnam the real world seemed too much like heaven — you know, rainbows everywhere, chocolate gumdrops growing out of trees. I was just not with it, was just not with the program.

So I lived for a while off the money I had saved in Vietnam, and then that emptied out. I learned I owed taxes — yes, they taxed the pay I received in Nam! By the time I got involved with James [Adams] I was two months late on my rent. I was sleeping a lot, I was depressed, and I often thought of destroying myself. I vaguely knew I wanted to destroy myself because I was so depressed — depressed that all we'd done over there was for nothing. Yeah, I finally came to the terms that Vietnam was for nothing. Our men were being slaughtered for nothing. Nobody gave a shit, nobody cared. That I knew. Plus I was feeling guilty because I wasn't over there.

When James came home, it was like a breath of fresh air. He asked me to move with him to Houston, Texas, where he had just gotten a job, and I said yes. Because I knew that if I went with him I had a chance to live. If I didn't go with him I figured I was going to die — I couldn't pay my rent, I couldn't hold a job, I couldn't do anything. And I couldn't relate to anybody. The only other person besides James that I felt understood me was John Lennon — at least he was on my side. This was around the time that he had those important songs out, "Give Peace a Chance" and "Imagine."

James and I had first met while Gail and I were on leave in Hong Kong. He saw me a couple times in Cu Chi after that, but I was determined I would not get involved with anybody. Well, after I got home I sent him a Christmas card and he wrote a heavy-duty letter back. And I thought, "Wait a minute — something's going on here." So we started writing heavy letters back and forth and when he came home we moved to Houston and got married.

All the time we talked about Vietnam — I'd keep him up till four in the morning, talking and crying about my guys, about this and that. I don't really think James heard half the stuff I said. All he could really do was shake his head and say, "Yeah, yeah — I understand."

In Houston I got a job in open heart surgery and couldn't do the work. I couldn't learn anything new, couldn't get along with anybody, because I felt too many people were incompetent. Which was true — there was a lot of playing around and nobody was as devoted to the patients as they should have been. There was another nurse who worked with me who'd been in Vietnam as well. I discovered her one morning because she was drinking Coke. "The only people who drink Coke for breakfast are people that served in Nam," I said. And she said, "That's right — how did you know?" "I just explained it to you — people don't drink Coke for breakfast." And there I was with *my* Coke. So we talked a little, about where we'd been stationed, but we didn't talk beyond that. And that was how it was with the other women vets I ran into. "Oh, you were in Vietnam? Where were you?" Nothing more than that. Up until the time, that is, that I came out of the closet.

What happened was, James and I moved to Hawaii. Helicopters used to fly over our house all the time. Well, the first time a chopper flew over I ran outside so I could be ready for the mass-cals. I waited and waited in the middle of the street, wondering why they weren't coming in to land. My daughter, Erika, I remember, came out of the house and wanted to know what I was out there for — and it was like going to another world, coming down from concentrating on those helicopters. So I look at my daughter and my daughter is thinking, "This is weird," and after that scene got repeated two or three times, I called up the vet center and talked and talked. That was really the beginning of me coming out of the closet. Later, of course, I talked to Lynda [Van Devanter] on the phone and that helped a whole lot. Lynda was also the first person to alert me to Agent Orange and all the physical complications related to it.

Like when I came back from Vietnam I had such a terrible case of cystic acne that James talked me into seeing a dermatologist. About two years later I had a breast tumor. The next year I got pregnant, was carrying twin boys, who died when I was seven-and-a-half months pregnant. None of it made sense to the doctors, and none of it made sense to me. And then in seventy-five I had a lot of knee problems and in seventy-nine my son, Daniel, was born without nerve cells in fifty percent of his large intestine and had to have a colostomy at eight months. I wish I had known about Agent Orange earlier — I don't know what I could have done, but I would have tried to do something.

What do I tell my kids about Vietnam? The truth. The confusion.

I've explained to Erika about one kid who had one leg missing, one arm missing, and one eye missing. When he came in to us he yelled, "You bitches leave me alone!" The captain got on his case, said, "You don't talk to them like that — they're women and you don't say those words to them!" Well, the kid had been hanging around with GIs and didn't know *bitch* was a bad word. He was a toughie, a real toughie, that kid. He ended up getting very attached to me and used to cry whenever I'd leave him. Well, I resisted getting attached to him — I resisted and resisted and felt real guilty for not allowing myself to give him what I wanted to give him. Because I didn't want to get attached, not to anybody. So I explained to Erika that this kid haunted me. That I did everything I should have done, that there was no way I could have adopted him — yet he got to me. That kid really got to my defenses.

Yeah, I had problems with children. Last Christmas is the first one I survived without going totally bananas at the sight of crowds of children. And that's because I'm really very well healed. I went to Salute One [the dedication ceremonies for the Vietnam Veterans Memorial in Washington], dealt with my grief at the Wall, and left a hundred pounds lighter.

Vietnam taught me a lot. It taught me that war is not the practical way of dealing with disagreements among countries, and it taught me that the men and women who served in Vietnam are very special people.

When I discuss Vietnam I find myself discussing the negative stuff. War *is* negative, and most of the time Vietnam was negative. But I want to emphasize that, as a nurse in a war zone, I found myself performing beyond my limits — as a result, I have more self-confidence, know that I can tackle any task, that nothing is impossible if you want it bad enough. I'm really proud to have served in Vietnam. No one can take that away from me or from the other vets.

I was lucky enough to witness the special friendships between men that you rarely see in so-called real life. I learned that men can be gentle, tender, and loving with each other. I learned that men and women can work together with mutual respect and admiration. But no matter what positive experiences we had over there, I know war is not the answer to anything. That's why I'll continue to work on peace issues for the rest of my life.

Soldiers aren't the only ones who die in wars. Like I tell my kids, grandmas, grandpas, mommies, daddies, and babies die in wars, too.

*Lily Adams is now a psychotherapist specializing in post trauma stress disorder. She is on the national board of directors of the Vietnam Veterans of America and is the chairperson for Vietnam Veterans of America's special committee on women veterans. Lily, James, Erika, and Daniel live in Roswell, Georgia.*

# Cindy Randolph (alias)

*Cindy Randolph was born and raised in Washington State. Her mother taught school; her father is a millwright at a pulp mill. "I was brought up Baptist. My parents were Republicans. They weren't overly strict, but their values were that you work hard, you save, you don't buy on credit, you go to school. If you do everything right, your life is going to be the all-American life and you'll naturally progress up. It was a big learning experience for me when I found out that that is not necessarily true."*

*Cindy entered the University of Washington at Seattle in 1964, graduating in 1968 with a degree in social work. From July of 1970 to July of 1971 she was in Vietnam with the Red Cross SRAO program. She was assigned to Danang, Qui Nhon, Cam Ranh, and Chu Lai.*

I REMEMBER READING an article in sixty-eight in *Cosmopolitan* that listed five ways for a woman to get to Vietnam. One was to be a stewardess and one was to be a nurse, another was to join the USO, and another was to join the Red Cross — anyway, there were like four or five ways to get there and I'd always loved traveling. So I sent off to the Red Cross for information about going to Vietnam. When I got the information, I said, "Oh, do I really want to do this?" And I didn't think I did.

Well, somewhere in the process I heard they were looking for a social worker at the local Red Cross. So, when I graduated, I applied for that job and got it. The first year, I got involved in disasters: I got sent off to Hurricane Camille down in Mississippi, and there I met several gals who had come back from Vietnam. That kind of rekindled some of my interest in doing it.

I think the other thing — maybe what actually pushed me over the brink to do it — was the work I did with military families. I was, in addition to getting sent to disasters, dealing with a lot of wives whose husbands were in Vietnam and a lot of guys who were coming home on emergency leaves. Those guys, I remember, were saying they weren't going back, that they didn't understand what the war was all about. Well, I'm very much the sort of person

who, when someone says the burner is hot, I have to touch it —
to find out if it really is.

I couldn't really understand what the war was about from reading the newspapers. And I couldn't really understand the demonstrations, though I was a part of that whole sixties thing, you
know. No, I was not antiwar. I guess I have to say I was actively
fence-sitting because I could hear both sides. Though, because I
was brought up conservatively, I think I was more inclined to
support the military.

So why did I, in the end, decide to go? Well, another explanation
is that my father came home traumatized from the Second World
War, and my family is still feeling that. My father has never been
able to resolve the difficulties he had in the war; even now, he has
nightmares continually. I can remember, all my life, waking up
and he's in there mumbling in German or maybe French, tossing
and turning in his sleep, you know. I think when you face that
kind of life-and-death situation, you're talking spiritual issues —
and if there's no place to talk and nothing to do with the pain, it
just sits inside you and rots.

So I think I wanted to be supportive of the military, even if the
war was an unpopular one. Because, no matter where these guys
had to go, they were going to have to go through things that would
traumatize them for a long time.

I'm trying to explain what I mean when I say I was actively
fence-sitting: it's not that I wouldn't have been willing to take
action against Vietnam, it's just that I understood that these fellows
were going to need support whether the war was right or wrong.
Because I believe you can be against a war and still support the
guys who have to fight it.

Well, the more I worked with these guys who were back from
Vietnam, the more it got clear in my mind that I couldn't be very
effective. Because they're sitting here saying how hot and dirty and
ugly the war is, and the wives are telling stuff that happened when
the guys came back. While I don't really know anything —

So, I signed up. I was twenty-three.

OK, we land in Saigon. I tend to get into a little drama at this
point — maybe everybody does — but I think the only thing that
occurred to me as we were landing is that a lot of people landed
and didn't leave in the same shape as they came. You know, I
remember looking around and saying, "I wonder which are the

ones . . ." I also remember thinking that a lot of the guys on the plane would go home in a box.

Well, the first death I experienced was — interestingly enough — an SRAO girl. This was two or three weeks after we left Saigon.

Anyway, Saigon. Saigon was all new sights and sounds. We stayed at a hotel in the Cholon area and there was a garbage depot or dump right outside our window. It was full of cans and yuck, and you could see all these rats running around. The dump had to be every bit as big as this room. The hotel was one of those hotels where they had the rotating fans, you know, like in the Humphrey Bogart movies. There were bunkers outside with Vietnamese soldiers and guns and all that. I never remember feeling put off by any of it — I mean, I know other people were like really overwhelmed by the heat and the smell, but I was always thinking, "Wow! This is really great! This is really an adventure!"

The first night we were in town I went to a correspondents' party, and that was the sickest I've ever been in my life. Actually, I don't remember drinking that much, but somebody told me on the way home that the stuff I thought was little chicken wings turned out to be pigeon. For some reason, that was the most offensive thought to me in the whole world. I mean, I'm quite open to eating almost anything, but for some reason, eating pigeon just sent me around the bend. It was terrible. I was taking care of both ends at the same time.

Getting that sick right off really sapped my energy, but I got through the orientation and was sent to Danang. Danang had a large recreation hall. We also did overnight stuff up at Quang Tri, on the border. Mostly we dealt with the Marines at Quang Tri, though there was some work with the Army.

OK, several weeks after we were in country, this gal that I came in with, Jeanne, was stabbed to death down in Cu Chi by — supposedly, they don't really know — an American serviceman. He broke into their building at about two or three in the morning and slashed her throat so she couldn't scream. This gal was from Ohio. She'd gone to Ohio State, had been a beauty queen. She was really a cute, vivacious young lady. Still, it's hard to imagine getting into a relationship that would get so passionate in only two or three weeks, and she didn't know anybody over there before she went. They never caught the guy who killed her. So what happened, really, no one knows.

I did have an experience the night she was killed that was somewhat extrasensory. Around the time it was happening to her, I woke up as if there were somebody in my room with a flashing knife. I couldn't go back to sleep and just had this foreboding feeling. It wasn't until the next morning, when we went to the center, that I knew what it was all about. Saigon called. They told us Jeanne had been murdered.

I remember going outside to the back of the center. I felt like I was going to get into some tears, when this Marine guy came out and asked me what was wrong. I explained that a friend had just been murdered, and he just looked at me and said, "Well, that happens to us every day. You should be glad that it's not you."

What I didn't understand then was that, in Vietnam, you didn't deal with or process feelings. You denied everything. Like the whole Nam language — you could carry on whole conversations and not use anything other than the slang of Vietnam. Vietnam was a world unto itself. The concept of going back to "the World," meaning the real world, always told me that we'd been exiled to some hellish place. Anything that happened in Vietnam wasn't real. You just got through it. You just survived it. And instead of behaving like human beings and supporting each other, there was a lot of sordid behavior — no, that's wrong. That isn't quite what I mean. What I mean is, healing can't go on when you're in the middle of that kind of situation: a situation in which there's no place for feelings, where you can't deal with feelings or let them surface.

The other thing that happened while I was in Danang is that I woke up one night aware that someone was breaking into our building. We were in a big old Navy nurses' barracks or Quonset huts; at the far end of our section there was a door with a bar across it and also a stand with a telephone. I was about three doors down from the end and my door was locked. But I had no idea whose doors were locked and whose doors weren't. I couldn't get to the telephone because the telephone was right in front of the door. And this was just after Jeanne had been murdered — so I was terrified. Absolutely terrified. Whoever it was — I have to assume it was a man — got in and walked down the hall. He walked the whole length of the building. I could hear him. I remember lying there, waiting. Finally he left. We never did find out who it was.

That memory has stayed with me because it was a real helpless feeling. I was just kind of waiting, wondering what was going to happen.

Other things happened at Danang. One day this little Marine came in — he looked about eighteen, like some kid you'd graduated from high school with — and he was looking real happy. I was checking out pool cues to him or something and asked what he was so happy about. He told me he'd gotten this mama-san that morning; he'd killed her. He was really jubilant about that.

I remember going, "What? How can you just say that?" And he said, "Well she was out in the rice paddies and, I mean, we were on patrol. Listen, she's just as much VC as anyone else —"

I had another experience in the center where this guy came in with pilot's wings on his boonie hat. Now there's no reason for a grunt to have pilot's wings on his boonie hat, so I said to him, "Where did you get those?" He said, "I got them off a VC." And I said, "Well, where do you think the VC got them?" Because, obviously, the VC got them off a pilot. I remember I just looked at the guy and asked him when those wings were going to change hands again. And he looked back at me like "How can you say that?" But to me, he was wearing those wings as a trophy. I wanted him to see that. I also wanted him to see how easily the same thing could happen to him. So I told him, "You know, you're wearing them like this is a neat thing, but it's not a neat thing. There are already two people dead. And you're wearing those wings with pride?" I think he got it then. It was painful for him to hear it, but I think he got it after that.

Remember I mentioned the Nam language — how telling the Nam language is? Well, sometimes, you know, guys would come in and we'd be playing cards or checkers or whatever, and these guys could hardly talk to a woman. Their experiences out in the field had been so terrible they could only use terrible language — could only communicate in primitive ways. It was often very difficult for them to carry on a conversation.

Recreation was the mechanism to help them communicate. I know a lot of people said, "What in the world are they doing sending these women over in these little blue dresses to play games with these guys?" But I think there was more therapy in our work than we'll ever know. I've worked on psychiatric wards since then, and what I've found out is that during times when someone is having trouble communicating, a lot of stuff comes out in just, say, the playing of cards. Yeah, a lot of yourself comes out, so that pretty soon there is some sort of a relationship developing. And that's how I understand the work we did in Vietnam. Some people believe we got paid just for playing cards, but basically I think I got paid for doing therapy.

There were guys that were hard to connect with, though. I'm thinking of the brothers now, the black guys — although I didn't have any trouble connecting with them, I know a lot of girls did. The brothers would hang out in their group, you know, and were always doing the dap, and I was certainly aware of the animosity between blacks and whites in the military. But I was usually able to relate in a very positive way with the blacks.

I'd say the people I had the least ability to connect with were the guys on drugs. You know, you'd go out to the fire bases and there would be guys who were really strung out, guys who were just sitting around listening to their boxes and reading comic books. They'd be flying high and they'd be hostile. If you tried to connect with them, they'd want you to connect in terms of the drugs and possibly sexually. Yeah, there would be those kinds of overtones. Although I'd done drugs before I left the States — I was part of that generation — I'd made a pretty firm commitment that drugs weren't going to be a part of my life in Vietnam. Because I don't see how I could have done my job on drugs. Some of the gals did get involved with drugs over there. Drugs made it easier for them to do what they thought was their job, but it didn't help them to connect with people. And that's what I saw our job as being: we were over there to connect.

I have to say that I really liked my job that year. It was especially good when you were with another woman you could program well with. The guys would really get into answering the questions and get into the competition set up between teams. I had a couple women I worked well with — there would be a lot of impromptu stuff, a lot of going back and forth and teasing, and that sort of thing would really energize the group. I liked working in the centers, but I liked going out on the fire bases pretty much. When you'd had a really good day, you'd come back feeling like you'd accomplished something and that you'd really connected with people.

One thing that's so bizarre to me is that, going out to the fire bases, I never felt fear. Like once we'd taken a Chinook out and had made three or four stops. At the last base, we finished programming and were waiting and waiting for the Chinook to come back for us — we were always supposed to be off the hills by four or five o'clock, and here it was seven or eight. Well, finally they come back to get us and when we get back to the hangar they show us the Chinook we'd gone out on that morning, what had happened just after they dropped us off. Well, the Chinook had a lot of holes in it right down the side where we'd been sitting.

When the guy was breaking in I felt fear, and I felt fear about some other things, but I never felt fear when we were going out to the fire bases. I guess that's a contradiction — I look back and it's so bizarre.

After Danang I was moved to Qui Nhon. Qui Nhon only lasted a few weeks; I was moved down to Cam Ranh as the program director there. Cam Ranh was the largest SRAO unit. It had nine or ten women. We did a lot of day runs, but we also did a lot of overnight runs up to Ban Me Thuot and Bao Loc on the Cambodian border. So scheduling was really heavy duty. But because Cam Ranh was an Air Force base, we weren't seeing much action. We did take some incoming and stuff, but it wasn't like up at Danang and Qui Nhon, where you had a lot of grunts, guys who were seeing the real stuff. What we had at Cam Ranh was a lot of Remington warriors. Even Bao Loc and Ban Me Thuot were like resorts.

Cam Ranh wasn't hard. But we did have a lot of drug problems at our recreation centers: heroin, marijuana, the whole shmeer. I don't think I could do anything for those guys, and I also don't think I felt pressured, at that point, to do anything but just be. I think I was sort of getting into some real depression.

Cam Ranh, I think, was when I started getting tired. I think stuff started snowballing — I had, maybe, a breakdown at Cam Ranh. I'm not sure about that, though; I'm not really sure what happened.

One day I had an accident going to one of the centers in a truck; my head got hit pretty hard. They couldn't find anything wrong other than they thought I had a concussion, and I went to bed for three or four days. And then one night I went to a movie — we'd had an activity at the centers and these guys had won a date with us to a movie — and standing in line, I collapsed. I just couldn't stand up.

They took me to the hospital. At first I was told I had a brain tumor, which was not the case but which kind of scared me. I think it was just exhaustion. I couldn't move, I was like paralyzed all over — yeah, I think it was not only exhaustion but also pushing down a lot of feelings. I think that was really what the paralysis stuff was all about. After I left Vietnam, I had the same paralysis for quite a while.

After Cam Ranh, I got transferred to Chu Lai as a unit director. That was great. Chu Lai was all forward runs. We didn't have a recreation center, but it was a great bunch of gals I worked with. We supported each other and worked hard and had fun, because there was just all this energy. So that was good, the last few months.

By the time I started working in the hospital at Chu Lai, I'd lost a lot of feelings; that, I think, is how I managed to get through some of the hard stuff about hospital work. For instance, I remember one guy in particular — I had to write letters for him — who wasn't going to be able to have kids and he hadn't told his wife yet. This guy had lost the bottom half of himself. The worst part for me, though — and I think this is true for the nurses, too — is that the bad cases were stabilized and then immediately med-evacked out. So there's a lot of unfinished business with those guys — you saw them in the most traumatized state and never worked that through to a point where it feels finished with you and them. I often wonder what happened to a lot of the guys I met. The enormity of what some of them were carrying was . . . well, I'd love to know where they are now and what they're doing.

But you know, seeing movies like *The Deerhunter* and *Apocalypse Now* — all the Vietnam movies, I've seen them more than once — somehow tends to give me some sort of completion.

Anyhow, that's life; you go on somehow. I mean, some people have the inner strength to do it and some people don't.

Which makes me think of something else: I was going out with this pilot, an Air Force pilot, who had flown like a hundred missions over North Vietnam. I remember lying in bed with him looking at his thumb and thinking, "We could lie here and make love and he's just dropped how many tons of bombs with that thumb?" You know, that's all it takes — you just push that little button to drop the bomb. That's incredible to me. It's really incredible. And this pilot was really removed from it. I mean, when they're up in the air, there's this distance between them and humanity. They don't see what their bombs are dropping on. They don't see the pain we're causing. What they're thinking is "This is my job." And, to me, that's incredible.

When I was traveling in Malaysia after Vietnam, I ran into this guy who was the first Marine conscientious objector to get discharged out of the military from Vietnam. We traveled together for a while and he was spending all the money he'd made in Southeast Asia when he was flying second seat in bombers. I think he probably did the most healing thing possible for him — it was like he was doing this whole spiritual number, getting rid of everything, including all the harm he'd done. I don't know how things ever finally worked out for him. I wonder. You know, every time I walk through an airport I'm always looking for him and other pilots that I knew.

There was another guy, too, that I often wonder about. His name was Mitch. Mitch was just this ambling, skinny kid from Tennessee. He was in the Army. When he first showed up at Cam Ranh we thought it was really funny because he hung around the center and would do absolutely anything for me — he had a particular puppy-dog thing for me. I mean, Mitch would clean, Mitch would paint — you needed something done, Mitch would do it. But it started looking odd — Mitch was on this Air Force base forever and ever. I never could get him to tell me what was going on.

Well, finally, after about a month, the MPs figured out that he didn't belong on this Air Force base. They picked him up; it turned out he was AWOL from his unit. So they put Mitch in one of those metal square boxes that they stored stuff in — those boxes get real hot — and left him there for a couple of weeks. After that they sent him back to his unit.

So then I'm up at Chu Lai, in the PX, and who shows up but Mitch. He's handcuffed and on his way to court. Anyhow, when the whole thing comes out, I learn that what had happened was that Mitch had been out as a grunt and had gotten in a firefight. Very few people made it, and the people who did were alive because of Mitch — he had really been heroic in getting people carried out and doing what needed to be done. He's also been slightly injured. So, in the hospital, they told him he was going to be sent back out to the field, and Mitch said, "I can't do it. I just can't do it again —" I guess, you know, that was why he was ambling around Cam Ranh Bay.

In the end, they decided not to discharge him dishonorably. I think he was put on probation and finally sent to a fire base where he wasn't going to be under as much pressure. But by that time Mitch was really disjointed, you know. I've always wondered what happened to Mitch. He didn't have much to go back to in Tennessee.

I mentioned before that I was aware of animosity between blacks and whites. Well, I also have to say something about the blacks and the Vietnamese. This may be racism on my part — I hope it's not — but I had quite a few experiences when the blacks were the worst of all in terms of racism toward the Vietnamese. They really were the worst when it came to putting their foot down on the Vietnamese, both in words and actions. Not that the U.S. — black or white — has anything to be proud of. My observation is that we made prostitutes out of Vietnam's women and pimps out of their young men and slaves out of their older people. To me, it's as simple as that. We did a lot of damage over there. We thought of them as "gooks," as less than human. And that attitude really turns me off.

When it was time for me to leave, I was ready. I turned twenty-five on July sixteenth, 1971, and — I was just trying to figure this out the other day; sometimes it takes a long time to figure things out — I was looking at these slides and there was this fellow who was a helicopter pilot. For some reason, he had an affinity for me. I'm not sure what it was all about, but I know he wanted to take me up on my fini [final] flight. So he and this other captain, we took this little Loach up. Do you know what a Loach is? It's a real tiny helicopter, sort of like a dragonfly. Anyway, we took this Loach up and we had this crate of hand grenades and we flew out over the ocean at Chu Lai where we could see all these sharks. This was an area where they went out for practice, only we weren't out for practice. We were out there just to have fun. So the guys radioed in and we got clearance, and I sat there in the back seat of that Loach pulling pins out of grenades and throwing them down at these sharks. I guess I was having a good time. In retrospect, though, I can't imagine myself trying to kill sharks. I mean, I believe you should live and let live. Those sharks weren't hurting anybody.

After I left Vietnam, as I said, I traveled with a friend. I had a real hard time during those six months of traveling. I don't know what was going on — I think it was delayed stress — but I cracked up when we were in Lebanon. I just totally cracked up, couldn't leave the hotel room for three or four days. I mentioned earlier this kind of paralysis that would come over me — from time to time I'd just go into this really deep, heavy place of just shutdown, when I couldn't communicate or talk to people. Well, I must have eventually left the hotel. I don't really remember, but I must have left because I'm here today.

In Seattle again, I got a job with an Employment Security office. It was really very, very boring. I think I was all at loose ends.

The one thing that sticks out in my mind about going back to Seattle is getting invited to a dinner at a girlfriend's house. Her parents were real ultraliberals. They were very anti-Vietnam and had friends at this dinner who bordered on communist. Well, one of the friends looked across the table — my girlfriend Judy had said I'd been in Vietnam with the Red Cross — and said, "It's people like you who perpetuate war." I just looked back at him. I couldn't say anything. After that I never talked about the war publicly, ever.

I do recall the first time I ever really talked to somebody in private. This was seventy-two and I was working for the Red Cross again. I was down in California on a disaster — one of the dikes on the Sacramento River had broken and totally covered this town with water. Anyway, there was a very antiwar guy named Greg, who was also working on the disaster, and after it was all over we went to San Francisco and I got really bloody drunk. I talked about Vietnam for hours, and he listened to me. So that kind of set a pattern — I'd say that from seventy-two to seventy-eight the only times I talked about Vietnam were when I got really drunk.

After California I got a job with the Red Cross in Oklahoma. So in Oklahoma I was getting my master's degree and working in a hospital at Fort Sill where there were quite a few guys from Vietnam. I liked working with them. From Oklahoma I went to England for a couple of years and worked with the Red Cross at an Air Force Hospital. Then I quit my job and came back here.

I think it was probably seventy-eight when I finally started talking about the Vietnam thing. All during that period of time, between seventy and seventy-eight, I was having acute depressions, depressions so bad I'd have to drop out for a week or two because I could not communicate with people. So it was around seventy-eight when things really started moving for me. I went to a Shalom Retreat, where they use bioenergetics — it's a really weird thing that happened, and I don't understand it — I was lying on a mat with about ten or twelve people around me. They were leading me into this breathing stuff, and whatever surfaced, you were supposed to just let surface. What surfaced for me was graves in Vietnam.

Well, I went into just total paralysis. It went on for about an hour. I was frozen, absolutely frozen, and the people I was with didn't know if I was coming back. I couldn't move my hands, my face, my legs — no matter how much effort I put into it. The only part of me that wasn't frozen was my mind.

And at that point in time I knew I had a choice. I could just go — and be in an institution forever. Or I could choose to come back and live. And that was the choice I made.

Not long after that I had a dream. In this dream there was an umbrella over my heart — it was one of those little Oriental paper umbrellas — and this umbrella was separating my head from my heart. In the dream I started crying and took the umbrella down. When I told that dream to my church group and sat there and shared my tears, that was really the first time I was able to share it all in a real way and have people hear me.

You know, listening to the news, hearing these guys talking about war in Lebanon — "We've got to go over there and blast the hell out of the Shiites" — that type of thing, I get real caught up in that. I think about my friends whose kids have just graduated from college, kids who are all gung ho now, who'd be the ones to go, even though they don't know what war is all about. And it gets sort of depressing, you know.

Right now, you want to know all about the bad side of Vietnam. But I can't say I'm sorry I went. Because there certainly was a wonderful side. Even a fun side — I don't know any of my friends here who waterskied down the Danang River! The incongruities are what made it so crazy. I mean, you could be sitting at a general's dinner table having this fantastic meal and then, the next day, be up to your waist in mud trying to program. Or you could be at the general's table the night before you went out to a fire base where there's a big, fat cook in a dirty white T-shirt dripping perspiration into the big metal kettle you're going to be getting your chicken gumbo from. I remember that, and I remember it being so goddamned hot. And I'm looking at that kettle and I'm looking at the cook, and I'm going, "Shit! I'm going to eat that?" So you go back and forth, back and forth. . . . You know, at the general's table they were always talking about the war like it was a chess game. It was not a chess game. It was ugly and it was dirty and it was real.

But despite all that, you were young, you felt powerful, you believed you could beat the odds and do and see it all. Going to Vietnam, you know, was one of the better highs in life. That's an unfortunate commentary on the war, but it says a lot about the shadow side of ourselves. And I think the only way we're ever going to have peace is if we can recognize our shadow sides. That's where I'm trying to get. I'm trying to understand and accept my shadow side more.

# Saralee McGoran

*Saralee McGoran grew up in Atlantic City, New Jersey. Her father was in the Army, in World War II, when she was born. When he came back "he went through lots of different jobs. He didn't get it together for many, many years — he worked construction, was a milkman; you name it. My mother worked as a telephone operator at the convention hall. She had only an eighth-grade education, and I think that made it hard on her. Apparently I was an unwanted child. I've heard my mother tell stories about the ways she tried to get rid of me and I think that had a bearing on what I call my suicide mission in Vietnam."*

*Saralee graduated from nursing school in 1960. She joined the Army six years later. From January of 1967 to January of 1968 she was an operating room nurse at the 12th Evacuation Hospital at Cu Chi.*

WHEN I WAS EIGHT YEARS OLD I met this guy who had been in World War Two. He was very young, like in his twenties. He was all crippled up and had contractures, severe muscle contractions that keep whatever part of the body is affected tightly clenched. Like, his fists were tightly clenched, and his arms were pressing forward onto his chest. I used to walk down the street where he was sitting out in his wheelchair and at first I was afraid of him. I wouldn't even look at him — I used to walk on the other side of the street. But finally I started walking on his side of the street and looking at him a little bit. Then it got to the point where I would stop and say "Hi" and move on. And then I started stopping to say "Hi" and we would talk. He liked Hershey bars and would always ask me to go get him one at the store. After a while he began to teach me about his contractures. He taught me how to pull his arms down, how to pull his fingers out, how to soften up his hands so that he relaxed. So that every time I would greet him we'd go through that ritual of pulling his arms and hands down, relaxing him, then going and getting the candy bar and spending time with him. Then one day he was gone. I don't know where he went or who took him or why. But it was devastating. A real painful loss.

It's only since I've started thinking about Vietnam, started dealing with it, that all this has come back to me. He was a young man who had been hurt by war, and he was teaching me about war. But I didn't know it at the time.

I guess I was about ten when I started going to the homes for crippled children. I used to talk to the kids and read them comic strips. I also got to know a lot of the nurses and doctors. And I used to ask them a lot of questions about what was wrong with this kid or that kid. By the time I was eleven or twelve, they were letting me use the medical library. I bought a medical dictionary for myself when I was fourteen years old. So you can see what my destiny was, where it was taking me. I think all those things kind of fit together. You know, like in a pattern.

Well, about the time I was thirteen or fourteen I was really convinced that what I wanted to do was become a doctor. I had an uncle who was an attorney. He had quite a bit of money and we didn't — we really were poor. But this uncle of mine was going to send me to medical school. He really believed in me. And then, the summer of my sophomore year in high school, he died. That was another big loss for me. I also knew it was the end of medical school. The only choice that seemed left was to be a nurse.

I went to the Albert Einstein Medical Center in Philadelphia. It cost four hundred fifty-five dollars for three years of nursing school. Because we worked, it was like slave labor. But it was good, because my family couldn't afford to send me — as it was, my mother had to cash in an insurance policy.

One night in nursing school a whole bunch of us were sitting around the dorm talking about our lives. One of the issues that came up was war. We kept asking what we'd do if there was another war. And almost every single one of us said the same thing: "If there's another war and I'm still single, I'm going to go." Those words came back to haunt me in 1966.

So I was twenty-six years old. I was in L.A., had worked on all kinds of different wards — I'd even designed a coronary care unit, probably one of the first in the country. I remember hearing the radio and T.V. reports about the war in Vietnam, and that's when I remembered what I'd said back in Philadelphia when I was nineteen. "Well," I asked myself, "was I serious about that? Would I" — I was still single — "really go to this war?" I thought some more about it and realized that, yeah, I would. After going to the Air Force and Navy I went to the Army recruiter, because the Army would send you over there fast. The guy said, "Wow! Sign right here!" What he actually said was that they really needed OR nurses in Vietnam and would I be willing to train to be an OR nurse and then go to Vietnam. And I said, "Sure. You train me and I'll do it." I knew they'd send me to school, that I could get my bachelor's degree if I wanted to when I got back. It sounded like a good deal. So I signed up.

I was sworn into the Army as a first lieutenant, because I had six years of nursing experience. I made captain a year later, when I was in Vietnam.

Basic training was at Fort Sam Houston, Texas. Then I went to San Francisco, to Letterman General Hospital, for the OR course. It took five months. That was when I first started to get to know about Vietnam, because I used to have to walk from my dorm down a long corridor to get to the OR. Lining this corridor were guys in wheelchairs. Young guys. One guy in particular caught my eye. He had red hair, blue eyes. Both legs blown off below the knee. At first, when I first starting walking that corridor, I was scared to death. I didn't want to look at those guys, didn't want to talk to them. It was the same pattern as with the war veteran of my childhood.

Gradually I softened up. I started to walk slower and take peeks. Then I'd sneak a couple more peeks. Gradually, over a period of time, I began stopping to say hi. It finally got to the point where I'd make extra time in the morning so I could stop and talk. I developed a kind of supportive relationship with this redheaded guy. He had a goal: to have his artificial limbs and be able to stand on them at his buddy's wedding. That was his treatment goal for himself. And I was able to stay around long enough to help him get up a long flight of stairs to where his buddy was getting married. He stood on his two artificial limbs as best man.

The redheaded guy had had his legs blown off by a nine-year-old girl. She'd thrown a grenade in the back of a truck.

I started hearing that kind of stuff at Letterman. I really don't know what effect it had on me. I mean, I think I was just a little bit — I think I was alarmed and upset, but I don't think it had

245

any kind of meaning to me personally. It just didn't. Not till I got there.

When we landed at Bien Hoa, what hit me was the heat. The heat just about knocked me over. We got out onto this airfield and the guys in the Air Force were flying F-101 jets, doing loop-de-loops in the sky. They were putting on a show for us — they knew a lot of us were nurses. It took me a long time to find my duffle bag because there were so many and they all looked alike, but I found it. We went by bus to a place called the Ninetieth Replacement Battalion at Long Binh. The buses were these green Army buses. They had wires, heavy metal wire mesh, across the windows. I didn't know why — it was, I found out, so grenades wouldn't come into the windows, and right away I knew this wasn't going to be fun. In the hootch at the Ninetieth it was real dirty and dusty and there were rats that ran across the two-by-fours at night. I didn't like it at all. It was spooky, scary.

That first night at the officers' club I noticed that everybody did a lot of drinking, so I learned about that right away, too. Yeah, there was always a lot of drinking when we weren't on duty. I only remember one time, though, when I drank when I shouldn't have. I don't remember the reason, but I was on call and having a real hard time. That's usually why I drank, to cope, no matter what. Like when we were working around the clock: eighteen, nineteen, twenty, twenty-two hours.

My initial assignment was to the Eighty-fifth Evac in Qui Nhon. But one of the things that happened when we were getting our assignments was that there was this very young nurse who started to cry. She was real, real upset. I went over to try to talk to her, but she was not to be comforted. Then, when I realized what she was crying about, I said, "Hey, I have the same MOS as you. If you're so upset, I'll switch with you. I don't care where they send me." So we switched and I went to Twelfth Evac in Cu Chi and this other gal went to the Eighty-fifth, which was a much better, safer place to go. That night at the officers' club I met two guys who flew dustoff. They were kidding around about a lot of stuff, about the war, about how we nurses were going to like it, whatever. Then they wanted to know where we were going. When I said I was going to the Twelfth Evac, their faces dropped. This one guy looked at me and said, "You don't want to go there. Get that changed right away." He started telling me all sorts of awful things about Cu Chi, how they were always getting hit, how the nurses worked all the time. He was right. It was awful, worse than he said it was. But what could I have done? I had to go there.

The next day they took me there by helicopter. They told me they couldn't land, that I had to jump. So I jumped maybe six feet. When I looked up, they were flying away real fast. Well, where was I supposed to go? I mean, here I was in the middle of this desolate land with just these little huts in the middle of the compound. I mean, I have no idea where to go. So I'm yelling up at the helicopter and one guy points toward a building. I walk up to it, go in and tell them I'm reporting for duty, and out comes this STRAC lieutenant colonel — STRAC. That was an expression we used when they were real starched and stiff, when they were real into the Army salute and protocol and all that. That's what a STRAC soldier is. So out this one comes.

I was real uptight; by this time I really was. When I get real uptight, I usually try to do something funny to break the tension. I had my ukelele case with me; it was a baritone ukelele. So this STRAC lieutenant colonel pointed at it and said, "What's in that case?" I said, "My machine gun. I thought I might need it over here." This guy — I mean, this guy couldn't take it at all. He just looked at me with fire in his eyes and dressed me up and down. Chewed me out. "Don't you talk to me like that" — you know. Finally we sort of got that all squared away and I apologized for being disrespectful to a superior officer and all that jazz. Then I went to where I was going to live and saw what I had: a metal bed with just a mattress, the most gosh-awful thing you've ever seen. That was it. In a space about three feet wide by maybe eight feet long, no cover on the doorway. And I looked at the bed, and I thought, "That's where I'm going to live for the next year?" Finally I asked around. I learned to do what everybody else did: scrounge. I went across the road to where they had an artillery battery, talked to some guys, borrowed a hammer, got some nails, wood, and Masonite and went out in the back of this hootch. Then I thought, "Gee, now what do I do?" I didn't know how to build anything. And there wasn't anyone there to help me. So I just punted. You know. I started putting that stuff together till it would stay together. In a-hundred-and-ten-degree heat, too. Made some shelves — I've got pictures, I can show you sometime.

The sheets they gave me stunk so awful I couldn't sleep on them.

I wanted to throw up every time I put my head down. Rice water. Brown rice water that the Vietnamese used. Couldn't stand it, I wanted to throw up for the first couple nights, so I found some green OR sheets that hadn't been opened and I just stole them. I washed them myself, too. Every week I hand-washed them in a great big metal basin with my feet, like in the old pioneer days. And I washed my fatigues myself, because otherwise they would have smelled just as bad as everything else. I think they probably had buffalo manure in the water or something. I don't know. But the Vietnamese have real poor sanitation.

My day there went from seven o'clock in the morning until seven or nine at night. Plus I was on call four nights a week. So when I was on call I could be working anywhere from twelve to twenty-two hours. It was a real busy area, near the Iron Triangle, near all the major operations at that time of the war. We supported the Twenty-fifth Infantry. So I did all kinds of surgery. Sometimes I actually had to function as a surgeon. Like, guys would come in with wounds all over their bodies — maybe they'd hit a mine, and there would be all these little pellet wounds. My job then was to make an incision and cut away the dead muscle and dead tissue — cut it away because if it's dead tissue, it will just get poisoned and gangrened. So we had to cut it away and clean it out, and then three days later we washed the wounds out again and then closed them up with suture material. And we'd do this for, like, four hours. Four hours on just one guy, because just one guy can have hundreds of wounds, wounds all over his body. So what we did was divide the body up and the surgeon would work on one half of the body and I'd work on the other half. We'd be like two surgeons. Imagine how long it would have taken if there had been just one surgeon doing all that.

So there were many times when what I was doing was actual surgery. Other times I was being a scrub nurse. When it was chest surgery or bowel surgery or abdominal surgery, then the surgeons really had to do that. Except for certain aspects of it. Like tying off blood vessels, suturing up. A lot of times, especially on a chest or bowel case, my left hand would function as a surgeon and my right had the function of a scrub nurse. I had to learn to do everything with one hand that I had used to do with two.

We were getting all kinds of casualties in. Guys would come in who had lost one eye, one arm, two legs. It wasn't uncommon to have a guy come in with wounds like that, plus with wounds all over his body. Or guys would come in with two or three wounds in their abdomen, or great big gaping holes in their abdomen and their back. You could put two arms in through the holes. American artillery did damage like that — yeah, we could always tell the difference, because American artillery created the worst wounds. They would be black. Plus the blast wounds and the holes they left were much larger than the other wounds that we saw. How do Americans get hit by American artillery? Well, it's when co-ordinates are called in, and artillery fires, and there are American guys in the way. Or if the coordinates were called in wrong. Or the artillery didn't fire far enough. For all those reasons. Also, a lot of times the South Vietnamese would get Americans caught in the crossfire.

It took me only about a week to realize that the war was wrong. That we didn't belong there. That it was gross, war was gross. And awful. And all the rest of the stuff. I don't know, I sort of learned about things. Like that the enemy would hide in the French plantations and that the Americans weren't allowed to fire in there. I learned about the rules, all kinds of rules. Like, there were some units that weren't issued weapons because maybe the second lieu-tenants didn't have the respect of the men, were afraid their own men would kill them — a lot of the second lieutenants were real paranoid, because they didn't know what the hell they were doing. So they wouldn't let their guys have weapons and their units would get overrun. They'd get slaughtered. It was terrible.

I don't remember names but I remember cases. You know, the things that were wrong with them. I have a lot of pictures in my head. One guy I see has a big gaping hole in his back. Another guy's whole insides are blown away. It's gross. I mean, it was all open tissue. And you know, we were so damn good at what we were doing, we could save almost anybody. And I'm not sure that was — see, in a conventional war, a lot of those guys would have died before they ever made it to a hospital. But with helicopters and us working on them, many of these guys lived that shouldn't have. Because it's hard to live your life like some of those guys have had to since. Like this one guy — another redhead. He was my breaking point. He was maybe seventeen or eighteen and he was just blasted. The whole bottom half of his body was just blasted to hell. He'd lost part of his penis and scrotum and his two legs. And he'd lost his legs so high that he really will never be able to walk because there was nothing to hook them onto. Even the tops of his legs were gone. He was half a man, really half a man. So while we were operating on him we were all sort of looking at each other and crying. The doctors were in tears, too. They were just sort of pleading, "What do we do?" But you know, we weren't trained to let people die. Not mentally. Not ethically or emotionally. We couldn't make that kind of decision. We got guys in like that and even though we could see the damage and the kind of future they were going to have, no one wanted to be the one to make the decision that this guy should die.

We worked furiously on that redheaded guy. We saved him. Even though there was such an enormous amount of blood it was unbelievable — the guy had a million clamps in him. I got through the day OK, but three days later, when he came back for his closure, I walked in and saw this blob on a stretcher. That's what it looked like to me: a blob with a sheet over it. So I walked over and I looked and it seemed real cold in there all of a sudden. I don't know why, but it seemed so cold. I remember that. My body remembers the cold. I picked up the sheet and got a glimpse of his red hair and blue eyes. And I couldn't look. I had lost it. I screamed and ran out the door. I remember screaming at the top of my lungs — all kinds of obscenities. And I remember being outside and there were helicopters going out on a mission and I was yelling "Kill kill kill!" and all kinds of awful stuff. I just walked around the hospital in my OR clothes, screaming and crying. I had lost it. No self-control at all. Couldn't stop screaming, couldn't stop crying. I walked all the way down around the wards and back down to where the OR was, and suddenly it dawned on me that the guy was all alone. So I went back to him. But in all honesty I don't remember a thing after that. The whole thing is gone. The only thing I remember is being in the chief nurse's office, yelling at her to get me out of there. I told her please to let me work on the malaria ward. The next thing I remember I was on R and R.

So I laid on the beach in the sun for three days. I ate pineapples. And when I got back to Cu Chi I'd built a wall that nothing or nobody was going to get through. I was different now. I was bitter. And I remembered how when I'd first gotten to Vietnam I'd met a lot of doctors that seemed cynical. At the time I hadn't understood it. But now I was just like they were. It was gross, the whole thing was gross: what we were doing, what they were doing, what people were doing to each other. Still, the last six months of my tour nothing or no one got past my wall.

The things we got used to. Because of where I worked I'd have blood on me all the time. We didn't have any hot water. If I took a shower during daylight hours, the water was sort of warm. But at night if you took a shower the water was just real cold. Because of the hours I worked, I always had to take showers at night. The water was pure hell. Icy hell. I hated it. But I was always covered with blood, American blood, and I hated that more. I wanted to get that blood off me.

Other things. Like if we worked eighteen or twenty-two hours, we weren't as sharp as we were if we worked eight. But the quality of work we were doing was almost as good. I mean, emotionally we were draggy and there was a lot more irritation and shit. We were all on edge. But you know, we sort of accepted it. We understood. None of us took the shit personally. And you know, when we worked those long hours the mess hall people would bring food in to us. That's one of the things I think about now that seems so gross — I'd be eating with one hand and doing stuff with the other. I don't mean when I was scrubbed in but when I was circulating. You had to keep going, and so you ate. I mean, three o'clock in the morning, you're eating a liverwurst sandwich while you're doing surgery. Gross. But we did it. That's how we got by.

Things like that made all the rules seem so useless. Like when the second chief nurse we had — she did some crazy, stupid things — made us put up white picket fences outside the hootches. Well, here we are in the middle of a war and of course it's ugly. Of course it's desolate. OK, I can understand she wants to try and make it look a little better — but white picket fences! Not only was it totally stupid, it was downright dangerous. When we got hit, people ran for the bunkers and somebody was bound to get impaled on one of those pickets. Also, we had rules about what time you had to be in. Well, hell, when you're in the middle of a war you don't need any damn rules like that. Chief nurses just had to administrate. They were usually older. Lifers. Brownshoe lifers, we called them. It's an expression. Our first chief nurse was really neat — she'd pitch in and help, you know, didn't have her head in the clouds — but our second one was a disaster.

Other rules. Like we weren't supposed to fraternize with enlisted men. But I tell you, my experiences were that enlisted men treated me with respect. Like a human being. I wasn't government property, someone to be pawed at or to just sleep with. The enlisted guys respected me. We could talk about whatever we wanted to. And if I wanted to get into a relationship with somebody, then it was done in a respectful manner. The officers were another story. An act of Congress or an act of God couldn't make a gentleman out of some of those creeps.

Like once — I'd been in country less than a month — the chief nurse called us in and said we'd been invited to some general's party. I got all excited. I thought it sounded good — she told us there would be really good food, plus we'd get to wear civilian clothes, dresses, instead of fatigues. Yeah, a lot of us thought that was pretty neat. So we get all ready to go and this major comes to pick us up in a helicopter. He has a Styrofoam case with champagne in it. Neat — a champagne flight in a helicopter! So we get to the place where they're having the party. There's a huge spread of food and real silverware and real plates. We ate a lot. That was nice after being in the mess hall. But then, afterwards, these generals — and these are big generals I'm talking, you know, the generals who headed up the big infantry divisions during that time — start trying to put their hands on us. This one guy wanted me to call him Big Daddy. He wanted me to be his girl, sit on his lap and stuff. He was real drunk and gross. Smoking cigarettes and sticking them in his nose and sticking them in his ear. Telling me that whenever he wanted me he'd send a helicopter to come get me. He didn't offer money, but still the whole thing was just sickening. Obnoxious. I knew right then I had to get out of there, so I said I had to go to the bathroom and went and found that major and told him to take me back. Well, he says he can't take me back till tomorrow. Now what am I going to do? So I go outside and walk around the compound. All of a sudden I hear something between the buildings — it scares me. But it turns out to be an enlisted man who worked at the hospital.

He seemed OK, like he was friendly — you know, it was hard to tell. But he seemed safe, so finally I told him what was going on, because I'd never been in a situation like this. I didn't know what to do. And the guy said, "Well, I have an idea. You can sleep on one of the hospital beds tonight." So he took me up to one of the wards where he was on duty and I slept in a hospital bed that night.

It was all real upsetting. I was real upset and scared. When I got back to the hospital the next day I told the chief nurse I wasn't going to any more officers' parties. Told her I'd rather work. Those guys were just too gross.

I did get involved with a couple of guys who were officers. One was a helicopter pilot. He got killed, I think. What happens is, some of these memories get real fuzzed over. Like, I can't remember his name. But I can remember the kind of helicopter he flew. The other guy that I went with was an Air Force pilot. He flew a single-engine plane and he taught me how to fly. I actually flew missions. The missions were to fly over convoys — it was a bird dog, a spotter plane — and protect them. So you fly up ahead and look over the terrain and if you saw any movement you reported it. If there were enemy there we'd mark the spot with a rocket, and jets would come or B-52's would come and they'd bomb it. Yeah, I used to fly some of those missions. I even used to do acrobatics and stuff in that plane. It was fun. Totally illegal. But anyhow, the guy lied. Told me he was single and wasn't. When he really got in too far with me, he got scared and asked for a transfer. I never saw him again. So mostly you were better off not getting serious with guys; they either got killed or left.

Remember I told you that going to Vietnam was a suicide mission? It was. For me, it was a test — a test of God and the universe and whether I was worthwhile and deserved to live. And the test was on. So I did a lot of crazy things, like flying those missions. Sometimes I went out to the perimeter. I did that at Christmas with a bunch of other nurses. Just went out to the perimeter to give all the guys a kiss, a Christmas kiss.

It was Christmas Eve and real quiet out there. It wasn't jungle, but it was spooky. Real spooky out there on the fringes, with enemy just on the other side. All desolate and barren. It was like being on a desert. I don't know if you've ever seen the sky out in the desert, but it's beautiful. It's like you can reach out and touch the stars — and Vietnam had the most beautiful skies I've ever seen anywhere in my life. So it was spooky but it was peaceful. The guys let us fire rockets and grenade launchers and we hung out awhile. We didn't know those guys, but they were nice. It was a crazy thing to do, going out to the perimeter like that, but see,

I figured that if they were going to get me they were going to get me. I was fearless. Totally fearless.

It was all part of my suicide mission. Like when we had attacks, which was pretty often, I'd get called out of the bunker to go to work because I was an OR nurse. Yeah, when our base camp was getting hit, that meant casualties; that meant work. A lot of the time I had to run from the bunker across an open space to get to the OR. The soldiers always tried to make me wear a helmet, but those helmets were heavy. They slowed me down. So I never wore a helmet. I just ran fast. Another time I was caught in a jeep with a guy I was going with. He was on call for his TAC, which was Tactical Area Command. When we were attacked — it was a mortar attack — his assignment was to go immediately to his station. I was with him, so he took me. And here we are driving down the road and the mortars are falling all around us, driving like a banshee to get to this place. We get in there and it's amazing. I sit real quiet and listen to them running the war. You know, it was the TAC thing where they're calling in coordinates, saying where the enemy is, where to fire, where not, where each company is. Then the guys started getting real nervous about me being in there and told him to take me back to the hospital. So we're driving down the road again with the mortars flying. And when I get back the chief nurse is angry because I wasn't supposed to be out in a jeep in the middle of the night. But it was part of the war and the suicide thing. Like I said, if they were going to get me, they were going to get me. That's how I set it up in my head.

Oddly enough, when I had about a month to go in country, I figured the test was over. That I'd won or something. That something must be OK, that there was a reason for me to be alive. So I started taking care of myself. When we had mortar attacks I'd actually go under the bed or stay in the bunker. And then, when it was time to go home, they'd hit Bien Hoa Air Base the day before and there were all sorts of people standing in line to get to the airplane. I was scared to death the day I was in line that they were going to do it again and I'd get killed right there, before I even got on the plane. I was reminded of the biggest group to go home from the Twelfth — there was a big mortar attack right before a big party we had in November, a dinner for the group going home. I'd written home for months and months and had been collecting tomato sauce, tomato puree, and stuff to make spaghetti. And it was a lot of fun, it really was. But the night before this dinner, we were hit. Our hospital was hit, right by the mess hall. I figured they'd gotten word of the party and had just made a mistake on the nights — if it had been the next night we would all have gotten hit. The night of the party I took a picture of all of us in the mess hall, covering up the holes the mortars had made.

Coming home was a real bummer. Yeah, just a real bummer. It was dark and cold when we got off the airplane. There wasn't anybody there. I'd been hearing about the protests and stuff and had a bad attitude about all that. Because I didn't want to come home to hostile territory — I was tired, real tired, and I was also real spaced out. I was surprised that there wasn't a welcome home. That there weren't any people waiting for us at the air base. Yeah, I thought there would at least be something there. A debriefing at least. But there was nothing. It was like coming into a vacuum and it was awful, really awful. I didn't know where I was, where I belonged, what the hell I was doing or where to go or how to get there. I remember I had to go through customs. It was all endless. And then somehow I was on a bus to San Francisco International Airport. The only thing that seemed friendly were the raindrops on the window. I was looking at the window, looking at the raindrops. And suddenly I was gone. I guess I was back in Vietnam.

Well, I went to Los Angeles, where a friend met me and some family. That was a nice welcome-home greeting. But I remember the next day we were driving to the hospital where I used to work — I wanted to see all my old friends — and a siren went by and I dove to the floor. There I was huddling on the floor on the passenger side with my friend looking at me kind of weird. She asked me what I was doing. I said I didn't know, that things felt weird. Another thing was, we went into a grocery store and the door flew open when I stepped on the mat — I didn't know what to do, I was real spaced out, shocked.

The other thing I remember about my leave was the party my dad gave for me. We had these people that he knew, and I didn't know anybody there except for me and my brother. There was all this drinking going on. And I was in and out of Vietnam. Finally I started thinking, "Who the hell are all these people?" They all wanted me to seem like some kind of hero, and, believe me, I didn't feel like a hero. And everybody wanted to talk about the war but nobody wanted to hear about it. Yeah, nobody wanted to hear but everybody wanted to talk. So I just went to bed and let them have their party.

After my leave was up I was assigned to Madigan Army Hospital in Tacoma, Washington. And back there I was safe. I felt OK. I belonged. Because I could be with the guys who had just come back from Nam — look in their eyes, look in their faces. And it could be real for us. Because it was real.

You know, in Vietnam I couldn't do that because I was an OR nurse. I couldn't have human contact with the patients. I couldn't look at their faces — if I did, I'd feel, and if I felt I couldn't function. So I did it at Madigan. I did everything for those guys, made sure they had everything. And as head nurse, I was convinced I had the best ward in the hospital. I was so proud of those guys. It was just like Vietnam, giving the best, only here they weren't dying. I felt a whole lot better there. I really did.

I don't know. Now, what I'm doing now — it's part of my own healing process — is I go out and talk to kids of all ages. Elementary school, junior high, high school, community college. I talk to them about the war, show slides. I let them know what my experiences were like, what the war was like. I let them know war isn't John Wayne, American pie, and glory stuff — that it's killing human beings, and it's awful. I go around quite a bit. Also to civic groups. And it's healing for me to do things like talk to you because then I get to put the pieces together.

You know, I'm thinking about that experience I had when I was eight, with the guy in the wheelchair. All he taught me. And I'm thinking that that was a very, very powerful experience that sort of brought me full circle with going to Vietnam. I opened up that guy's arms, I opened the tightness of the contractures and softened up the hard places. That's what happened with me, too — I went to Vietnam and then I tightened up, couldn't talk about it for like twelve or fifteen years. And then the softening up. It was when the Iranian hostages came back. I started crying, didn't know what was going on. Eventually I went down to the vet center and got some help, got in touch with my feelings again. It was like pulling that guy's arms down. Opening up to the softness that's really there behind the wall, the softness that I really am. It's the part of me that I lost touch with through that awful experience in Vietnam, because I had to build a wall just to take care of myself.

I'm working with kids now. Working with vets, too. And when I think of myself going down that path to become a healer, a wounded healer, I know everything has come full circle.

*Now a therapist, Saralee McGoran lives in Auburn, Washington, with her ten-year-old son. Her fourteen-year-old daughter lives with Saralee's former husband. Both her children have birth defects; Saralee believes the defects are Agent Orange–related.*

# Afterword

THE HOUSE IS WEATHERED-LOOKING and barnlike, one of those New England houses that resemble a natural phenomenon. Inside, boards and boxes serve as living room furniture. Toys and clothes litter the hallway. The kitchen is crammed with plants, cookbooks, and dried things in mason jars, so crammed it's hard to navigate. The woman I've come to interview seems in her element here.

And I remember a house on a hill, surrounded by others like it: narrow, once-elegant, run-down. It's in a block that hasn't yet been gentrified, where trucks grind their gears through the intersection and twice an hour the city bus lumbers around the corner, its right rear wheels leaving a track on the edge of the yard. The woman I've come to interview is an exotic here. Her movements are quick, intense. She isn't afraid of silences. And she's used to being watched. Sometimes, watching her watching me, I see her as she was in Saigon: nineteen, hair to her waist, the girl in the photograph.

Now I'm sitting on an enormous lawn. It has rained most of the morning, and overhead the leaves are very green and bright. I look at the fish pond and the canna beds and the moving balls of gnats, and then I look again at the woman I've come to interview. She's wiry and tough as a snip of tungsten filament. She tells raunchy stories easily, even casually, and knows how to make me laugh. Nonetheless, there's something distracting about her hands. They seem to have a life of their own. It's as if, like a deaf person, she's actually talking with her fingers.

Picture a house in the middle of a mazelike subdivision. The drapes in the front windows are pulled against the three o'clock heat. Inside, the rooms are dim and overfurnished with squat Oriental objects, against which she herself appears startlingly tall and blond.

These are the scenes the reader doesn't see. These are the absent descriptions, the immediate foregrounds of the stories. For every interview there are takes like these: the women as they looked to me, the women as I remember them. And most of the time I remember them at home.

In the course of doing these interviews, I crisscrossed a big chunk of the map. I interviewed women in vet centers, in offices, in motel rooms, but whenever I could, I interviewed them at home. At home, other people's lives make tangible sense. Their words attach themselves to things you can see, hear, smell, feel, so that the lives become realer and solider than your idea of them. And the danger I most wanted to avoid was this: turning people into abstractions or caricatures. Taking the goods and running. Selling people out. So I tried to interview these women in their own territories, among the things of their lives. In addition, I sent them drafts of their interviews; it was the only way, in good faith, to do this book.

Here, then, is how I worked. I taped interviews, had them transcribed, edited them, mailed them out for corrections and comments — no one signed a release until she had read and, in most cases, emended her interview. For a journalist, this is risky. You can't predict who will water down her language, qualify candid stories, or strike significant references. You can't predict who will rewrite her life, tempering everything with nostalgia. And you can't do anything about people's jobs, kids, divorces — whatever it is that keeps them from getting back to you.

This method of working accounts, in part, for the shape of the book. In addition, decisions about scope always had to be weighed against the demands of narrative; some women were good storytellers, some not. Finally, had more black women granted me interviews, the book would have been more balanced.

I first began thinking about American women in Vietnam after reading Mark Baker's *Nam*. This was in 1981. In 1983, while interviewing some male veterans for a piece on post trauma stress disorder, I began to ask where the women were. Still, when I began this book last April, I didn't have so much as a phone number. What I did have was a passionate curiosity and a certain faith in randomness.

As it turned out, I was in the right place at the right moment: ninety miles from Jeanne Christie the week an excerpt from one of her letters appeared in a *Time* review of *Dear America: Letters*

*Home from Vietnam.* I called Milford, Connecticut, directory assistance, learned she was unlisted, and then called a vet I'd interviewed two years before. A few more calls and I had Jeanne's number. With Jeanne I was on my way. She opened her files to me, gave me the run of her Rolodex, and briefed me about the dedication of the memorial in New York.

After New York I traveled on an oral passport. I went up and down the Eastern seaboard, through the Deep South, to the Midwest, and across Texas. In addition to names and phone numbers, the women I interviewed shared scrapbooks, photo albums, mementos. They gave me clippings and articles. They fed me. And they floored me with their trust; without their continued trust, this collection would have been impossible.

Of course the work had built-in frustrations. For instance, there are bits and pieces I wish were in here, fragments that — for all kinds of reasons — I had to exclude. One woman talked about a botched suicide and how, after meeting another woman who had been in Vietnam, she came to terms with her urge to self-destruct. It's a story that stayed with me. (Paging through my journal, I see the note it inspired me to jot down: "Sometimes your history is absent until you need it — in bad times it can come back to you, providing you with images against which the present begins to make a livable pattern.") Although she told the story beautifully, she asked me not to use it. Other women, concerned about what one called "the too-tough image of the female vet," deleted hard-hitting bar scenes and references to drug use. Still others cut descriptions they thought might get them in trouble with the military.

A story I particularly miss is that of the woman who worked as a decoder in Saigon. She wrote me: "Thank you for the chance to tell my story but I am not really ready [to go public] yet. . . ." And I regret the Navy nurse who thought I'd butchered her life and the former Red Cross woman who told me my editing made her seem "shallow and negative." I also wish I had been able to include an interview with the only Red Cross woman who volunteered for a second tour in the field; for reasons unknown, she never got back to me.

Another problem was people not liking the way they talk. I don't mean people who wanted to delete their "fucks" and "shits" — that, all things considered, was a minor snag. I mean people who don't like their English. I'm thinking, in particular, of a black Navy captain who denied me permission to use her interview because she thought she sounded as if she "hadn't gone to school a day." Getting her letter was one of the low points of the entire project. All I could think about was the two rainy days I'd spent on a miserable strip in a miserable Southern city where there's nothing to do but drink beer, eat fast food, and listen to C&W.

There were other low points. Some had less to do with the work than with being on the road; others had to do with being in the Deep South, a part of the country that invariably taps collective memories I'd rather leave buried. In a Motel 6 near Fair Play, Georgia, I wrote: "No use — I woke up exhausted after sleeping maybe an hour. Now I'm sitting on the bed watching Oral Roberts. I hate this place. I hate the people along the highways in the rest areas and Waffle Houses, the ones with the god/guns bumper stickers, the ones who drive with their headlights on.* I hate them because they remind me of my roots."

I hit another low point in a Ramada Inn in Abilene, Texas. There the women pushing linen carts along the corridors were Vietnamese. I told myself interviews with Vietnamese women were beyond the scope of this book: I had contracted to do a book about Americans. That was when I began to get depressed about the narrowness of the effort. I wanted to bag the book and I wanted out of Abilene.

Many interviews clearly caused people pain. I'm thinking of a former Army nurse, who, moment by moment, seemed to disintegrate. After half an hour all she could say was "It was horrible" — over and over. I had sensed almost immediately that the interview would be unusable. Afterward, I didn't even listen to the tape. Her story, I knew, was both too jumbled and too sketchy; other pain-riddled stories I had been able to piece together, but she had simply disappeared from hers.

There was also the disappointment of interviews I didn't get. Three black women, all military or former military, said no right off. (I'm not the one to write it, but there's a book to be written about black women in the military.) And I kept hoping to talk to a former CIA woman who had retired, my contact said, "down in the Shenandoah"; at one point I expected to get a tape in the mail, but it never materialized.

* This was during the June, 1985, Beirut "hostage crisis."

Most accessible were the women who had been in Vietnam with religious organizations. Although I did meet one woman at the New York dedication, these women aren't really part of the network. I found Marjorie Nelson, Julie Forsythe, and Linda Hiebert not through other women who had been in Vietnam but instead by calling the American Friends Service Committee. Neither Marjorie, Julie, nor Linda fits the "civilian veteran" slot very neatly. Unlike the other women I interviewed, they were critical of U.S. military policies and institutions when they went to Vietnam; they seem to have escaped the debilitating ambivalence that so often dogged women whose shakier belief systems were rocked by the war; they had people to talk to when they came back. Marjorie even talked to journalists (including Susan Brownmiller, for *Against Our Will: Men, Women and Rape*) about her time as a POW.*

This is not to say that other women weren't generous and forthcoming. They were. Some astounded me with their willingness to talk. And, on this score, I have no big quarrel with the military. Lifers Sidisin, Splawn, and Jordan — as well as a lifer whose story, by August, struck me as redundant — were more than cooperative.

There is an unmistakable high that comes with getting a good story in person. Although sometimes you don't know what you've gotten until you've listened to the tape, often you can tell by the way you feel sitting there at the kitchen table. Your brain is filled with pictures. You're absorbed in hands-on details. For, in a good oral narrative, words have shape and weight. You can touch them. You can wear them like a second skin. At moments like this you forget about the fast food and the Motel 6s. You forget you were lost on the Jersey Turnpike, lost in Ohio, lost out of West Palm Beach. You forget about airport coffee shops and backwater commuter flights. You forget all the tense moments in phone booths. In your excitement, you even forget you're the one who will have to make the whole thing hang together.

Finally, there is the excitement of getting a note like this one: "I very much like what you did with the interview. I especially appreciate your ability to help tell a story. Thank you for helping me 'tell' mine."

---

* In light of the recent made-for-television movie *Intimate Strangers*, it is worth noting that no American *military* women are known to have been captured.

# Acknowledgments

I want to thank the women whose stories are collected here. I am particularly indebted to Lily Adams and Jeanne Christie, whose lists and packets of Xerox copies made my task vastly easier. In addition, I want to thank all the veterans — civilian and military, male and female — who shared their memories with me, wrote to me, and gave me their time and support.

George Allen deserves a special thanks for a long afternoon of talk. David Elder of the American Friends Service Committee deserves a special thanks for providing me with names and phone numbers, as does Claire Garcia at the Memphis Veterans Outreach Center. I also want to thank Sandra Okamoto of the *Columbus Ledger-Inquirer,* Vincent Coppola at *Newsweek*'s Atlanta bureau, and Nancy Price of the *Jacksonville Times.*

Grace Sevy generously shared her work with me. At the Department of Defense Center for Military History, Major Cynthia Gurney, Mary Haynes, Geraldine Judkins, and Colonel Bettie Morden helped me with research. Pat Martin of the Mennonite Central Committee, Howard Jost of Church World Services, and Father Robert Charlebois of Catholic Relief Services answered questions and provided me with research material.

I am grateful to Lough O'Daly for sharing her Smith Scholar's thesis on American women in Vietnam. Lough also gave me invaluable criticism, guided my research, and kept me company during the last half of this project.

Rick Berg put me onto the idea of an oral history. David Black gave me encouragement. My agent, Melanie Jackson, was enthusiastic from the beginning, and my editor, Ray Roberts, never doubted that all this talk would add up to a book.

Finally, I want to thank Tetty Gorfine for helping me find my own words. And I want to thank Danny Czitrom for reading, criticizing, arguing, advising, encouraging — for being there in more ways than I have words to tell.

# ✿ Selected Bibliography

Adair, Gilbert. *Hollywood's Vietnam*. New York: Proteus, 1981.

Arlen, Michael J. *The Living Room War*. New York: Viking, 1966.

As, Berit. "A Materialistic View of Men's and Women's Attitudes towards War," *Women's Studies International Forum, 5*, nos. 3 and 4 (1982): 367–376.

Avery, Paul. "Mildred Harrison's Viet Nam Ordeal," *Ebony* (June 1966): 88–96.

Baker, Mark. *Nam*. New York: Quill, 1981.

Boettcher, Thomas D. *Vietnam: The Valor and the Sorrow*. Boston: Little, Brown, 1985.

Bonior, David, Steven M. Champlin, and Timothy S. Kolly. *The Vietnam Veteran: A History of Neglect*. New York: Praeger, 1984.

Borton, Lady. *Sensing the Enemy*. Garden City, New York: Dial, 1984.

Butler, David. *The Fall of Saigon*. New York: Simon and Schuster, 1985.

Capps, Walter H. *The Unfinished War*. Boston: Beacon, 1982.

Coppola, Vincent. "They Also Served." *Newsweek* (November 12, 1984), pp. 35–36.

Cranston, Alan. "Senate Okays Women Veterans' Week," *The Stars and Stripes: The National Tribune* (August 16, 1984), p. 6.

Earley, Pete. "Nurses Haunted by Memories of Service in Vietnam," *The American Nurse* (February 1982), p. 8.

Edelman, Bernard, ed. *Dear America: Letters Home from Vietnam*. New York: Norton, 1985.

Elvenstar, Diane. "Mary Comes Marching Home," *California Living* (December 14, 1980).

Emerson, Gloria. *Winners and Losers*. New York: Harcourt Brace Jovanovich, 1972.

Englade, Ken. "After Shock," *Savvy* (November 1984), pp. 97–100.

Enloe, Cynthia. "Black Women in the U.S. Military," *Sojourner* (November 1985), pp. 16–17.

———. "Women in NATO Militaries: A Conference Report," *Women's Studies International Forum, 5*, nos. 3 and 4 (1982): 329–334.

Fallaci, Oriana. *Nothing, and So Be It*. Garden City, New York: Doubleday, 1972.

Figley, Charles R., and Seymour Leventman. *Strangers at Home: Vietnam Veterans since the War*. New York: Praeger, 1980.

FitzGerald, Frances. *Fire in the Lake*. Boston: Atlantic–Little, Brown, 1972.

Gitlin, Todd. *Inside Prime Time*. New York: Pantheon, 1983.

# SELECTED BIBLIOGRAPHY

Glasser, Ronald J. *365 Days*. New York: Braziller, 1971.

Helmer, John. *Bringing the War Home: The American Soldier in Vietnam and After*. New York: The Free Press, 1972.

Herr, Michael. *Dispatches*. New York: Knopf, 1977.

Holm, Jeanne. *Women in the Military: An Unfinished Revolution*. Novato, California: Presidio, 1982.

Horne, A. D., and John Wheeler, eds. *The Wounded Generation*. Englewood Cliffs, New Jersey: Prentice-Hall, 1981.

Huston, Nancy. "Tales of War and Tears of Women," *Women's Studies International Forum*, 5, nos. 3 and 4 (1982): 329–333.

Karnow, Stanley. *Vietnam: A History*. New York: Viking, 1983.

Kirk, Donald. "It Was 2:00 A.M. Saigon Time," *American Journal of Nursing* (December 1965), pp. 77–79.

Knightley, Phillip. *The First Casualty*. New York: Harcourt Brace Jovanovich, 1975.

Lifton, Robert Jay. *Home From the War*. New York: Basic Books, 1973.

Lynn, Barbara. "Good Samaritans in Vietnam," *Ebony* (October 1968), pp. 179–185.

Lynskey, Jerrold J. " 'You Learn a Lot — About Men and Life,' " *Army Digest* (September 1969), pp. 4–7.

MacPherson, Myra. *Long Time Passing: Vietnam and the Haunted Generation*. New York: Doubleday and Company, 1984.

Miller, Carolyn. *Captured!*. Chappaqua, New York: Christian Herald Books, 1977.

McCarthy, Mary. *The Seventeenth Degree*. New York: Harcourt Brace Jovanovich, 1974.

Norton , Mary Beth, et al. *A People and a Nation*, II, 780–982. Boston: Houghton Mifflin, 1982.

O'Neill, William L. *Coming Apart: An Informal History of America in the 1960s*. Chicago: Quadrangle, 1971.

Rogan, Helen. *Mixed Company*. Boston: Beacon, 1981.

Salisbury, Harrison, ed. *Vietnam Reconsidered*. New York: Harper Colophon, 1984.

Santoli, Al. *Everything We Had*. New York: Random House, 1981.

———. *To Bear Any Burden*. New York: Dutton, 1985.

Saywell, Shelly. *Women and War*. New York: Viking, 1985.

"Secretary on the Edge of War," *Ebony* (June 1966), pp. 27–34.

Shea, Frances T. "Stress of Caring for Combat Casualties," *U.S. Navy Medicine* (January/February 1983), pp. 4–7.

Stiehm, Judith Hicks. "The Protected, The Protector, The Defender," *Women's Studies International Forum*, 5, nos. 3 and 4 (1982): 267–376.

———. Editorial. *Women's Studies International Forum*, 5, nos. 3 and 4 (1982): 345–346.

Terry, Wallace. *Bloods: An Oral History of the Vietnam War by Black Veterans*. New York: Random House, 1984.

Theiler, Patricia. "The Untold Story of Women and Agent Orange," *Common Cause Magazine* (November/December 1984), pp. 29–34.

SELECTED BIBLIOGRAPHY

Van Devanter, Lynda, with Christopher Morgan. *Home Before Morning.* New York: Beaufort Books, 1983.

Walker, Keith. "The Forgotten Veterans," *California Living* (May 15, 1983).

Walsh, Patricia. *Forever Sad the Hearts.* New York: Avon, 1984.

"The War in Vietnam," *Newsweek* (March 28, 1966), pp. 40–42.

Wheeler, John. *Touched with Fire: The Future of the Vietnam Generation.* New York: Franklin Watts, 1984.

Willenz, June A. *Women Veterans: America's Forgotten Heroines.* New York: Continuum, 1983.

Young, Perry Deane. *Two of the Missing.* New York: Coward, McCann, and Geoghegan, 1975.

Zinn, Howard. *A People's History of the United States.* New York: Harper Colophon, 1980.

# ❦ Glossary

AFR  *Armed Forces Radio*

AFSC  *American Friends Service Committee (a Quaker organization)*

AIT  *Advanced Individual Training (for military specialization)*

APC  *Armored Personnel Carrier*

ARC  *American Red Cross*

ARVN  *Army of the Republic of Vietnam (South Vietnamese)*

AWOL  *Absent Without Leave*

BOQ  *Bachelor Officers' Quarters*

Charlie  *Viet Cong, either individual or collective (from American military communication alphabet; originally "Victor Charlie," for VC)*

CIA  *Central Intelligence Agency*

DOD  *Department of Defense*

DMZ  *Demilitarized Zone*

DROS  *Date Eligible for Rotation from Overseas*

E-4, E-5  *Pay grades below that of officer (E stands for "enlisted")*

ETS  *Expiration of Term of Service*

era vet  *veteran serving elsewhere during Vietnam War*

evac  *evacuate (send back to the United States, or move to another location)*

GI  *ordinary soldier (from Government Issue)*

grunt  *infantryman*

hootch  *general term for hutlike living quarters (from Japanese for "house")*

ICU  *intensive care unit*

IV  *intravenous (injection, fluid, or apparatus)*

IVS  *International Voluntary Services*

lifer  *career member of the armed forces*

Loach  *LOH (light operation helicopter)*

LZ  *landing zone*

MACV  *Military Assistance Command, Vietnam*

MASH  *Mobile Army Surgical Hospital*

MEDCAP  *Medical Civil Assistance Program*

# GLOSSARY

medevac  *medical evacuation*

MI  *Military Intelligence*

MOS  *Military Occupational Specialty*

MP  *Military Police*

NCO  *noncommissioned officer (of rank between private first class and second lieutenant)*

NVA  *North Vietnamese Army*

OB  *obstetrics*

OOF  *("Oh-Oh-F," Actually 00F), a Military Occupation Specialty abandoned in 1974. It was the equivalent of Drill Sergeant.*

OR  *operating room*

PFC  *private, first class (next-to-lowest Army rank)*

POW  *prisoner of war*

PRG  *Provisional Revolutionary Government (South Vietnamese)*

PTSD  *post trauma stress disorder*

PX  *Post Exchange (department store run by military for servicemen and their dependents)*

R and R  *rest and recuperation*

Remington warrior  *member of a noncombatant, "safe" unit (for Remington typewriter)*

ROTC  *Reserve Officers Training Corps*

round eye  *Oriental term for Occidental, especially female*

SEAL  *Sea Air and Land Team (demolition experts)*

short-timer  *someone whose term of service is almost over*

SRAO  *Supplemental Recreational Activities Overseas (Red Cross program)*

SSG  *staff sergeant*

STRAC  *Strategic Army Corps; someone who is strong on preparedness, protocol, etc.*

TAC  *Tactical Area Command*

UHI  *Utility Helicopter-1*

USAEV  *United States Army Engineers, Vietnam*

USAV  *United States Army, Vietnam*

USO  *United Service Organizations (largest organization for entertaining service personnel)*

VA  *Veterans' Administration*

VVA  *Vietnam Veterans of America*

VVAW  *Vietnam Veterans Against the War*

WAC  *Women's Army Corps*

the Wall  *the Vietnam Veterans' Memorial in Washington, D.C.*